The Hagley Wood
Tree Murder

The Hagley Wood Tree Murder

Reviewing the Case of Bella in the Wych Elm

By Keith Swallow
with Rachel Joy

THE CHOIR PRESS

Copyright © 2023 Keith Swallow

All rights reserved. No part of this publication may be reproduced or transmitted in any form or by any means, electronic or mechanical including photocopying, recording or any information storage or retrieval system, without prior permission in writing from the publishers.

The right of Keith Swallow to be identified as the author of this work has been asserted by him in accordance with the Copyright, Designs and Patents Act 1988

First published in the United Kingdom in 2023 by
The Choir Press

ISBN 978-1-78963-353-5

Whilst every effort has been made to trace and obtain permission from copyright holders for all images used in this book, the author and publisher will be pleased to hear from anyone who has not been appropriately acknowledged, and to rectify any errors or omissions in future reprints.

Map data from OpenStreetMap - openstreetmap.org/copyright

Contents

Author's Preface — vii

Part I: Events and Their Reporting (Chronology) — 1

Chapter 1: A Murder is Announced – The Body in The Tree — 3
Chapter 2: Initial Investigation — 17
Chapter 3: The Writing on The Walls — 31
Chapter 4: Witchcraft? — 51
Chapter 5: Some New Leads — 55
Chapter 6: Una Hainsworth, Jack Mossop and the Dutch Spy — 66
Chapter 7: More Spies — 75
Chapter 8: From Beyond the Grave — 82
Chapter 9: Later Developments — 87

Part II: Analysis — 103

Chapter 10: Officialdom – The Forensics and Police Enquiries — 105
Chapter 11: The Travelling Community — 128
Chapter 12: Provenance of the Wall Messages — 153
Chapter 13: Una Hainsworth's Story — 168
Chapter 14: Other Spy Ring Theories — 193
Chapter 15: The Occult and Related Angles — 201
Chapter 16: The Deceptions of Wilfred Byford-Jones — 206
Chapter 17: Other Sources of Confusion — 236
Chapter 18: Loose Ends — 245

Contents

Part III: In Conclusion 255

Chapter 19:   Summing Up 257
Chapter 20:   The Area Today 269

Appendices: 281
A – Timeline 283
B – Transcript of West Mercia Police Case Closure Report (2005) 295
C – List of Persons Reported Missing to (Birmingham Police),
      May 1940–August 1941 305
D – Sequential "Bella" Wall Messages 307
E – List of Customers Calling at Williamsons, Early Monday,
      27 March 1944 309
F – Summary of Police Enquiries at Addresses in Hagley Road,
      Hasbury, 2 August 1944 311
G – Transcript of Victor Crumpton Letter 313
H – Transcript of Statement of Vivienne M. Coss 314
I – Transcript of First Anna of Claverley Letter 317
J – Transcript of Second Anna of Claverley Letter 318
K – Statement Provided to Police by Una Ella Hainsworth
      28 December 1953 319
L – Bibliography, Film, TV and Radio Broadcast Detail 322

Index 325

Author's Preface

My introduction to the Tree Murder case (as it was initially coined by the press) was through my travelling work as a systems auditor. Much of my time was spent in Birmingham, and I grew bored with lodging in city centre hotels. In the summer months I would, when possible, stay further out so that I could at least have a couple of daylight hours to enjoy the countryside after work. One of the places I opted to stay was the hotel attached to the Badger's Sett pub, close to Wychbury Hill and the Clent Hills. I grew to love the Clent Hills, although I noticed how quickly the sun went down here, and how they would then take on a quite eerie appearance.

One evening, in the Badger's Sett, I heard an obviously new employee talking to a colleague about some strange experiences he had encountered in the pub. "Oh, so you've met Bella, then," his colleague remarked. She proceeded to tell him about "Bella", and how her ghost now haunted the pub. I thought little of it at the time, assuming that this was merely the time-honoured tradition of winding-up the newbie. But, when I got back to my room, I decided to run "Bella" and "Hagley Wood" through a search engine, and was amazed by the results thrown up; not least because I had never heard of the case before – and I have long held an unhealthy interest in unsolved crimes. For those unfamiliar with the story, it is quite extraordinary – involving allegations of witchcraft and espionage, as well as murder. I soon realised that, not only was I staying almost opposite Hagley Wood – on which the saga centres – but, as a regular visitor to the Lyttelton Arms and also the Hagley Obelisk (whilst walking up Wychbury Hill), I was familiar with two of the other prominent locations within the mystery. It cried out for further investigation.

Whenever I unearthed a new account of the crime, I was astonished at the contradictions that emerged. Further, there were many obvious errors within the reporting. The most basic of details have been corrupted, and even the tree at the centre of the case is not the wych elm as legend has it. There was one obvious person to turn to: Rachel Joy, a

Author's Preface

work colleague with a gift for genealogy and related research. Together, we have trawled archives, contemporary newspaper articles and standard genealogical records[1] in an attempt to get to the bottom of this mystery. Part I of this narrative considers the facts of the case as they were reported at the time, the events and the sequence in which they occurred; Part II details the way in which these facts were misrepresented and grossly distorted by a number of journalists and authors; whilst Part III draws conclusions. Included within the appendices are transcripts from some of the key police witness statements that were made available to the public via the Worcestershire Records Office in 2016.

For some of the research into individuals, we have used genealogy websites and archives, cross-referenced to key family detail. This process has been aided – fortuitously – by the tendency of many families of the time to give the mother's maiden name as a middle name to each offspring. In some cases, it has been necessary to purchase birth, marriage or death certificates to conclusively prove links; but this has not been done for those individuals on the periphery of events. Another caveat that should be invoked is that, for much of the period involved, certification of births, deaths and marriages denotes only the quarter in which registration took place. Given the requirement to register births only within the first six weeks, some of these will have taken place in the quarter prior to registration. Accordingly, where dates quoted are not specific, some leeway must be allowed. I must also add a few words of thanks to Pete Merrill, an acknowledged expert on the case (and who, along with his son, Alex, has already written two volumes on the subject). It has been invaluable to "bounce" ideas off somebody like Pete, who has a thorough knowledge of the case. Similarly, I should like to thank Gigi Jakobs (who has a family link to an aspect of this case) for her help.

Many of the photographs and copies of documents used in this book are from the police files, and I am most grateful to West Mercia Police for their permission to use. Further photos are my own, or have been supplied by individuals (some being via a Creative Commons – CC – licence), who are credited as appropriate. I should also particularly like to thank Glen Hayes and Jon Hardy of *The Pristines* for permission to use

---

[1] General Register Office (GRO), parish and census records; and trade directories.

Author's Preface

View from the Nimmings Wood in the Clent Hills, looking down towards the Wychbury Obelisk (field, top left) and the Badger's Sett / Gipsy's Tent (right centre).

their photographs or images. In a very small number of cases, I have used pictures which appear on public websites, but where I have, despite my best efforts, been unable to identify the copyright holder. If I have omitted anyone I apologise and request that those affected contact the publishers in order that amends can be made in any subsequent reprints.

Examining this case has also identified a number of interesting social conditions which demonstrate just how much society has changed in the intervening period. Perhaps reflecting a particular trait of the West Midlands, many people seem to have spent their whole lives in the area in which they were born, and many members of extended families often lived cheek by jowl, sometimes occupying much of a whole street. This is evidenced by the Jones and Willetts families taking up a large part of the same neighbourhood in Halesowen, and by the number of families with the surname James living in Trafalgar Road, Moseley. Our research suggests that there were up to three branches of this family resident there; however, in this and other cases, the commonality of the surname means that direct ties are sometimes hard to prove. A number of protagonists also seem to have been able to change birth and marriage details, without being challenged. In some cases, this was for reasons of vanity (to make them appear younger), but in others it was to avoid the stigma of having given birth outside of wedlock, or to preclude the need

Author's Preface

to obtain parents' permission to marry. These are issues which would puzzle many younger people today.

Other interesting insights into social history include the reliance on the postal service at the time in question: letters were written with a request that the recipient meet with the writer the following day, with clear expectation that the former would both receive the letter on time, and be available at such short notice. There would have been no opportunity to decline or rearrange meetings but, in pre-mobile phone times, this was the way that business was often conducted. Further, there are two examples of potential victims being eliminated from enquiries because witnesses recalled receiving Christmas cards from them more than two years before. Today, even though fewer Christmas cards are sent by post, receipt (or lack) of one is hardly memorable. Similarly, the many different pubs that feature heavily in the saga is a reminder of an era when the public house really was a community hub, the centre of local social life.

A sad footnote to this case is the number of individuals who clearly suffered from mental health problems, of varying degrees. And the rampant and endemic racism and sexism of the day was, unfortunately, never far from the surface, epitomised by a key witness being dismissed as "a Dago" within police reports, and pub landlords being listed (in directories and census returns) as "innkeepers", whilst their hard-working wives were classified as mere performers of "unpaid domestic duties". But a more obscure insight into rural life of the time is given by a witness who recalled members of the travelling community "frequently searching the hedges for hedgehogs" – a much-prized source of food. The same witness also reported employing a man who he believed to be an army deserter but was happy with the arrangement as the man was a good worker: public opinion and sympathy was certainly split when it came to war service.

During this account, I have at times been quite critical of some journalists who reported on the case and related matters. I should like to acknowledge that these were different times, and there were different expectations – as well as controls – over reporting. This also applies to the newspapers' and editors' supervision of their staff. Some of the newspapers involved are still operating, and I should like to make it clear that there is no implied criticism of their current practices.

Author's Preface

Lastly, something that has been a revelation to me over the course of my more recent research has been the beauty of the surrounding countryside. My previous experience of the West Midlands had been mostly limited to Birmingham and the environs of the A456 between there and Hagley, but this project has given me the opportunity to explore the Shropshire settlements to the north, and the interconnecting rural roads. The villages of Beckbury and Claverley, in particular, I find to be most attractive, despite being only a few miles from an industrial centre. And I'm not ashamed to say that I took the opportunity to indulge in another interest of mine – sampling a few pints of excellent real ale in some of the lovely unspoilt country pubs that have managed to avoid the brewers' axe.

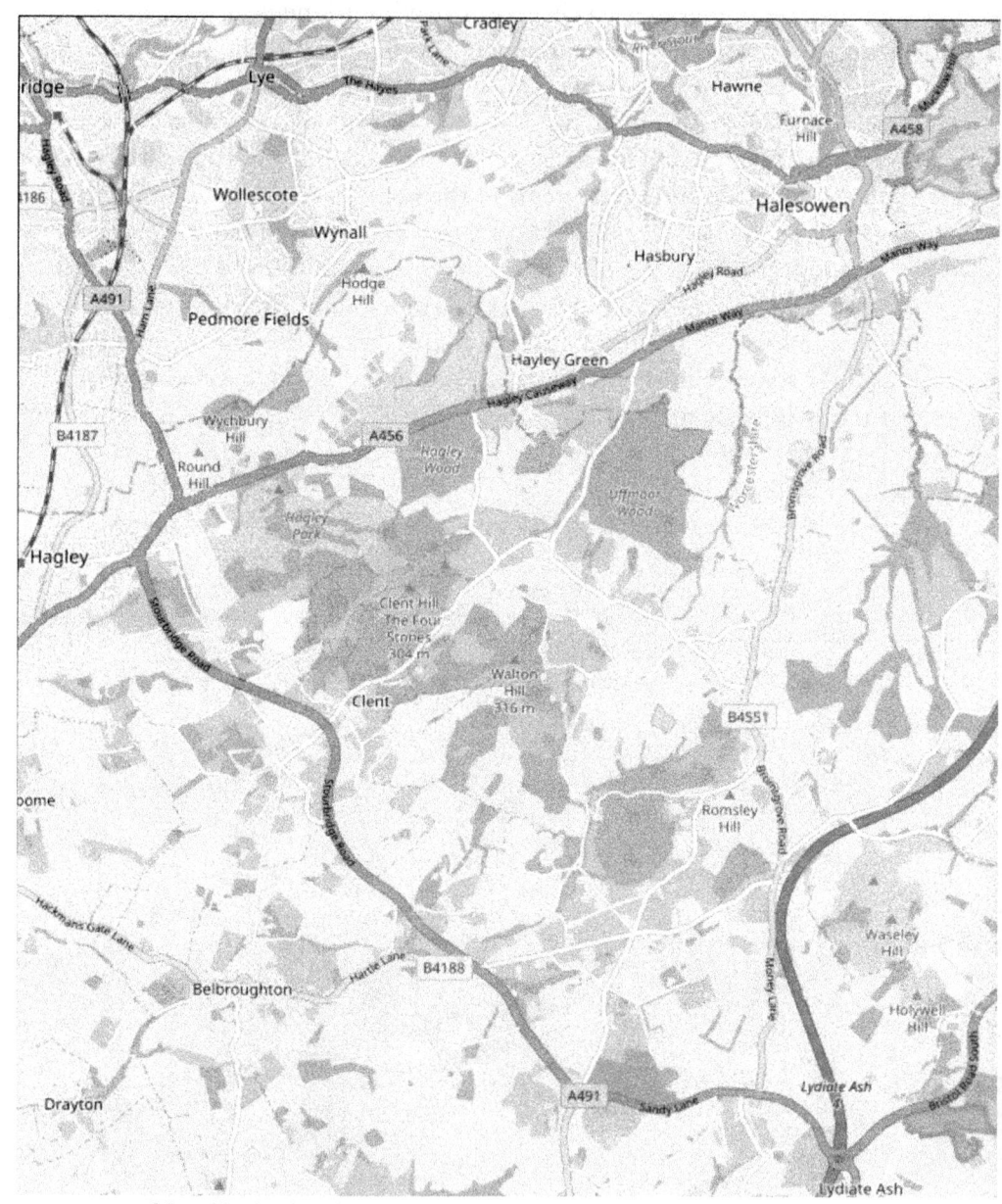

Map of key locations that appear within the narrative. (openstreetmap.org/copyright)

PART I:
Events and Their Reporting (Chronology)

CHAPTER 1

A Murder is Announced – The Body in The Tree

Discovery

It was Sunday, 18 April 1943, a week before Easter. Four teenagers from the nearby Stourbridge districts of Lye and Wollescote were in Hagley Wood, close to the A456 road which links Kidderminster and Birmingham. They were not bad lads; bored, perhaps, because of the hardships and rationing of war – and seeking a bit of excitement. They were regular visitors to the Clent Hills, where they would send their lurcher dogs rabbiting, to supplement the family pot at a time when austerity was starting to bite quite hard. Their journey should have taken them around the outside of the woods, as these were – and still are – private, being part of the estate of Lord Cobham. But the youths inevitably took the shorter route through the woods. This also gave them the opportunity to do what many lads of their age did to amuse themselves: some foraging, hunting and a bit of bird-nesting. The latter – the collecting of eggs from birds' nests – may now seem rather barbaric (as well as being illegal), but was then as common a pursuit as stamp collecting – another pastime in which today's youths rarely indulge.

The youths were Fred Payne, Bob Farmer, Thomas Willetts and Robert Hart, with three dogs in tow. The acts that they were undertaking were not illegal in themselves on common land, but the four were fully aware that they were on a private estate – and thus open to charges of poaching. Having just found a blackbird's nest containing four eggs within a tree, when they noticed a similar tree nearby, they made a beeline for it. This is the point at which the story starts to get interesting, but also where significant disparities begin to appear within accounts. The first piece of conventional wisdom is that the lads stumbled across it in the early evening of a sunny day. This would appear to have been the

Events and Their Reporting (Chronology)

The police file copy of the widely published photograph of the tree in question (left) and another from their archives. It is unclear whether these do, in fact, depict the same tree. The likelihood is that the latter picture was taken on 19 or 20 April 1943; although neither is of good quality, the foregrounds would suggest that they may have been taken at different times of the year. (West Mercia Police).

case, although the *Birmingham Daily Gazette* of 24 April reported that it was 12.30 p.m., and some sources portrayed it as being a dark evening.[2] Newspaper articles all agreed that the tree in question was a wych, or "witch", elm (*Ulmus glabra*), and this has become wrongly accepted as fact. The tree, with hundreds of thin, whippy tendril-like branches emanating from it as a result of some rather poor pollarding, was actually a witch hazel (*Hamamelis*); the two are similar in appearance and often mistaken, although such semantic issues were clearly of little interest to the boys.

Fifteen-year-old Bob Farmer started to climb the tree,[3] and discovered

---

[2] It seems to have depended largely upon the angle that the individual journalist was trying to develop.

[3] The alternative version is that it was Farmer who had discovered the blackbird's nest in the first tree, and that he directed Robert Hart to look in the subsequent location.

a hole which showed the centre of it to be hollow. Peering inside, he saw a skull. The lads were not unused to seeing dead animals, and he at first assumed that it belonged to a badger or fox. Prising it out with a stick, however, the group soon rightly deduced that it was of human origin, with some flesh and hair still attached. Rapidly returning it to its original resting place, they sprinted out of the woods and continued to run home. Because they had been trespassing, they swore to keep their find a secret. Such a secret, however, weighed heavily on young minds. Once again, there is more than one version of how the truth emerged. Several sources have it that the youths, after fleeing the woods, encountered Fred's[4] older brother, 17-year-old Donald Payne, in the vicinity of Oldnal Pits and took him to the tree to show him; another that all four told their parents. But most reports state that it was Tom Willetts, described as the youngest of the group, who was the one to crack, and he told his father. This is probably closest to the truth although, at 18, Willetts was some three years older than Bob Farmer.[5]

The *Birmingham Daily Gazette* subsequently reported[6] that Tom Willetts' father phoned Sgt Richard Skerratt from Clent, who took the young Willetts back to the wood to show him the tree and its contents. He then notified Supt Hollyhead at Stourbridge. But other sources suggest that Mr Willetts first contacted Sgt Lambourne, a close personal friend, who was on duty that day at Hagley Police Station – and police records seem to confirm this (albeit that contact may have been on the following day – Monday, 19 April). Lambourne's measured response was to first go to the home of Robert Hart. Hart then guided the police to the spot, where the sergeant confirmed that the find was indeed human – and that the rest of

---

[4] As a sad footnote, Fred Payne would die some six years later, from a long-standing illness. But his family additionally suffered through the action of a local journalist, who – for dramatic effect – would later write that his death was brought on by the shock of what the teenagers discovered.

[5] Over 50 years later, in an interview with the *Wolverhampton Express & Star*, Bob Farmer confirmed that this was the case. He was to say: "If it wasn't for Tommy Willetts opening his big mouth the skeleton would probably have never been found." Some reports state that Willetts was 17 rather than 18, but probably because years of birth rather than exact dates were supplied to the press; similarly, the ages supplied for Fred Payne (14) and Robert Hart (15) may be "out" by a year.

[6] 29 April 1943.

the body appeared to be still encased within the tree. By this account, Lambourne was soon joined by Sgt Skerratt, PC Jack Pound from Hagley, and Sgt Jack Wheeler. This does appear to be the most likely version of events, although still other reports suggest that the police may have taken all four youths back to the wood.

 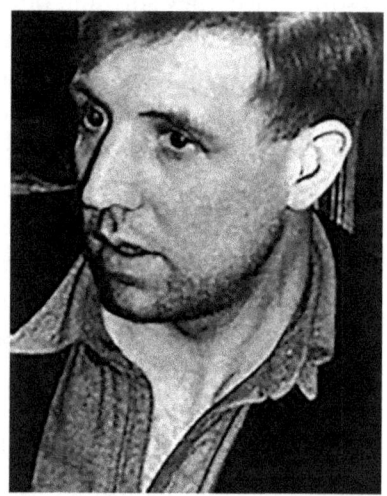

Robert Hart (left) and Thomas Willetts, pictured two years after discovery of the body. (Photos courtesy Wolverhampton Express & Star)[7]

There has been debate as to exactly where within the wood the tree was sited. This is partly due to the subsequent widening and minor re-siting of the main Hagley–Birmingham Road, and partly because of tree replanting in the south east corner of Hagley Wood. To get into the detail of this is a little distracting (and it is well covered in other books on the subject). In terms of ease of access and later developments, however, it is worth noting that it was probably around some 125 yards from the edge of Nimmings Field (the southern edge of Hagley Wood)[8] and about 40 yards from the eastern edge of Hagley Wood Lane. Although now hardly a major thoroughfare, Hagley Wood Lane was then even less

---

[7] There have been subsequent suggestions that the newspaper may have used the wrong caption and that one photo instead depicts Bob Farmer.

[8] Sometimes simply referred to as "Nimmings".

prominent. The *Birmingham Daily Gazette* described it in the following terms: "Hagley Wood is accessible only by foot. But a narrow, winding lane, little more than a cart track, runs alongside it and is easily accessible by car to a point where a five-bar gate affords entrance to the wood."

Securing and recording the scene

Detective Superintendent Sidney Inight was soon placed in charge of what clearly appeared to be a murder investigation. He was assisted by Detective Inspector Thomas Williams, and they jointly determined that the remains were too tightly wedged in the tree to be extracted, and might be further damaged by forcible removal. They took the sensible decision to call in the recently established Home Office forensic science laboratory. This was based – rather handily – at nearby Birmingham University, although nobody from there was available to attend that day. In the interim, a "volunteer" was sought to guard the scene throughout the night. The short straw was drawn by Squadron Leader William Douglas-Osborn, a former special constable who was home from the RAF on a short period of leave.

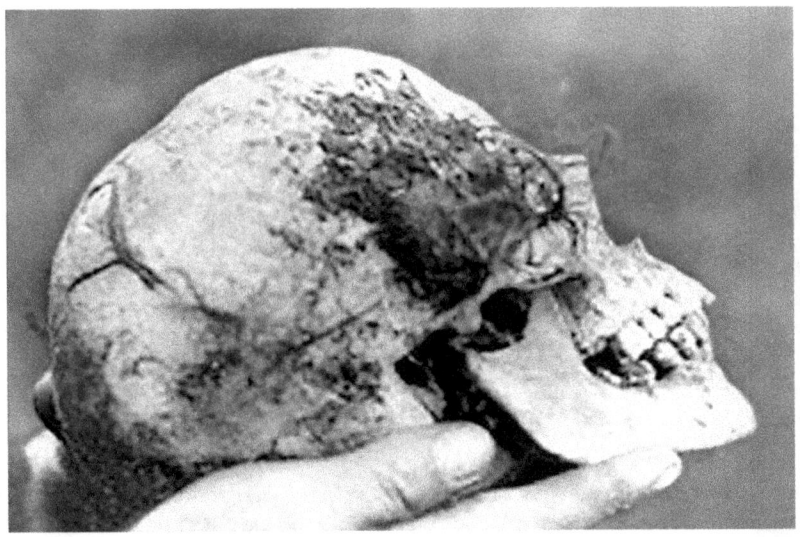

The skull recovered from the cavity of the witch hazel tree, with tuft of hair still intact. (West Mercia Police)

Events and Their Reporting (Chronology)

It must have been a relief to Douglas-Osborn to be released from his duties the following morning (20 April), although this is not the last that we hear of him in the saga. Det Supt Inight, DI Williams and PC Pound took over, but had little to do until the evening, when Professor James Webster (head of the science laboratory) finally arrived on the scene.[9] Having clambered up a ladder to inspect the inside of the tree, it was Webster who determined that the best means of extracting what was left of the body, without causing undue disturbance to it, was by demolishing the tree. Jack Pound – as the lowest-ranking officer, and who had also previously worked in forestry – was charged with undertaking this task with an axe. Once extracted, the skeletal remains were sent to Webster's laboratory.

Before the tree was destroyed,[10] however, measurements were taken and recorded, which showed it to be:

A hollow tree with the main trunk being 5½ feet high with the hollow or bole being lower down at about 3½ feet from the ground. The bole aperture was 24 inches at its widest points, the inside was funnel shaped, with the aperture reducing to 17 inches lower down.[11]

Police photographs purporting to show the bole of the tree in question (left-hand picture, centre); and after extraction of the body. (West Mercia Police)

---

[9] Some accounts relate that Webster did not arrive on scene until 6.40 p.m., although his own report states that he extracted the body at 6.30 p.m.
[10] Police papers certainly suggest that the tree was completely destroyed, although some later articles appearing within the *Black Country Bugle* suggest otherwise. See Chapter 9.
[11] Webster's report.

A Murder is Announced – the Body in The Tree

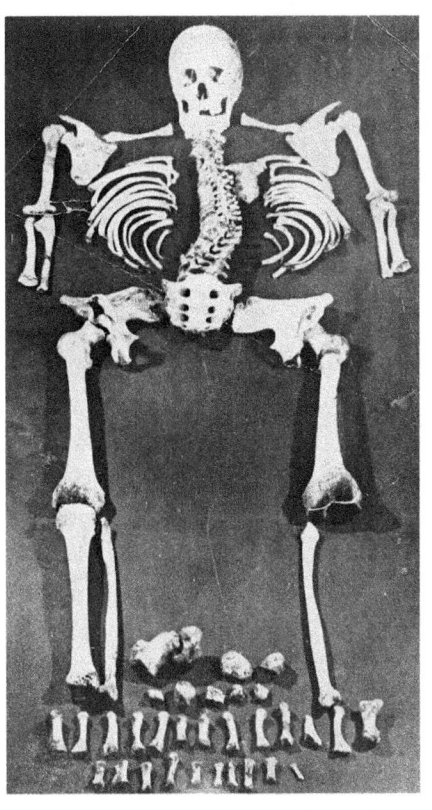

The re-assembled skeleton of the victim, as pieced together by Professor Webster's team. It was from this exercise that the missing bones were identified. (West Mercia Police)

Much has been written about where the bones were discovered and what else was found in the base of the tree, and most of this has been accepted as fact without reference to source documentation. Unfortunately, police records are patchy – and all those specifically relating to the search of the surrounding wood have gone missing. Those later records that have survived quote Webster as saying that, at the time he retrieved the disarticulated skeleton from the tree on 20 April, it was incomplete, and that he had spotted and recovered a human shin bone some 12 yards away. The forensic report confirmed that a subsequent search (largely entrusted to an assortment of special constables, Home Guard members, servicemen and Boy Scouts) uncovered a left pelvic bone, a right femur and a right fibula (the suggestion being that these were within about 15 yards of the tree, i.e. just beyond the 12-yard radius covered by the team that retrieved the body). These were handed over on 22 April and, from these, together with those bones retrieved from the bole of the tree and surrounding area on 20 April, Webster was then able to piece together the bulk of the skeleton. This rather macabre jigsaw-puzzle exercise confirmed that all the bones recovered were part of the same skeleton, which was now complete, with the exception of the right tibia (shin bone), part of the hyoid bone, a patella (kneecap), and some of the small bones of the hands and feet. In addition to the bones, the search had found a shoe matching that which had been recovered from within the tree.

The victim

From the skull and disarticulated skeleton, Professor Webster postulated that the victim was in all probability around 35, but within a wider range between 25 and 40 ("my impression is that she is on the 40 side of 35 rather than on the 30 side of 35").[12] She had been dead for at least 18 months, but no more than three years. As with her age, Webster tried to narrow this down further, advising that the most likely time of death within these parameters was between April and October 1941. No second opinion was obtained and, in a separate testimony to the regional police group, Webster later added the caveat that the body could have been there for a "very considerably longer period". The wide age range which Webster had put forward at this stage, though, would place her date of birth between 1901 and 1916.

Webster acknowledged that his calculations in relation to the minimum period of interment were based only partly upon how long it would take flesh to naturally fall from the bones in such conditions, and that he was influenced by the rate of tree growth through the items of clothing in suggesting a possibly longer time. In this, both he and his assistant – biologist John Lund – were clearly making the assumption that the clothes did belong to the victim. In later concluding that the body could not have been forced into the tree when rigor mortis had set in and that the interment probably took place before then (when the body was still warm), Professor Webster would also concede that the task *could* have been undertaken after rigor mortis had passed. This opened up the further possibility of the body having been initially stored elsewhere and subject to a faster (or slower) rate of decomposition. If so, it had to be considered that the body may have been in the tree for less than 18 months.[13] Webster's assessment of the victim's height has also been the

---

[12] DI Tommy Williams would later say that the victim was "about 37 years of age in 1941".

[13] This would assume that the clothes were not necessarily linked to the body, or that Webster's knowledge of plant growth was flawed.

subject of great debate over the ensuing years. Whilst initially asserting that the skeleton was that of a woman some 5' in height, he would shortly afterwards amend this estimate, saying that it had been based on her wearing shoes, and that her actual height would rather have been 4' 9½"–4' 10".[14]

Analysis of the teeth and dentition provided what many saw as the most useful lead for the police. The teeth were generally in good condition, except for a premolar and a molar which were carious – one of which extremely so. This may have given the woman some pain in the latter stages of her life, or resulted in bad breath. There was no evidence of any fillings having been administered, nor of a dental plate being fitted. Webster later advised that "she has definitely had one extraction in the lower jaw ... the tooth was extracted long[15] before her death", but this information does not feature within the forensic report. It has been subsequently reported that there was pronounced disfigurement of teeth within the jaw, but Webster's report merely states: "The only other point about teeth is that in the lower jaw there is some definite over-lapping of the incisors and the upper front teeth tended to project rather more than normal."

The wisp of hair clinging to the skull as well as further, much larger, clumps found in the tree, allowed Webster to conclude that the victim had had brown, mousy hair. "I cannot tell you if this was bobbed or waved and so on, for the very simple reason that whilst it looks a complete mess, it consists of a number of broken pieces due to the action of the weather." From her clothing, he deduced that she "obviously [was] not in the 'higher flight'", but "nor [was] she a ragamuffin ... she is, moreover, a type of person who may have been rather neglectful as to her appearance and habits". He acknowledged that he was indebted to Special Constable Goldfar in respect of analysis of the clothing, which

---

[14] Although DI Williams consistently stated that he was confident in Webster's estimate of height, he did later acknowledge that the woman could have been somewhat taller.
[15] This has appeared as "not long" in many accounts, which gives a completely different meaning. A later report by Webster suggested that the extraction had taken place at least one year earlier. This is itself a little puzzling, as elsewhere it is made clear that John Lund led this part of the investigation, and a two-page report under his name was issued on 23 April 1943.

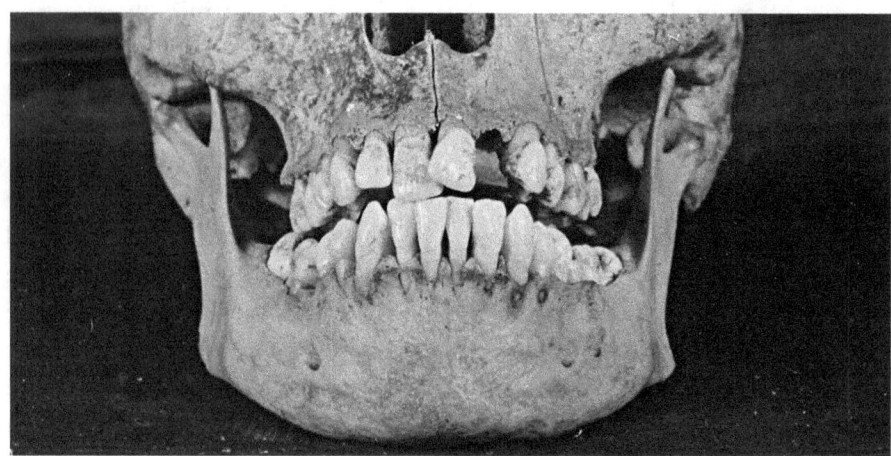

"Bella's" distinctive dentition. Although this photo would suggest that the extraction may have been from the upper (rather than lower) jaw, Professor Webster made it clear that a tooth had fallen out from the upper jaw after the skull had been recovered. (West Mercia Police)

suggests that he – understandably – paid less attention to this area himself. He reported (based on Goldfar's work) that the woman had little remaining clothing, although there was sufficient to develop a picture of what she had been wearing. Closest to the body would have been a taffeta[16] slip which, due to being hemmed at the top and bottom by hand, was determined to be home-made. This was probably fashioned from a coat lining, although DI Williams did put forward an argument that it could be part of a nightdress, possibly signifying that the woman had put her clothing on over the top when fleeing an air raid. Its colour was described as being either peach or fawn, but Webster further indicated that, in his opinion, the latter was nearer the mark. A piece of material had been found stuffed into the jaw of the body, and it was identified as a portion of this garment. The knickers were blue lock-knit, and Webster advised that the victim had also worn a corselette which was "definitely not old-fashioned". He was confident that stockings had not been worn. The skirt was mustard-coloured, and it was noted that the cardigan was of slightly better quality than the other clothing, and was ribbed. This was described as being of "five ribs in one inch in navy, and three ribs making up half an inch in mustard or khaki". Buttons were cloth covered

---

[16] Whilst taffeta is often of high quality, it was observed that this item was not.

whilst the belt was a slightly darker shade of blue[17] than that within the cardigan. Generally, the clothing was deemed to be summer[18] rather than cold-weather wear – which would support the contention that death may have occurred around July 1941 (the mid-point of Webster's range). It was further noted that there were no labels attached to the clothes.

The artist's impression of the victim circulated by the police, although it is unclear in which newspapers it appeared at the time. Professor Webster additionally concluded, from analysis of wear, that the ring had probably been in use for about four years.

Whilst the clothing may have been of poor quality, the shoes – which police again concluded must have belonged to the victim – were not. These were size 5½, and initially identified as "black leather Gibsons" – although it was soon established that they were in fact blue, having become discoloured due to exposure to the elements.[19] There has, however, been inconsistency throughout the case with variations (such as midnight blue, and other colours) also being attributed. There is certainly no indication that any bones were found within them – put forward as significant by some commentators on the case – but the shoes could easily have become detached when the body was being forced into the tree.

---

[17] The detail on the artist's sketch, however, differs in relation to the belt colour.
[18] John Lund would later similarly describe her as having been "lightly dressed", although Webster also said that "she was dressed in full outdoor clothes". This could, alternatively, have indicated the limited finances of the wearer.
[19] A police memo of 24 April 1943 confirms that: "the shoe is a blue Gibson shoe and not black, the discoloration is due to exposure to the weather".

Events and Their Reporting (Chronology)

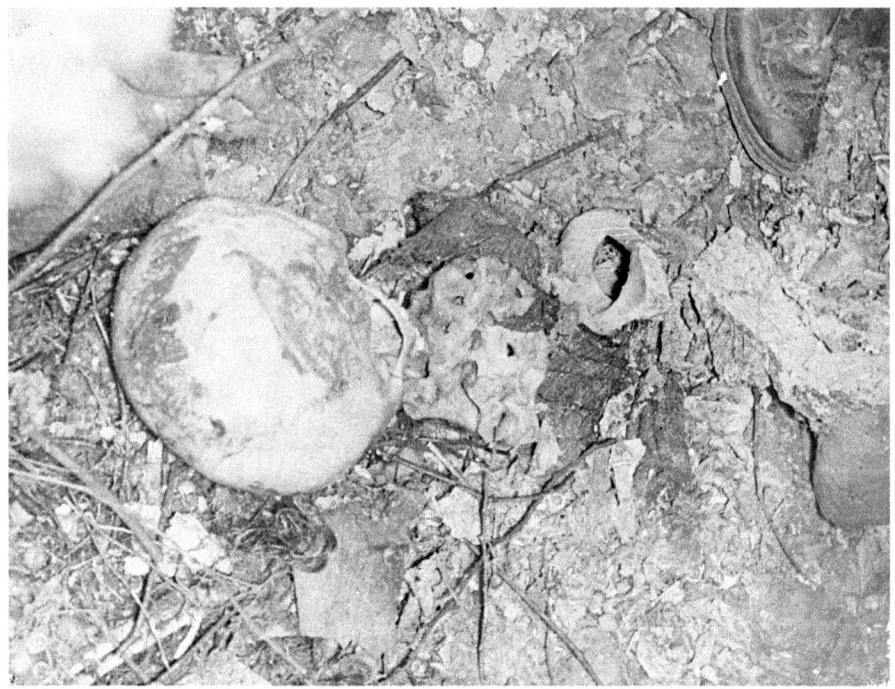

A crime scene photograph showing the one shoe (at top right), sitting above the leaf litter in the base of the tree. The skull is to the left. (West Mercia Police)

There were other issues which may have also confused members of the public, and hampered the police in their work. Webster had reported that the woman's pelvis had markings frequently associated with pregnancy or childbirth, but was keen to stress that this was not conclusive. Some newspapers reported on this basis, however, that the victim was a mother, and this may have prevented individuals coming forward (if a missing person was known to be childless). The police sketch also indicated that the victim was wearing a "mock wedding ring." Quite what this means is perplexing – the ring was undoubtedly cheap, but "mock" seems an inappropriate word.[20] There were certainly those who interpreted this as meaning that the victim was unmarried, which may again have clouded the issue. Another explanation that may be valid

---

[20] Within the *Police Reports* journal of 30 April 1943, the ring is described as "faceted" (having many sides). It may be that this was misinterpreted as "fake"– hence "mock".

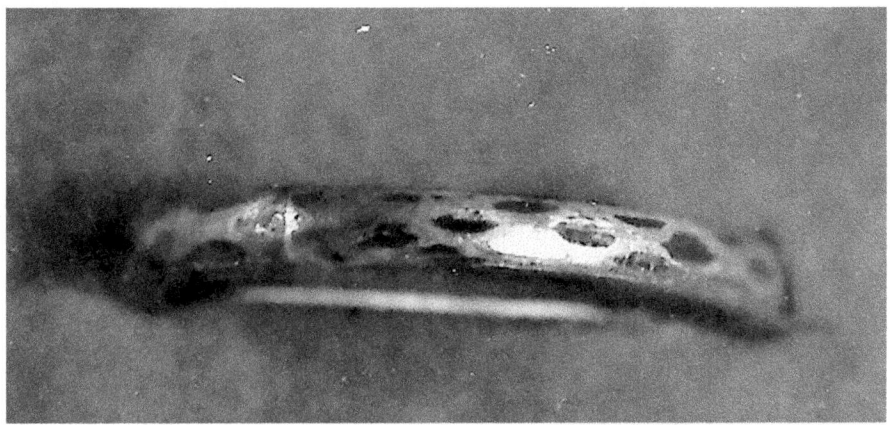

The wedding ring worn by the victim. (West Mercia Police)

is that prostitutes of the time sometimes wore cheap gold rings to give the impression of being married, to facilitate booking hotel rooms. The sketch that was issued did not have the approval of all involved, with Webster himself expressing concerns that it did not fit well with his view that the victim had been "neglectful as to her appearance". Further, he pointed out that he had given no indication as to her build, or her hairstyle.

Facial features

Surprisingly, the prospect of using facial reconstruction from the victim's skull was considered by Professor Webster at this time. Although the technology was very much in its infancy in the 1940s, in his briefing to the regional police representatives, Webster referred to the one successful use of this approach, in the United States, but clearly went on to decide against going down this route. The likelihood is that this would have been on the grounds of cost.

Cause of death

The measurements of the tree, as recorded above, made it a very tight fit, and suggested that the body must have been forced into the bole. From this, one of the more obvious inferences drawn by both Webster and, subsequently, the coroner, was that it was unlikely that death was the result of suicide. Accordingly, the verdict of murder "by person or persons unknown" was felt to be both appropriate and fully in keeping with the available facts.

From the remains, Webster could find no evidence of violence, or of disease. Based on the rather flimsy evidence of the strip of taffeta stuffed into the mouth cavity, he tentatively surmised that asphyxiation *could* be the cause of death, but certainly did not commit himself on this score. An alternative possibility was that the killer(s) may have stuffed the cloth into their victim's jaw to stifle her screams whilst some other form of terminal injury was being inflicted. The youths who had made the discovery later conceded, however, that, in their attempts to lever the skull out of the tree with a stick, some of the fabric had become entwined around it and may have been forced into the jaw – either then or when, in their haste, they replaced the skull in the tree. Certainly, given the decomposition and the ravages of time (not to say the impact of animal activity) it would have been surprising for a gag to have remained in place for any length of time.

The formal inquest on the body was held on 28 April, at Stourbridge, with the coroner reviewing the evidence assembled by Professor Webster, John Lund, and the police. A verdict of murder against some person or persons unknown was returned, and this much was reported in the media – although no copy of the coroner's report has been retained. What has survived are the reports by Webster: "Human remains found in a hollow tree in Hagley Wood on the main Birmingham–Kidderminster Road" (23/04/1943); and by Staff Biologist Lund: "Clothing Examination" (21/04/1943), which informed the coroner's inquest. Further significant facts and opinions were later supplied by Webster and others at a police conference held on 3 May 1943.

CHAPTER 2

Initial Investigation

Early on, the police pursued a number of different lines of enquiry, including investigating rumours circulating within the community. One doing the rounds was that the murder was the result of "moon madness"[21], partly based on the fact that, pre-war, the proximity of the Bromsgrove Lunatic Asylum had made many locals familiar with the occurrence of mental illness.

Some of the initial rumours, however, arose from the presence of so many American servicemen in the area. This inevitably led to speculation, particularly amongst those who famously resented that the "Yanks" were "overpaid, oversexed and over here". These US servicemen were certainly known, in common with local youths, to take girlfriends and prostitutes into Hagley Wood. If one were looking for a parallel, then the murder of Florrie Porter in nearby Bromsgrove in October 1944 provides a good example. Porter was not a prostitute, but her demise demonstrated the dangers facing women in wartime. It was widely suspected (probably known) that a particular American serviceman (GI) was responsible, but the US Forces transferred him before he could be questioned by police. Coincidentally, Florrie's autopsy was undertaken by Professor Webster, and this murder also remains officially unsolved. Sadly, there were similar cases of military forces' personnel murdering civilian women throughout the course of the war, both in the Midlands and throughout the country. As with the Florrie Porter case, the military would sometimes not only refuse to cooperate with the authorities, but actively conspire against the deliverance of justice. Despite local prejudice, however, there really was no evidence to suggest any GI involvement in this particular crime.

---

[21] Referencing the phenomenon that a full moon can result in some strange behaviour (and from which the word "lunatic" derives).

Whilst the police did entertain this possibility with the Bella case, the view of many officers was that the protagonists were probably local; the murder being the result of either a family argument or a sexual assault, and that somebody would come forward to report a family member, colleague or friend missing. A related theory was that the victim may have entered the wood to take cover during an air raid. Hagley Wood was quite regularly used as a perceived place of safety during air raids, and it was possible that she had met her killer there in such circumstances. This was supported by Webster's report of the taffeta stuffed in her jaw: could this have been part of a nightdress and indicate that the victim had fled from an air raid that may have subsequently destroyed her house – notwithstanding the presence of other clothing?

Clues

Although there was no obvious link between the body and persons reported as missing around the perceived time of death, the police did appear confident that they would soon be able to identify the victim. The reason for this optimism was based on their having the dentition and clothing evidence to fall back on. X-rays were taken and circulated to all local dentists in the hope that one of them would be able to recognise the dental work as his own. Unfortunately, this initiative led nowhere, so enquiries were extended to all dentists nationally but with a similar lack of success. Although the woman had (relatively) recently had treatment of some sort, the police now felt that this lack of response, combined with the two carious teeth and absence of fillings, pointed to her not having been a regular patient. Many people were then unable to afford professional dental work, resorting to "back street" practitioners when in extreme pain, particularly during wartime when money was even shorter.

The expected leads from the victim's clothing also failed to result in anything significant. The items were to reveal nothing that would help with identification: although they appeared at first glance to be distinctive, the lack of labels was frustrating. But, because they and the ring were indicative of a woman of limited financial means, the police now turned their attentions to the travelling community. PC Arthur J. Pound rather belatedly recalled that, sometime in December 1942, he

Initial Investigation

had encountered a Gipsy encampment in the Nimmings Field. He remembered that there was one horse-drawn caravan about 15 yards from the entrance; and that 10 yards further away and higher up the field were two canvas tents or bivouacs. Previous papers were traced and – within a memo – [22] PC Benbow of Severn Stoke had recorded both the presence of a travelling family (the Smiths),[23] and that the local farmer had confirmed that he had granted them permission to camp. The same memo recorded that some clothes and other belongings had been found nearby, and only some 115 yards from the tree that was the body's resting place. It listed the items found, which included shoes and a knife. The routines that the family followed now allowed them to be traced, living in a caravan between Kempsey and Upton upon Severn, working for a farmer called Sanders. Family members were interviewed and Arkus Smith (aka Butler) advised that he had at one time owned a knife fitting the description given. This had been used for tapping roots, and Smith had volunteered that he could identify it if required. Similarly, the clothing was found to have once belonged to the same family. The police determined from this that there was no connection to the Hagley Wood body, although the rationale for this conclusion is not clear.

The police now turned to records of other unusual activity in the area dating to the time of death parameters as indicated by Professor Webster. There was one that stood out: in July 1941, an employee from a local industrial company had been returning home to his lodgings in Hagley Green when he reported hearing a woman's screams coming from the direction of Hagley Wood. Very soon after, he met a schoolteacher walking in the opposite direction who confirmed that he, too, had heard the screams. They decided to phone the police who duly arrived and, with the assistance of the two men, searched the wood. Although they found nothing, the search had confirmed the presence of Gipsies within the wood. Some sources have suggested that the pub almost opposite the wood – the Gipsy's Tent – was so named because of the large number of

---

[22] Dated April 1943, and part of the initial police investigation.
[23] It transpired that the family name was actually Butler, but they chose to be known as Smith, which was the maiden name of one of their number. This is one of many illustrations of the close-knit nature of the travelling families, which often inter-married and used names fairly indiscriminately.

Events and Their Reporting (Chronology)

Travellers within the wood at the time, but this was not the case. The name was not unique amongst pubs across the Midlands, and this particular establishment had borne it from the 19th century. Although the police would frequently be told that there had been no other Gipsy families using the woods, this was not the reality and, mirroring the distrust that many felt at the time, the public were now quick to point the finger. Suggestions were made that the victim may have been ostracised by her community, and the ultimate penalty imposed. Interestingly, police records identified that they had been called out to another dispute involving Gipsy families nearby in 1941; the officer concerned, however, had described this incident as having been of a fairly trivial nature.

The view that the victim was probably of limited financial means also led the police to pursue the theory that she may have been a prostitute – "a pick-up for lorry drivers on this busy [Kidderminster–Birmingham] road", as *Tit-Bits* magazine delicately put it. The same magazine also recorded that "a check-up was made on all the women known to be friendly with truck-drivers". That this could hold the key to solving the case increasingly became the view of a number of police officers on the case, but no prostitutes were identified at this point as being missing from their usual patches.[24] Some commentators have claimed that this possibility was ruled out because the victim was too old to fit the profile of a prostitute, but this does not fit with research into the characteristics of prostitution – particularly during wartime – nor with evidence within police files.

Another theory put forward – that the woman was murdered when a lover discovered she was pregnant – was quickly dismissed, because the inquest had heard that, although there was evidence to suggest that she had been pregnant at some time in the past, the woman had not been with child at the time of her death. Of course, this did not rule out a man killing her in the mistaken belief that she was pregnant. But, as more and more people came forward to report previous sightings of Travellers in the woods, the police began to look more closely at that angle.

---

[24] Although this was felt to be the case at the time, some retrospective claims to the contrary would be made.

Initial Investigation

As identified within Chapter 1, the victim's shoes did not fit in with the perception that the woman was of limited means. The police spent a lot of time investigating this angle, and established that the type retailed at 13s 11d – a sum equivalent to around £40 at 2020 prices, and about which DI Williams later said: "this was a fair price to pay for a shoe at that time". The indication that they had been subjected to six months' hard wear was viewed as potentially significant, too.

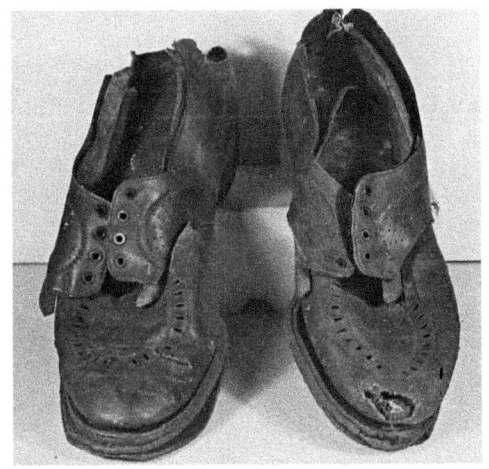

The crepe-soled shoes found with the victim. Confusion as to their colour runs through this case.
(West Mercia Police)

Through thorough research and numerous visits to Lancashire, the police were able to determine that the shoe model in question had first been produced in April 1940,[25] by Maden & Ireland, in Rossendale. It had been manufactured for wholesalers Clarence Bray of Sileby, Leicestershire. W. M. Wilford of Leicester had taken 6,000 pairs and added the reference number; they in turn supplied to just four outlets. Whilst some of these had placed large orders, only 132 pairs were of size 5½. Within this element of the investigation, DI Williams interviewed Leonard Pass, a boot repairer based in Wednesbury. He had regular dealings with Messrs Allen, a nearby shoe retailer, and ran a credit scheme for purchasers who could not afford the full cost of shoes. He had kept details of all credit sales and repairs undertaken over the previous five years, and Williams – together with DC Sutherland – examined over a thousand of his invoices. These identified four pairs of blue Gibsons. Whilst none was of size 5½, Pass confirmed that each of the purchasers of these four pairs was known by him to be still alive.

---

[25] Records of police enquiries identify both April and July as being the earliest likely date of manufacture. Given that they also show a consignment being despatched in May 1940, it is assumed that April is likely to be the correct time.

Events and Their Reporting (Chronology)

Hagley Wood, as seen from Wychbury Hill (2018).

It was reported that, in total, the police managed to account for all but six pairs of this shoe – and these had apparently each been sold to unknown customers from a Dudley market stall. Slightly conflicting reports had it that all the shoes were traced except for four further pairs sold on Wednesbury Market, and another source claimed that one pair had been bought by a housewife who had exchanged them with a passing Gipsy for a cup and saucer.[26]

The only name that came to light as a result of the shoe line of enquiry was that of Ethel Prosser. Her photo appears in police files, along with an official memo of 5 May 1943. From this it would seem most likely that she was identified as a purchaser of the crepe-soled shoes in question. The memo is cross-referenced to a further document, which unfortunately is missing from records. No

---

[26] We have been unable to find this account within police records or contemporary reports. The version is, however, recounted by Donald McCormick in his book *Murder by Witchcraft* – see later.

other photographs of women identified from this part of the inquiry have been retained on police files, and it may be inferred that, at some point, Ethel Prosser was considered to be a "possible" for the murder victim.

A trawl of contemporary newspaper archives does not provide any clues to Ethel Prosser, either in terms of criminal activity or even as the victim of domestic violence. But, given that the police were following other leads more than ten years later, it is unlikely that there was any enduring belief that she was involved. Her picture (opposite page) is taken from the police file (courtesy West Mercia Police).

Missing persons enquiries

The police would subsequently claim that, by the end of 1945, some 3,000 missing person enquiries had been followed up. It would also be reported that this figure included all those who had lived within 1,000 square miles of Hagley Wood. Unfortunately, few of the results of these enquiries have survived, and the names of those successfully traced are largely unknown.

One of the few documents that may shed some light on this exercise is that which appears at Appendix C. This is a list of persons who had been reported missing to the Birmingham Police force, covering the period May 1940 to August 1941. It is not known whether this is a complete list (the indications are that it was probably an extract), nor whether all the names were fully investigated; however, it is assumed that such lists must have formed the basis of investigation work. There is one name on this list which attracted a significant level of police attention and resource: Dinah Curley (aka Dinah O'Grady). Following a particularly heavy bombing raid on Birmingham in May 1941, the Birmingham Citizens' Society received an enquiry from a resident of Manchester, concerned about the whereabouts of this woman, believed to have been living in the Birmingham area. Such enquiries were fairly routine, with worried relatives learning of bombing raids and, not having heard from their loved ones, seeking confirmation that they were still alive. Although protocols were not set in stone, in most cases where the subject of an enquiry could not be quickly traced, details would be passed on to the relevant police force. In this instance, the concern had been raised by a woman calling herself Mrs M. Lavin.[27] For reasons not fully apparent from their files, the fate of Ms Curley was considered serious enough to warrant police investigations which would last over a year and which would also involve a number of other forces. Despite the lack of anything to back this, the police case Closure Report[28] summed up the "evidence" as showing that Curley probably did not exist – and that a member of the Lavin family was trying to exploit the situation for personal gain (the basis of which is not explained). Contemporaneous police documents, however, strongly suggest that, for a time, there was a belief that Dinah Curley may have been the murder victim.

Other specific lines of enquiry which the police are known to have followed at this time are listed below.

ANN FORREST
One of the most promising early leads in this area resulted – not for the only time – from an overheard pub conversation. In this case, the pub in question was the Cross Keys, at West Hagley, and the informant a Mrs Hannah Bolton – a domestic worker of 36 years of age, who was employed in the same village. She had passed on what she had heard, on the evening of 10 April 1944, to a civilian police clerk (a Mr F. St C. Stanley). Enquiries identified the originator as being Mrs Dorothy Lewis, of Hayley Green near Halesowen, who had stated that the dead woman matched the description of a Gipsy[29] who had once camped on farm land with a man that she (Mrs Lewis) took to be her husband, and two children. The relationship between the two adults was allegedly extremely volatile, with violence frequently involved: on more than one occasion, the woman was seen fleeing the tent with blood oozing from a throat wound.

It transpired that Mrs Lewis had formed the view that this could have been the murdered woman. Although West Hagley is a short distance from the deposition site, it was only when Mrs Lewis

---

[27] Incorrectly spelt "Levin" in some accounts.
[28] See Appendix B.
[29] In official documents, the family were described as "showmen".

Initial Investigation

subsequently saw a similar tent pitched in a field next to Hagley Wood (opposite the Gipsy's Tent pub) that she formed the view that there could be a connection with the murder. When questioned by the police, however, she became less sure of her facts and the owner of the field was initially adamant that nobody had camped on the site at the time in question. This view was apparently supported by members of the Home Guard who had regularly patrolled the area. Further police investigation identified that 53-year-old farmer Percy Cutler had originally hosted the Gipsy family at Spout Farm in West Hagley, and that Mrs Lewis had been a fellow tenant. Cutler advised that Mrs Lewis had complained to him at the time about the couple's arguments, and that the screaming had scared her; Cutler had evicted the family because of the upset they were causing his other tenants. He described the man as being "about 40", 5' 8"–5' 9" in height, and with light hair. The woman was "about 35 to 40 years" old, 5' 5" with light brown hair. Significantly (and presumably with police prompting), Cutler also described a "nice set of even teeth" and recalled that she had worn "a thick prominent ring with stone setting".

Diligent police work allowed Sgt Skerratt to establish that a constable had been called to one of the incidents reported by Mrs Lewis, and track down both the officer and his pocket book. An entry in this, dated 6 July 1941, showed that the person in question was identified as Forrest Swaley. It would transpire that the name was actually Swaley Forrest, although further checks revealed that the individual registered as such was only eight years old! More delving revealed that there had been a number of lost identity cards within the family and that, after these had been reissued, there had been some interchanging. The underlying purpose was probably for reasons connected to by-passing food rationing controls, but there is little doubt that the man interviewed over the incident had been James Forrest. His wife was Ann Forrest, and their children Mary Ann and Hamilton.[30] Whilst the couple had subsequently separated, Ann Forrest was contacted and confirmed that she had had frequent quarrels with her husband whilst living in the tent,

---

[30] Swaley was probably a nephew of James Forrest.

and that on at least one occasion she had run out of the tent whilst only partially dressed, to escape her husband's rage.

Mary Wenman / Lee[31] / Beaver[32]

Another prominent line of enquiry in relation to the Gipsy or travelling community was the reported disappearance of Mary Wenman. And it may be that the actions of Private William Fletcher suggested to the police that he could have been involved in – or knew more about – the murder. Fletcher was seemingly one of three people to have raised concerns about the whereabouts of Mary Wenman, in light of reading about the Hagley Wood victim in a newspaper. The second was his army chaplain (on Fletcher's behalf), whilst the third was another soldier, Private Haywood. By apparent coincidence, Haywood had served in the same battalion as Fletcher, although the police soon smelled a rat and, after making use of their forensic investigation unit, were able to confirm that the letter purporting to come from Haywood had been written (or at least dictated) by Fletcher in January 1942. Haywood would later confirm that he had had no knowledge of the letter, and Fletcher admitted that he was bored and wanted to rekindle a previous relationship. This was his alleged reason for telling the police that he was concerned about Wenman's mental health, and saying that she was at risk of suicide. It further seems that Fletcher had fathered a child of Mary Wenman; he was later to tell police: "before I joined the army, I thought Mary Lee was pregnant". His friend, Nalie "Titch" Smith, said that he knew that Fletcher was "probably" the father of Mary Wenman's child.[33]

---

[31] To add to the confusion, the family often spelt the name as "Lea", and this is reflected in some police documents.

[32] For avoidance of further confusion, she is referred to as Mary Wenman throughout the rest of this narrative. A police memo of 14 May 1943 states "Mary Lee's correct name is definitely Mary WENMAN."

[33] It does appear that it was soon after having Fletcher's child that Mary married Henry Beaver.

Initial Investigation

Two of the three letters in question: that purporting to be from Haywood (left), and an extract from Fletcher's own correspondence. (West Mercia Police)

Police enquiries led to the Star Inn at Halesowen, where Fletcher and Wenman used to meet,[34] but were hampered by Fletcher's insistence that Mary's surname was Lee or Lea, which the woman had only rarely used herself. One of the travelling community which used the Star Inn as a "base", a woman by the name of Ellen Drummond,[35] advised that Charles Henry Lee had a married daughter who had not been seen since around summer 1941. She could not recall her name but stated that she was about 5' 3" in height and around 25 years of age. From such a description, this could have been Mary Wenman.

The fact that there are 113 related documents in police files demonstrates just how seriously this line of enquiry was taken, but Wenman was eliminated from enquiries after Traveller sources confirmed that she had been seen alive in the autumn of 1942

---

[34] The Star Inn (sometimes shown as the Star Hotel) was a regular haunt of a number of Traveller families, and this was not the only time that it would feature in police enquiries. Located in Halesowen's Bull Ring, it was long ago demolished.
[35] Daughter of Frances Dickson, married to David Drummond.

(during both the pea- and hop-picking seasons). Notwithstanding, a later police memo[36] recorded that, "although there was good evidence that she was seen alive and well at Pudge's Farm, Bishops [sic] Frome, some 12 months after the discovery of the skeleton", she had "never been specifically interviewed".

One of the other locations that featured prominently within this line of enquiry was Illey, to the south-east of Halesowen. Many seasonal workers would camp at Illey House Farm during the fruit- and pea-picking seasons. Police documents refer to this as being host to a permanent Gipsy encampment, which closed around 1940. Intriguingly, in view of the number of times that this surname crops up in the saga, the owner was an Alfred James. The same police memo confirms that, in 1939, members of the Lee family were staying here, although nobody could recall a Mary Lee / Wenman being amongst them. Fletcher himself, however, would later confirm that he would regularly escort Mary home from the Star Hotel "to Illey Lane".[37]

Illey House Farm, Lower Illey, pictured in 2009. (CC-BY-SA/2.0 - © Roy Hughes - geograph.org.uk/p/1213241)

---

[36] Written by DI Tommy Williams, 05/10/1945.

[37] Illey House Farm is in Illey Lane, and was about a mile and a half from the Star. It is likely that, at this time, Mary was using the name Wenman.

Initial Investigation

Much later, a researcher and prominent writer on the case – Joyce Coley – would report that, following the discovery of the body in the tree, rumours that it belonged to one of Mary Lee's party were rife – particularly in the Hasbury area. Some of these rumours hinted at a dispute over "pitches" between related groups. With the closure of the Illey Farm site, the pressure to find new and suitable sites would most certainly have increased.

VIOLET GOODE
On 3 April 1944, DC Venables, attached to Old Hill station in Staffordshire, received information from a special constable that a bus driver had overheard a conversation in which a man claimed to know who had committed the murder. This exchange had taken place during the lunch hour of Thursday, 30 March 1944, and involved a man who identified the killer as an associate living within the town. Remarkably, the discussion had also taken place in Halesowen's Star Inn. The alleged killer had reportedly fallen out with his wife, owing to his association with a Birmingham woman. This was about two years before the body was found, and the man had then left the district and not returned.

The police were able to trace the bus driver, John Bache, who was able to give a good description of the man who had been doing the talking. He was in turn identified as 49-year-old marine store dealer, Edward Hall. Hall reiterated the story that Bache had heard, although now changed the timing of events. According to him, Harry Truman had been in a fairly unhappy marriage to May Gladys Taylor, the sister of a Halesowen JP. Truman was allegedly a poor husband, keeping his wife short of money whilst freely spending on himself and a succession of other women. It seems that one of these other women may have become pregnant by Truman, and that his wife confronted her and demanded that she stopped seeing him. This had no effect, so Mrs Truman left the family home, taking their two daughters and obtaining a separation order. This was in June 1935. Subsequently, Truman left his mistress and returned to his wife. Hall did not know the name of the mistress, but clearly held the view that hers may have been the

Events and Their Reporting (Chronology)

body in the tree, killed so that Truman could get back together with his wife.

DC Lee, who took the statement, was clearly not impressed with Hall, commenting that: "he is not a man in whom a great deal of reliance can be placed." Nevertheless, some further investigation work was undertaken which confirmed that the Trumans had become reconciled in 1938. These timings therefore mitigated against the "other woman" being the victim. She was subsequently identified as Violet Goode – alive, well and living in Stourbridge.

CHAPTER 3

The Writing on The Walls

In the absence of any clear progress, some new developments now significantly shifted the focus of the police investigation. The catalyst was the appearance of the first of what would become popularly known as the "wall messages", which were to turn the case into a cause célèbre.

On 28 March 1944, police were notified of graffiti that had appeared on a wall in the fruit market area of Birmingham. This was in Upper Dean Street, near the junction with Pershore Street, on empty premises next to Messrs Williamson,[38] and close to Messrs Francis Nicholls Ltd. Memos suggest that this was initially spotted by a Mr White of Stourbridge, who in turn alerted DC Kedward. The writing, in 3-inch-high letters, read: "WHO PUT BELLA DOWN THE WYCH ELM – HAGLEY WOOD". An article in the Birmingham *Evening Despatch* of 30 March 1944, under the headline: "Hagley Wood Bella – new mystery chalk mark appears", brought this firmly into the public domain, and reported that "this was the first time any name had been given to the woman." But, even as the *Despatch* was going to press, a similar message – "HAGLEY WOOD BELLA" – appeared in the vicinity. This was outside the wholesale premises of Messrs White (and there may have been a connection here to the aforementioned Mr White). The Birmingham police, aware of the possible significance of the first message, alerted their counterparts in Worcestershire, and an investigation was set in motion. This was quite thorough in parts, and included the compilation of a list of all customers who had called into Williamsons' premises overnight (as per Appendix E). Each was subsequently interviewed. A vigil was also undertaken in case the scribe returned, although surviving records suggest that this lasted only some 30 minutes. As a result of enquiries, a young warehouseman by the name

---

[38] Williamsons was located at 19 Upper Dean Street.

of George Bond confessed to having written the words. He subsequently withdrew his confession and, after taking handwriting samples and diagnosing that he was only semi-literate, the police concluded that he was not a viable person of interest.

The first Birmingham fruit market message (left), and what is believed to be the second – although not identified as such within police files. (West Mercia Police)

Whilst they were still looking into this, however, the police were approached by a local man, James Rowley, who claimed that the first of these messages, reproduced in the *Birmingham Daily Gazette*, was very similar to one: "WHO PUT LUBELLA IN THE WYCH ELM", that he had seen on a cottage wall at Haden Hill, Old Hill (just to the north of Halesowen), towards the end of the previous summer. Probably because of his youth (he was just 20), it would seem that the police treated his claim with some caution at first, possibly believing that Rowley may have been jumping on the bandwagon to achieve a bit of fleeting fame amongst his peers. Nevertheless, leads were still in short supply, and DI Williams himself visited the site and found that the writing was still there. He duly examined and photographed it. By coincidence, he ran into an acquaintance there, schoolteacher John Cox. Cox – a more reliable witness in the eyes of the police – confirmed to Williams that he had also been aware that the message had been there for a significant length of time.[39] Williams formed a theory that the writer could have been an

---

[39] It is interesting to note that there are some differences between Cox's written statement and Williams' report of their meeting. Williams describes Cox as a headmaster, whilst Cox states his role as that of schoolteacher. And Williams reports that Cox was aware of the message being there only prior to Christmas, whilst his own statements show this as being since "late summer".

employee of the firm Gaskell & Chambers,[40] which had recently moved from Dale End (Birmingham city centre) to Hayseech (to the north of Halesowen and just a quarter of a mile from the message seen by Rowley and Cox).[41]

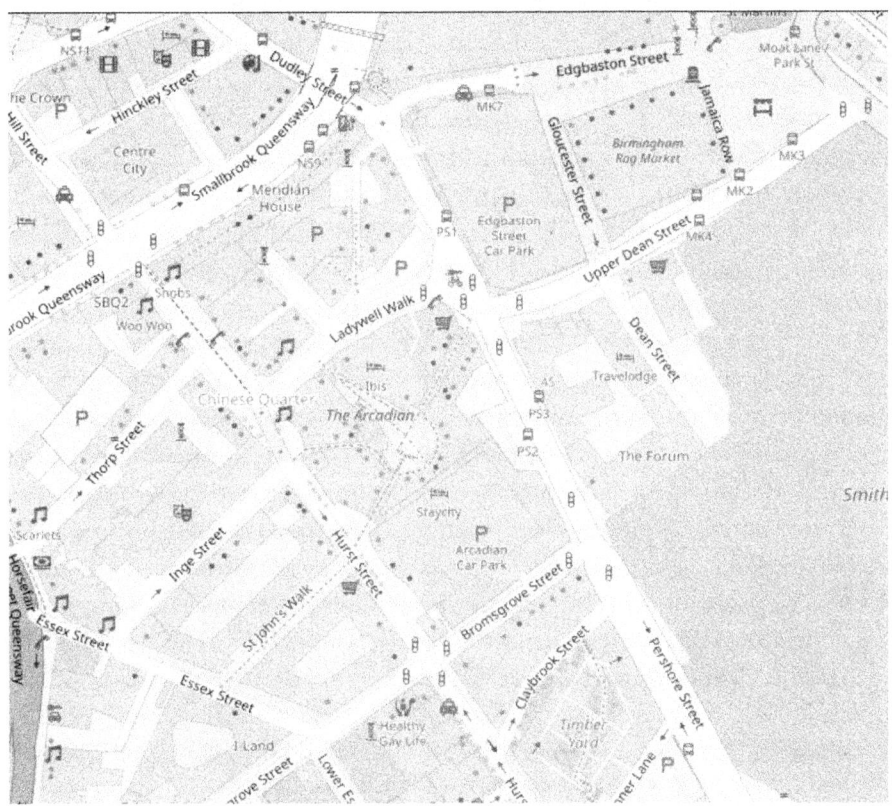

The fruit market area of Birmingham. The first wall message that came to light was in Upper Dean Street. (openstreetmap.org/copyright)

The *Sunday Pictorial* of 2 April 1944 claimed that: "It is believed that whoever wrote the first [i.e. Haden Hill] message[s], disappointed

---

[40] A firm which historically made fittings and equipment for pubs, but which had diversified in 1939 to produce armaments, mine detectors and other devices required by the War Office.

[41] This seems a little counter-intuitive, given that the Birmingham graffiti clearly seems to have been written some considerable time later.

because the clue had not been seized, went into Birmingham and repeated it, altering the spelling of the name to *Bella*." Just why the name was shortened to Bella was not explained, but the police papers suggest another belief that the originator may have been involved in farming – based on the proximity to the fruit market and the fact that the writing was probably undertaken in the small hours, when only traders in farm produce would have a bona fide reason to be in the vicinity. Rather more obviously, they also concluded that the work was probably that of an adult, as some of the messages were too high up the wall for a child to have been responsible. At this point, DI Williams sent photographs of these three messages to the forensic science laboratory at Cardiff, for analysis. Director, Dr Wilson Harrison replied, expressing his view that they were probably all written by the same hand.

The list of customers who had called in at Williamsons on 27 March ran to 14 names, and one immediately stood out because of the concurrent investigation of wall messages at Old Hill. This was a Mr H. Edmonds, who lived at Halesowen Road, Old Hill. Investigation identified this to be Horace Henry Edmonds, born in 1898. When interviewed subsequently, Edmonds claimed that he had not seen the (fruit market) message until someone drew his attention to it. There is little other mention of him within police files, except for a manuscript note by DI Williams which states: "Telephoned DC Venables Old Hill who knew Edmonds and was quite satisfied that he knows nothing of this matter."

Another lead was provided by the *Birmingham Daily Gazette*, which tipped off the police that a man named Jones had visited their offices on 25 March 1944 and asked to see their files on the Hagley Wood murder. There was no shortage of men named Jones living in the Birmingham area but Williams, clinging to his belief that the culprit may have worked for Gaskell & Chambers, asked Halesowen's Insp Bache to instruct DC Lee (already familiar with the case) to identify anyone of that name there. This drew a blank, but other enquiries led by Sgt Renshaw of the Birmingham force managed to track down the individual in question to 106 Reservoir Road, Erdington. His full name was John H. Jones, and he freely agreed that he had been the newspaper office visitor. On 5 April, DI Williams, along with Sgt Renshaw, visited Jones at his home. He turned out to be 20 years of age, employed as an electrician at the BSA in Small Heath, and a member of the local Home Guard. Williams was clearly not impressed by the young man, whom he described as "a peculiar youth". It transpired that Jones had been discussing a number of unsolved murders in the local pub, and had developed his own theory about what may have happened in this case. Despite Williams' view that he was of limited intelligence, Jones clearly thought that he was better placed to solve the case than the police – although his ideas seemed to have been based largely on an article that he had read in a journal called *Armchair Science*. He claimed that the reason for his visit to the *Birmingham Daily Gazette* offices was to determine whether the police had overlooked any leads.

The most alarming part of Jones's story, however, was that in August 1942, on returning from Clent Youth Hostel where he had been staying with his sister, he had passed Hagley Wood, where he claimed to have experienced a feeling that "something terrible was going to happen". Williams had initially viewed Jones as a possible candidate for having written the chalked messages, as the first of those in Birmingham had coincided with his visit to the newspaper office. Samples of Jones's handwriting, allied to his inability to spell, however, dispelled this notion and Williams soon concluded that the youth could not have had any involvement in the writing – or the crime.[42]

With the wall messages now firmly in the public consciousness, further daubings would appear in the region with some regularity, although their authenticity has to be called into question. Without doubt, the police were right to disregard a number as the work of mischief-makers, fantasists, bored teenagers and the mentally unhinged. One such message was found at Mucklow Hill, in the north-east of Halesowen. On a wall adjoining Messrs Walter Somers' premises, and opposite the Laminated Springs works, this read: "WHO PUT BELLA IN THE WITCH ELM HAGLEY WOOD JACK THE RIPPER? / JACK THE RIPPER / ANA BELLA DIED IN HAGLEY WOOD?", and was initially examined by DC Lee on 12 April. He determined that the likelihood was that the message had been written sometime between 10

---

[42] The handwriting sample was also forwarded to Dr Harrison of the forensic science laboratory, who shared Williams' view.

a.m. and 4 p.m. that day. DI Williams later pronounced that he was satisfied that the writing was quite different from that seen at Old Hill and Birmingham, concluding that workers on a lunchbreak had been responsible.

Police concluded that this message was not connected to the others – although the reference to Jack the Ripper is an interesting one. This message was not photographed, and this is DC Lee's handwritten note of its contents. (West Mercia Police)

The next three messages however – two of them in the Belle Vale area of Halesowen – were deemed by Williams to be by the same hand as the Old Hill and fruit market daubings[43] – and two potentially provided a huge clue.

Sun Street pub, pictured in 2014. The old Sun Passage, to the right of the pub, still remains despite recent large-scale redevelopment of the area.
(CC-BY-SA/2.0 - © Gordon Griffiths - geograph.org.uk/p/3903567)

---

[43] It does seem that Williams also submitted these to the forensic science laboratory for analysis, although their findings are unknown.

The Writing on The Walls

It was on 1 August 1944 that 24-year-old Stanley Arthur Ray reported a chalked message underneath a railway arch (Sun Passage)[44] at Heath Town, near Wolverhampton. He later provided the following statement to police:

> I am 24 years of age, a civil servant, Chemist employed at Mander Bros. by Ministry of Supply. My home address is 133, Stanley Fields Road, Selly Oak, Birmingham 29.
>
> At about 12.30 p.m. on Tuesday, August 1st 1944, I was walking along Sun Passage, right under the archway, from Heath Town towards the Railway Station, when I noticed on the left-hand wall of the archway some works [sic] written in chalk.
>
> After an examination I found them to read "Hagley Wood, Lubella, address was opposite Rose & Crown, Hasbury."
>
> Being a native of Birmingham and knowing of the Hagley murder, I thought this may be of some importance and reported the matter to the Police, same date.

The next day, DC Lee, during the course of his duties, discovered two more messages in Halesowen. One, chalked on a decaying five-bar gate in Shelton Lane, Belle Vale, opposite the Shelton Inn. It read:

ADDRESS WAS OPPOSITE ROSE AND CROWN HASBURY HAGLEY WOOD LUBELLA

One of the messages that appeared in Belle Vale at the start of August 1944. (West Mercia Police)

---

[44] Now Sun Street.

Events and Their Reporting (Chronology)

Also in Shelton Lane, on a nearby wall were the following words:

HAGLEY WOOD LUBELLA WAS NO PROSS

although, in one police document this is wrongly transcribed as reading: "I USE TO HAGLEY WOOD LUBELLA WAS PROSS". Having spoken to other civilians in the area, the police determined that at least one of these messages had been there for no less than two weeks, and that the poor lighting in Sun Passage had prevented it from being more widely noticed.

The police responded by visiting Hasbury, and interviewing the families living at those houses with even numbers between 394 and 410 Hagley Road (inclusive). According to their initial interpretation, only these could meet the criterion of being "opposite the Rose & Crown" public house. The task was entrusted to PC Albert Pitcher, who visited all the occupants on 2 August. His notes record that he was satisfied that all who had lived or stayed at these addresses over the past five years could be accounted for, with one exception. This was a lady with the surname James, recorded as being a distant relative of the inhabitants of No. 404 (the Allsops),[45] and with whom she sometimes stayed. The Allsops had not seen her for four years, and the fact that her forename was Bella initially caused great excitement.[46]

Shelton Lane, Belle Vale – as it is today. (2021, CC-BY-SA/2.0 - © Ian S – geograph.org.uk/p/7058557)

---

[45] Although spelt "Allsopp" within a number of police documents, census records show this to be the correct spelling of the family name.

[46] The James family lived next door at 406. Whilst this might suggest confusion on the part of the police, the close-knit nature of such communities at this time meant that family connections were plentiful.

The (now rebuilt) row of houses opposite the Rose & Crown. That on the far left (top photo) is No. 400; lower numbers are at the far end of this shot. Number 404 Hagley Road (door in the centre of bottom photo), stands on the corner with No. 400. Photos from 2018.

The next day, a senior team comprising DI Williams, Insp Bache and DC Lee followed up with a visit of their own. Williams' report[47] shows that they spoke to Mrs Allsop, and confirmed that Bella James would have been aged between 60 and 70; later enquiries found her to be alive and living at Kidderminster. Suggesting that PC Pitcher's remit may not have been sufficiently wide, Williams' party next visited a timber yard directly opposite the Rose & Crown. This was J. T. Willetts & Son, a father and son business. Williams' report does not identify the specific individuals he spoke with, although it would seem likely that the main contacts would have been Walter Willetts (listed as director of the timber yard) and his son, (Arthur) Ernest, living at Nos 392 and 390 Hagley

---

[47] Police findings from these two visits are summarised at Appendix F.

Events and Their Reporting (Chronology)

Road respectively. Williams' report is most interesting, and includes the following:

> I have known the Willetts family for a long time and they have both promised to pass to the police an[y] conversation which they may hear having any bearing upon this case and have also promised to get in touch with us should they get any information about the person who may be chalking these messages about the district ... Mr Willetts agreed that the person who put the body in this particular tree must have had a good knowledge of the Wood or else was extremely fortunate in the fact that at the time when this offence was committed he was very near to this hollow hole of the tree and was able to find ready at hand a means of disposing of the body. He in fact adheres to the view that the woman was taken to the Wood and that some person attempted to have intercourse with her against her will and that her death occurred as the result of some violence being used and he says it is not a local woman.

No members of the Willetts family interviewed could recall anyone by the name of Lubella, or anyone else remotely resembling the description of the dead woman; nor could they offer any insight as to who may have been responsible for chalking the messages in the locality.[48]

The Rose & Crown, Hasbury, pictured in 2018.

---

[48] It is also worth recording that Walter Willetts' father, John, was one-time landlord of the Rose & Crown. It really was a very tight-knit community!

Another similar chalked message in the vicinity some three months later gave an even more specific clue. Appearing in Station Road, Old Hill, Oldbury, on a wall extending from the railway bridge to the entrance of timber merchants Messrs W. H. (William Henry) Palmer & Co., it read:

HAGLEY WOOD LUBELLA
ADDRESS WAS 404 LOWER HASBURY
HALESOWEN

The message at Oldbury which seems to offer a firm clue. (West Mercia Police)

This was first noticed by PC Laycock on 2 November, and his subsequent enquiries would reveal that, in all probability, it had appeared between 29 and 30 October 1944. But, walking up Station Road towards Gorsty Hill, Laycock, discovered "similar chalk marks on a wall opposite the mouth [*sic*] of Coombe Hill" (just off Station Road). These read:

404 LOWER HASBURY
HAGLEY WOOD LUBELLA
ADDRESS WAS

The message (alone amongst the daubings to this date) had been written with black lettering. Laycock was unable to ascertain when this had first appeared, but it was generally assumed that it had been written around the same time.

There is (and was) no such property as 404 Lower Hasbury, but the police were fully aware that the addresses of Hasbury houses on the Hagley Road were commonly referred to as such – and, indeed, even appeared as Lower Hasbury within census records. Number 404 was, of course, where the Allsops lived. On their first two visits, the police had only recorded that Mr and Mrs Samuel Allsop were resident here, and Samuel had been reluctant to disclose details of a further relative. In the light of this new development, DC John Lee was sent back to make further enquiries, and identified that the couple had had a daughter, who had died short of her second birthday. More significantly, he reported that they also had a son, named after his father. Whilst Samuel junior was serving in the RAF and based at Newmarket in Suffolk, he was in the habit of regularly returning to the family home when on leave. It does appear that the police now briefly considered Samuel Allsop junior as a potential suspect, and spoke to his previous employers. They described him as shy, but well-mannered and inoffensive. DC Lee concluded: "I have been able to ascertain nothing of a doubtful character in the history of either this young man's parents or in the history of the young man himself."

Other leads

Police next undertook analysis of the chalk used on each of the early messages, and thought that they had made a breakthrough when confirmation was provided that it was all of similar origin, manufactured by the same firm. However, it transpired that the firm in question had a virtual monopoly in supplying it to pubs throughout the country, for use by darts players.

In early November 1944, the police received a letter from a man signing himself "Mr Wood", who claimed to be the writer of the central Birmingham wall messages. The letter had been dated 31 October, but the postmark showed the following day (time 4 p.m.). "Mr Wood" offered to meet the Chief Constable at "Market St of [sic] Collshill St [sic]"[49] at 5.30 p.m. on 1 November. It is a moot point whether the letter writer had meant to post it the previous day, but clearly the police had no opportunity to meet that deadline. Subsequent investigations identified that the letter had been posted in the Head Post Office District, which stretched from King's Norton to Aston (a linear distance of some 8 miles), and the police tried unsuccessfully to match the signature to local lodging house records. They also made similarly unproductive enquiries in Smithfield Market. Unfortunately, there was no further communication from the mysterious Mr Wood.

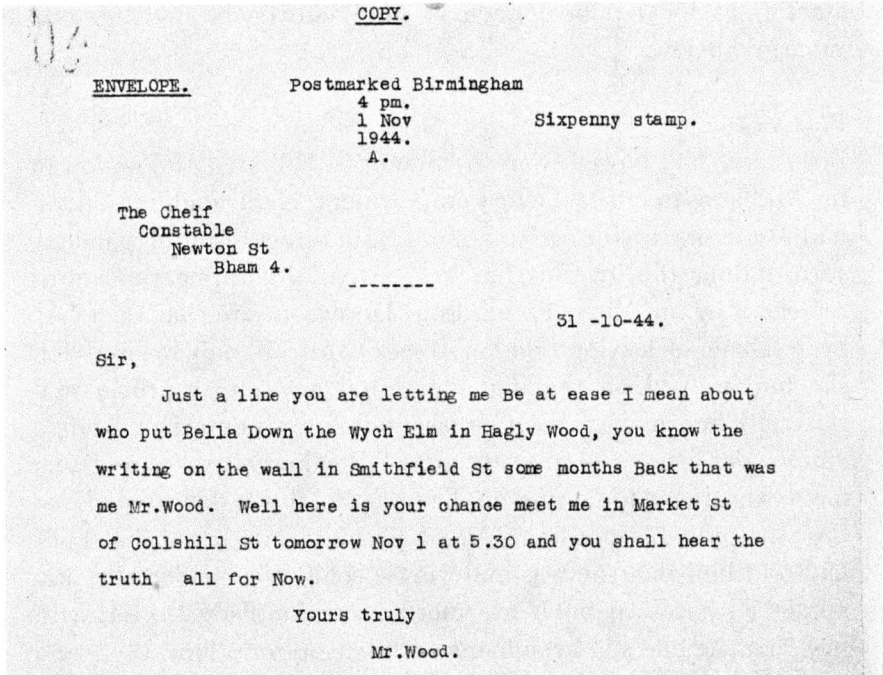

The police file transcript of "Mr Wood's" letter. This is far from the only document where, disappointingly, the original does not appear to have been retained. (West Mercia Police)

---

[49] Market Street ran from Coleshill Street to Hick's Square, between Doe Street and Howe Street. Along with a host of other roads in this part of Birmingham, it disappeared after the war, making way for redevelopment and the expansion of Aston University.

New missing person enquiries

In the light of these wall messages (which are summarised at Appendix D), the police received a number of fresh reports from members of the public concerning missing persons with a forename that could be construed – in any form – as Bella. Police reports also identify that electoral records were trawled for any woman named Bella or Isabella; and that Food Offices and "other places" were visited, with the same checks being undertaken.

Some of the names put forward were in direct response to an article within the *Sunday Pictorial*, which asked anyone with information to contact their local police. Each arising report was investigated, as summarised below.

BELLA LUER

Bella Luer had moved from the Stamford Hill area of London to the Midlands to pursue factory employment. Her friends in London had lost contact with her, and it was as a direct result of publicity surrounding the graffiti that her potential disappearance was reported, by an Alfred Richardson. He was aware that Luer had been talking of leaving London to seek work, but only realised that she had moved on reading a national newspaper article that reported her having been prosecuted for absenteeism from a gunpowder factory (on the outskirts of Reading). A woman of that name was traced to Goring-on-Thames, but it was determined that this was probably not her.[50] Alfred Richardson advised that Luer had told him that she was marrying a soldier (coincidentally, also named Richardson), but her former London landlady, Dora Harris, said that she had still been living with her up until June 1942, and that she had also received a Christmas card from Luer later that year. These dates seemed to preclude her from being the murder victim, and the police appear to have taken a similar view. Surprisingly, concerns as to Bella Luer's whereabouts were also raised by a factory manager (Mr I. J. Levaine) in the Punjab. Bella

---

[50] A *People* newspaper article of 9 May 1943 contains a reference to a Bella Luer, who was charged with absenteeism from her war work in a factory.

Luer was described by Dora Harris as then: "about 24 [making her date of birth c.1920], about 5' 4"–5", mid-brown hair which had been dyed from fair, slim build, a good set of teeth, her own not false". She was also described as being of Jewish stock.

BELLA TONKS
Bella Tonks had very little to connect her to the murder but for her forename, although it was claimed that she was fond of walking in the Clent Hills. She was tracked down to Staffordshire, where police reports state that she was living under her maiden name. Given that Tonks seems to have been her maiden name, this is surprising; however, a witness (Mrs Skinner) gave evidence that clearly placed Bella Tonks as being between 56 and 58 at the time of the murder, which anyway ruled her out of contention.

BELLA BEECH
The background of Bella Beech paints a sad picture of how war tore apart many families. Following the national publicity, a concerned family friend in London contacted the police. Some three years earlier, the friend had paid a visit to the Beech home and found that this, and most of the rest of the West Ealing street in which it formerly stood, had been destroyed by a bomb. Bella Beech's mother (Emily) had been killed and, whilst her father (Donald) survived, he would die soon after in an asylum (one can probably surmise as to what caused his mental deterioration). Following lengthy investigations, which also involved Ipswich County Borough Police, it was ascertained that Bella had gone to live with her twin brother in Birmingham. In one of the many coincidences which seem to characterise this case, his house was in the Dean Street area, very close to the fruit market. But Bella Beech was still very much alive.

BELLA LAWLEY
The single most promising lead in these new enquiries was a tip-off given to police by a Birmingham prostitute in April 1944. She advised that a fellow sex worker named Bella had gone missing

three years previously, after working on the Hagley Road. The informant was interviewed by police, and a detailed description obtained. This description was very much in keeping with what was known of the dead woman, and many at the time and since have felt that Bella Lawley could well have been the murder victim. Although it is strange that the informant had waited three years to divulge this information, she claimed that it was only the recent publicity that had made her aware of the case.

The police clearly believed that Bella Lawley was a credible candidate, and devoted a significant level of resource to finding her. But their investigation tracked her down (via her former Trafalgar Road landlady)[51] to her parents at 93 Gorsemoor Road, Heath Hayes (near Cannock), where she was living under her maiden name of Shemwell.

A suspect?

Most of the information that the police received or gathered to this point had been in relation to potential victims rather than suspects. But, within a few weeks of the new interest sparked by the discovery of the wall messages, the name of a suspect from outside the travelling community was put forward for the first time. The individual implicated was a railwayman, Arthur W. Edgington. In April 1944, the police had received two anonymous messages mentioning Edgington, although their subsequent enquiries identified him as an inoffensive individual with nothing to link him to the murder. His estranged wife suffered from mental illness, and the police concluded that these letters came either from her or a third party acting on her behalf. There is nothing to suggest that the writing in these letters had any similarity with that of the wall messages, although the police did record that there was some likeness to an original letter concerning the murder. It is clear that the police at no time felt Edgington to be a viable suspect.

---

[51] Yet another Mrs James, who recalled that she had received a Christmas card from Bella in 1942, but had heard nothing since.

The Writing on The Walls

One of the anonymous letters implicating Arthur Edgington. (West Mercia Police)

The strange behaviour of Victor Crumpton

The wall messages reached their peak in 1944, but then died down. It would not be another nine years that the *Birmingham Daily Gazette* was to run a story headlined: "Scrawl clue to 'Bella' is false". Chronologically, this followed very closely another revisiting of the case by the *Wolverhampton Express & Star*. This had in turn generated a letter to Sidney Inight, on 23 November 1953. Part of this read:

> Several years ago "Staffs County Police" Old Hill were put to much inconvenience with "chalking on a wall" at Belle Vale (Barrs Road end). PC B. Horrobin who after months of vigil whilst on night duty with various colleagues, himself caught the offender; there was no conviction – so no record. According to PC Horrobin's own graphic account to me, it was about 4 a.m. and his second visit this night to area; with no results. Suddenly footsteps were heard coming up road from Halesowen direction so the officer in his place of concealment commanded [a] good outline of [the] wall in darkness.

Events and Their Reporting (Chronology)

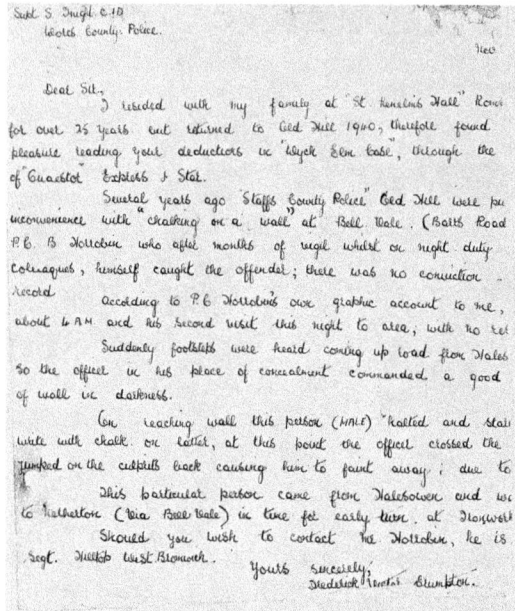

Victor Crumpton's letter to Sidney Inight. A transcript of its contents appears at Appendix G. (West Mercia Police)

The sender was Frederick Victor Crumpton, who was well known to police, although not for reasons of criminality. Born in 1909, in Old Hill (then part of the parish of Rowley Regis), he was the second child of Frederick and Laura Crumpton. In correspondence with Crumpton, Tommy Williams[52] challenges the number of different forenames that he uses. In reality, however, it is mostly Victor that he employed, presumably to avoid confusion with his father. Frederick Crumpton senior had founded the Old Hill grocery firm of Crumpton and Windsor, and for a time was a very successful businessman. As a result, the family were able to move to the splendid St Kenelm's Hall, Romsley (Halesowen)[53] in around 1913, when Victor was just four or five years old. By 1939, however, financial pressures meant that the Hall had to be sold on. Victor, now 30, was still living with his parents up until this time, but then returned to Old Hill. It is unclear whether this was alone, or with the rest of his family.

---

[52] By now promoted to the ranks of Detective Superintendent (Det Supt).
[53] This is close to Hagley Wood, with Hagley Wood Lane leading into St Kenelm's Pass.

The Writing on The Walls

Victor never seemed to hold down regular employment, and in the 1939 Register was shown as an assistant to his father. His younger brother, Rex, was a van driver for a time after leaving school, but in 1940, as a leading aircraftman, became a war hero when his exploits as a rear gunner earned him a Distinguished Flying Cross (DFC). Victor himself would appear to have served in the war, although it's not been possible to definitely corroborate this. Whilst at Old Hill, Crumpton was in the habit of accosting any constables that he encountered. He clearly suffered from mental health issues: in the unfortunate vernacular of the time, police described him as being "slightly mental". He was clearly aware of his own frailties and, in a police statement, claimed that he had suffered a serious wartime head injury (sustained during a "beach landing" training operation). He further claimed that he had been given electrical shock therapy by way of treatment, and that this had badly affected him in later life. Again, the lack of documentation or records prevents independent confirmation that this was the case. He subsequently entered into a chain of correspondence with the police, and the level of interest that they afforded him suggested that they considered his possible involvement in, or knowledge of, the crime. Using Professor Webster's timings, he would have been around 33 years of at the time of the Hagley Wood murder.

Halesowen (Belle Vale and Hawne) in 2007.
(CC-BY-SA/2.0 - © Darren Jackson - geograph.org.uk/p/482959)

Events and Their Reporting (Chronology)

Particularly disturbing was that, early in the morning of 7 December 1953, Stourbridge PC John A. Davies encountered Crumpton behaving in a very odd manner. Crumpton was happy to engage in conversation with him, and recounted that he had lost his wallet in Hagley Wood at 4 a.m., when looking for the tree which was at the centre of the case. He claimed that he had made the visit as a result of a wager, and further divulged that, in the excitement of the moment, he had lost control of his bowels. In his memo of the same day, PC Davies declared that he knew Crumpton and wrote that he "suffered from the mental complex of 'split mind'", adding that he was a one-time resident of Barnsley Hall Mental Hospital at Bromsgrove.

Crumpton's story does not end here however. The police files contain details of ongoing correspondence between him and Tommy Williams. These letters mainly date to after Crumpton had again been committed to an institution, and verge on the banal. They include Crumpton giving details of a football match he had played in and his efforts at poetry, as well as his hopes of marriage. More intriguingly, he provides details of "missing persons" who might have held the key to the "Bella" mystery. These seem to consist almost entirely of his former nurses that he had not seen for a time. Where one was concerned, he had even proposed marriage, but had seemingly been rebuffed.

CHAPTER 4

Witchcraft?

At the outset, the circumstances around the location of the body made it inevitable that speculation would thrive and wild theories circulate. One such was that witchcraft was involved. The police did consider this, but quickly ruled it out. Local newspapers were keener to pursue the angle, but with very little to go on.

All this would change, however, with a macabre but unconnected murder some 40 miles to the south, at Lower Quinton. It was here, on Valentine's Day (14 February) 1945 that the body of elderly farmworker Charles Walton was found, pinned to the ground with his own pitchfork. This had been driven through his neck, and his billhook had been used to carve a cross on his torso. There were some obvious reasons to believe that this may have been a ritual killing, and it did mirror a similar murder that had taken place in the same village 70 years previously. Some older residents suggested (on being prompted) that black magic was practised in the community, and the press – understandably – had a field day. Despite the local police force calling in the famed Insp Robert Fabian of Scotland Yard to investigate, the case was never solved. This is surprising in as much as there is strong evidence to suggest that Walton died at the hand of his employer, Alfred Potter. Walton was known to be a believer in witchcraft and to dabble in black magic; he also spoke freely about both the earlier murder, and the pagan symbolism of impaling a victim with their own pitchfork (the blood of the victim believed to make the soil into which it drained more fertile). He was openly in dispute with his employer over money and, if Potter was, indeed, his killer, this would also have been a rather neat way of trying to throw police off the scent. It has certainly been postulated that events were staged by Potter after the murder to make it look like an occult killing. It is interesting to note, too, that Insp Fabian reported that he found every door in the village closed against him; this rings true, but probably due to a natural suspicion of outsiders rather than a bid to suppress any genuine black magic involvement. In later newspaper interviews, local people displayed incredulity at the notion that witchcraft was being practised at this time (with the exception of that initiated by Walton himself).

All that connected the murder of Charles Walton and the body in the tree in Hagley Wood was (a slight) geographical proximity. That remained the case until the intervention of Professor Margaret Murray of University College, London. She was a foremost Egyptologist, and best known in that capacity, but was also an anthropologist and archaeologist, and a student of witchcraft. In relation to the latter, she had already had two books published (*Witch-Cult in Western Europe* in 1921, and *The God of the Witches* in 1933); and others of the same genre would follow. Citing both crimes as examples of ritual killings, Murray implied that, if there was not some crazed occult serial killer operating in the vicinity, they at least demonstrated that witchcraft was alive and flourishing in this part of the country. Specifically in respect of the Hagley Wood murder, she had the following to say:

> I believe the dead woman here was another victim of the devil-worshippers. Like Walton, her body was found in an isolated place. I also believe that many of these murders with peculiar twists are the result of the devil-worshippers.

Later, author Donald McCormick, in his book *Murder by Witchcraft*,[54] which went over much of the same ground, collated a number of Murray's articles from the local press and also augmented these with his own notes of an interview with the academic. These are insightful, with Murray confirming her view that the "severed" hand of the Hagley Wood victim was evidence of Hand of Glory practices. This is the belief of occultists that a hand taken from a dead body (but usually that of a murderer who has just been hanged) has magical properties. Possession of a Hand of Glory can supposedly reveal the location of buried treasure, undo locks and even put people to sleep. At the time, as a result of Murray's interviews, this became a popular theory in relation to "Bella".

---

[54] This book is considered further within Chapter 7.

Witchcraft?

Professor Murray in her younger days. (Wikimedia / Creative Commons licence)

In relation to the secreting of the body within the tree, Murray commented:

> ... the very act of placing a body in the hollow of a tree is associated with witchcraft. The cult of tree-worship is an ancient one and it is linked with sacrifices. The skeleton alone was left, so one cannot be sure whether the body was marked in any way. The wych elm is also significant in terms of witchcraft lore. Whoever committed this murder must have known about the hollow in the tree. The other curious fact about this case was that there were many other hollows where the body could have been more easily hidden.

At this time, the wall messages were still fresh in many minds, and Murray was not going to miss out on an opportunity. She went on to say:

> As for the chalk writings on walls in Midland towns, these may have been simply the work of a hoaxer or hoaxers. Indeed, they probably were. But Luebella, one of the names used, is a witch's name, and so for

that matter is Bella.⁵⁵ Coincidence perhaps, but strange all the same ... It is also a coincidence that the first of these chalk writings was found on a wall in Halesowen, a Midland town that has in the past produced some occult phenomena.

Police pursual of this line of enquiry was probably due to both a lack of alternative leads, and a wish to placate the public. As can be imagined, it also reopened a rich seam for both local and national newspapers. Anyone who had a view either way was invited to comment, and there was no shortage of interviewees putting themselves forward.

Operation Cone of Power

Later still would come claims that the murder could have been connected to *Operation Cone of Power*. This was the rather unlikely use of witchcraft to keep the Nazi threat from the shores of Britain. It was an event staged on various dates between May and August 1940, and supposedly involved covens from all over the south of England. Other historians refer to a specific event held on 1 August of that year, the eve of Lammas Day (a significant event in the pagan religion of Wicca). Then, a coven based at Highcliffe-on-Sea in Dorset instigated such a ceremony with the intention of "staging a magical assault on the mind of Adolf Hitler". These events were subsequently documented by one of the adherents to Wicca, Gerald Gardner, in a 1954 book entitled *Witchcraft Today*.⁵⁶ Gardner was an otherwise strait-laced man who, before his retirement, had been a civil servant. In his book he claimed that, not only had this group of 17 witches successfully staved off a German invasion, but that there were historical precedents, with both a 1588 Spanish invasion and an 1805 Napoleonic threat being repelled through the same means!

---

⁵⁵ Others have also linked the name Bella to witchcraft, but for the reason that the plant belladonna (deadly nightshade) is used within numerous spells. It is apparently a key ingredient for allowing broomsticks to fly! This does seem tenuous, at best.
⁵⁶ For which Margaret Murray penned the introduction!

CHAPTER 5

Some New Leads

Following the excitement of the discovery of the wall messages in 1944, and Professor Margaret Murray's pronouncements the following year, things went quiet for a time. But the media were keen to keep the case alive, and interest would be dramatically reignited in 1949.

Claims of a breakthrough

Particularly significant was the *Hull Daily Mail* running a story on 4 October that year which suggested a major breakthrough:

> The information given by a man recently is just one of the many pieces of information that have to be sifted ... Worcestershire CID do not expect any developments in the next few 2 or 3 days.

It seems that this story emanated from yet another pub conversation which hinted at the involvement of the travelling community, and which was notified to the police. This had taken place a few weeks earlier, at Halesowen's Lyttelton Arms.[57] The landlord denied all knowledge of any such exchange, but George King and William (Bill) Fletcher were identified by others as the instigators, and both, in due course, gave statements. The heated exchange had involved not only the two men but, additionally, Fletcher's brother-in-law – Eddie Shearwood – and some female friends.

The main thrust of what was discussed in the Lyttelton Arms was

---

[57] This is not the pub of that name which would later feature much more prominently in the case, but would appear to be the Lyttelton Hotel in Church Street, Halesowen – now known as Pick's. Even more confusingly, Fletcher, however, referred to this as the Old Lyttelton Arms in his statement. There was another pub of this name in the town, since demolished.

that, prior to being called up to the army for war service, Shearwood had been employed by a local slaughterhouse. In this capacity, he had been called out to collect a dead horse from a field adjacent to Hagley Wood. When he arrived, some young men from a nearby Gipsy encampment came to help him, returning to their camp when Shearwood was securing the horse prior to driving off. But, before he left, a violent fight broke out between the men, who attacked each other with cartwheel spokes and a crowbar. Shearwood noticed a woman who tried to break up the fight being knocked down, and not getting back to her feet. He had later related this incident to an army colleague who had recommended that he speak to the police – on the basis that the body found in the tree could have been that of the woman. Shearwood had not done so, claiming that he had subsequently forgotten the incident up until now.

DC Hancock, who took the statements, noted in his report that he knew Shearwood slightly, and that he considered him to be "the type of person who has to tell a better tale than the rest, when he is in a pub in conversation". William Fletcher's statement confirmed there had been a certain amount of "leg-pulling" that night at the pub. However, a similar story had apparently appeared in a local newspaper, and King remarked that it had also been spoken about in an Oldbury pub.[58] Fletcher further revealed that Shearwood had mentioned entering the wood after being "taken short"; and that he had had found a woman's black shoe and searched for the other – but without success.[59]

The general consensus was that Shearwood had, indeed, exaggerated the story, but the police nevertheless convened a meeting at Hagley Police Station (on 2 October) which involved four of the senior officers involved in the case, and in which Shearwood himself participated. He convinced police[60] that he had been correct in his assertion that he had seen a number of Gipsies encamped in the Nimmings Field about 120 yards

---

[58] It has not been possible to trace the article, and there is no record of which pub this may have been. Reading from other papers, it may be that this was also in Halesowen (possibly the George) rather than Oldbury.
[59] The inference being that this could be related to the other shoe found in the bole of the tree with the victim's body; but the matching shoes had already been found by now.
[60] This is confirmed within a memo from Tommy Williams of 5 October 1949.

Some New Leads

from where the skeleton of the murdered woman had been found. As a result, further enquiries were undertaken with the following parties:

- Messrs Spalding (horse slaughterers) of Oldbury – Shearwood's former employers;
- John (Jack) Palmer, licensee of the George Inn, Halesowen – who had also been involved in the removal of a horse from the area;
- Charles Palmer (brother of above), landlord of the Hill Tavern at Clent;
- Alfred (Fred) Reece – farmer of Pen Orchard Farm, Clent;
- Mrs Flora Elizabeth Reece – wife of Alfred;
- Felix Tate – farmer, of Holliers Farm, Hagley (some 2–3 miles away);
- Mrs Prudence May Tate – wife of above, who regularly walked up Hagley Wood Lane to visit her parents (the Palmers) at Spring Farm, Clent;[61]
- (Charles) Harry Willetts – retired farmer, who had previously (at the presumed time of the murder) been a tenant of that part of Hagley Hill Farm, which included the Nimmings Field; and
- Sarah Annie Lorrie Porter – widow of Toll House Stores, Birmingham Road, Hayley Green, Halesowen; and who had served a number of Gipsy customers at her shop.

These enquiries confirmed that a dead horse (Jinnie) belonging to Fred Reece had been collected from a field adjacent to Hagley Wood Lane at around the time in question, and Jack Palmer recalled having dragged the horse (presumably by tractor) onto the road for collection.[62] Records were retrieved and, whilst they did not positively identify which Spaldings' employee had been involved with the animal collection in question, they strongly pointed to the date being 23 December 1942. Palmer also told police that he believed that one of the Spaldings' drivers was a relative of Bill Fletcher.[63]

---

[61] This was / is just to the east of Hagley Wood Lane.
[62] Jack Palmer had, at the time, been living at Spring Farm.
[63] In all likelihood, this was a reference to Eddie Shearwood.

Events and Their Reporting (Chronology)

Mrs Tate's testimony was that she had not seen Gipsies camping in the precise area in question. Others had also asserted that Gipsies were not allowed to camp there, but some remembered differently. Mrs Reece had seen them, and Jack Palmer confirmed that they had been there when he moved the horse (although they had not approached him or offered any assistance). Further, Harry Willetts confirmed that he had given permission for these "gipsies" to camp on "his land",[64] after Felix Tate had asked them to leave his site. Willetts went on to say that this was the only time that "gipsies" had camped in Nimmings Wood, and that they stayed for some 5–6 weeks. He could remember little about them; indeed, he was able to provide more detail of their horses! His statement, however, did go on to say:

> I seem to remember it was said [that] a gipsy woman was missing when they went away, but I can't remember who said it, except that it seemed general talk, and I've thought about it since, and I seem to think it referred to another lot of gipsies who stayed actually in Hagley Wood Lane – lower down, and then there was some talk afterwards that the gipsy woman had been found and she had gone away to have a baby.

Mrs Tate additionally advised that she had noticed a "very nasty smell at a point in the bend in the lane about 40 to 50 yards above the [Birmingham] Water Track which appeared to come from the direction of the wood". She could not, however, precisely date when this was, other than that it "may have been SIX [*sic*] or more years ago"[65] and "certainly before the skeleton was found"; she had assumed at the time that it had come from a dead animal.[66]

---

[64] Willetts was only a tenant, and presumably not empowered to sublet.
[65] That is to say dating to around 1943.
[66] It is possible that the smell did emanate from a dead horse, although Mrs Tate may not have been aware of the fate of Jinnie at the time.

Some New Leads

The Hill Tavern, Clent, in 2010.
(CC-BY-SA/2.0 - © Chris Whippet - geograph.org.uk/p/2128342)

Mrs Reece also told the police: "I remember after the skeleton was found in the wood it was being said that there was one gipsy missing when they went away. I don't know which gipsies the remark referred to and I don't know who said it." It would certainly be helpful to know whether any Traveller did give birth around this time, but the lack of records and informality of arrangements makes this almost impossible to determine. All that police interview records relate is that, when they briefly investigated whether a particular Traveller – Lennie Smith (married to Danny Smith) – could be the murder victim, they ascertained that she had a daughter called Lallie who had given birth around then. But this would have been in February 1939, so arguably too early to have been of significance.

All this also brought back into focus the incident that PC Arthur J. Pound had investigated in December 1942, when some clothing and other belongings had been found near to where "Bella's" body was later deposited. As recorded within Chapter 2, the routines that the family followed had allowed these articles to be linked to Arkus Smith / Butler. This line of enquiry also confirmed that Arkus Smith, Daniel Butler, Wisdom Smith, Ellen Smith, Ivy Butler and a young woman with the surname Davies (who appears to have been Wisdom Smith's common-law wife) were all part of a larger travelling group.

Something that troubled Tommy Williams was that he felt there was some familiarity with two of the main protagonists responsible for this story coming to light (Shearwood and Fletcher), and in this he was proved right. Firstly, Eddie Shearwood had previously made a formal complaint to the police that money he had collected whilst playing the piano at the same Lyttelton Arms had been stolen. Secondly – and more significantly – his brother-in-law was the same Bill Fletcher who had both written to the police and forged a note from a fellow soldier in respect of the "missing" Mary Wenman.

John Swindon's account

It can't be denied that, during the war, there were plenty of people using Hagley Wood who were not authorised to do so. Some of these were fleeing air raids, others were not. In the light of fresh publicity, a 58-year-old library caretaker – John Swindon – of 71 Church Road, Smethwick, now came forward, with a retrospective sighting of a couple entering the wood. Despite the passage of seven years, he could precisely date the episode in question to 16 June 1942.[67] The reason he could be so sure over the date was that this had been the first day of the fishing season. Swindon, who had boarded a bus at the King's Head, Bearwood, en route to Bewdley, had noticed a soldier and a woman alight almost opposite the Gipsy's Tent and enter a coppice adjacent to Hagley Wood. He was understandably vague on some of the detail, but gave the age of the soldier as between 34 and 38 years, with the woman being of a similar age but shorter in height. As Swindon hadn't seen them board the bus, he assumed that their journey had started before his. There is nothing within the police files to confirm that this lead was followed up – although it is difficult to see what could have been done at this late stage. If his sighting was out by a year, the date would be a good match in terms of Webster's assessment of the time of death.

---

[67] It seems that he may have first stated 1943, before amending his statement.

Some New Leads

Kenneth Patten

It was still October 1949 when police took down an extraordinary statement from Mrs Vivienne Coss, who had also come forward with new information. That the police saw this as potentially significant is underlined by the fact that it was Tommy Williams himself who took the witness statement – a transcript of which can be found at Appendix H. Coss was a 28-year-old housewife, who had originally related her story to a Mrs Garrett; she in turn had told her husband, ex-Major Charles Garrett – who felt it warranted police attention. The incident she described dated to October or November 1942.

Hagley Hall, pictured in 2018.
(CC-BY-SA/2.0 - © Philip Halling - geograph.org.uk/p/5728173)

At this time, Coss had a milk delivery round in West Hagley and, as a result of this work, struck up a casual friendship with a man who introduced himself as Pat Graham.[68] Graham had a female friend by the name of Sheila,[69] who was employed at Hagley Hall and often entertained him there. At one point, Graham told Coss that he had a van

---

[68] It seems that Graham at some point undertook some vehicle maintenance work for Mr Parsons, owner of the dairy which employed Mrs Coss.
[69] From Coss's statement, it seems that she gained the impression that Sheila was Patten's girlfriend.

hidden in Hagley Wood, which he had unofficially "borrowed" from his principal employer – Rolls-Royce. In her statement, Coss related that she had been told by police that they were looking for Graham, and that later the same day Graham had appeared at her door in an anxious state. She divulged that the police were after him; he was not surprised, and volunteered that it was probably in relation to tyres that he had procured without a permit. He then asked if Coss would lend him her dog and give him a lift to an unspecified location later in the day. Coss was understandably reluctant to do this, but Graham was insistent, and refused to leave her house, staying until nightfall. In a wish to be rid of him, Coss then agreed to drive him to Hagley Wood Lane. During the journey, he acted very strangely and started to sing hysterically, and Coss was understandably unnerved. Coss dropped Graham in the lane with her dog in tow, and he instructed her to drive back alone. Coss's statement advises that Graham refused to give any reason for his actions: "he [said that he] could not possibly tell me, but [told me] that one day I might know". Coss also recounted that, after she had dropped Graham off, a bus went past and he took great care to hide his face from its passengers. When Coss went to collect her van from the dairy the following morning, her employer reunited her with her dog – which he said had been returned by Graham at 10.30 the previous evening. Coss claimed that, when news broke of the discovery of the body in 1943, she did not contact the police because she realised that the time frame did not fit. The newspaper reports of a breakthrough in the case had made her think again, and Major Garrett persuaded her to come forward.

Hagley Hall, seen from the obelisk, on the opposite side of the A456 (2018).

Some New Leads

Police enquiries soon established that the name Pat Graham was a pseudonym, and they must have been intrigued to ascertain that the man in question was actually one Kenneth Francis Patten, a known petty criminal.[70] Tracking him was not difficult, as he was serving a sentence at HMP Wandsworth. To add to the confusion, the name Vivienne Coss meant nothing to him – he had known the informant as Biddy Williams![71] The subsequent interview with him was undertaken by Metropolitan Police officers, rather than those close to the case, and Patten – who flatly denied that he had ever asked Coss to drive him to Hagley Wood or taken her dog – convinced them that he was not of any interest in this respect. A review of their own files reveals that Patten was arrested at the time of the incident to which Coss referred. This was not in relation to motor vehicle tyre irregularities, however, but for theft of a mackintosh from Hagley Hall. PC Pound had travelled to Manchester to effect the arrest, and confirmed that he had seen the (a?) woman named Sheila at the same house, thus eliminating her as the potential murder victim.

Another missing person

The most explosive development in the case would not come until 1953 and in the interim, matters again quietened down. Between 1949 and then, there are few references within either newspaper or police files. An exception, though, was the report of a missing woman by the name of "Billy" Gibson. In February 1951, Mr Leon Hughes, a resident of Hasbury, contacted the Worcestershire Police, expressing concerns over the well-being of Ms Gibson. Hughes was clearly a concerned citizen, rather than an amateur sleuth or somebody with mental health issues, and the police felt that there was sufficient evidence to warrant enquiries. A formal reply to Hughes stated:

> With regard to the height of "Billy", I make her about 5' 4½", whereas, according to Professor Webster, the woman in the case was 5' in height.

---

[70] The name "Pat", presumably, being a contraction of his (real) surname.
[71] Marriage records show that Vivienne M. Williams was her maiden name; she married a Neville Coss in Bromsgrove in 1943.

It should be said here that although I have the highest possible regard for the opinion of the Professor, when another expert made a reconstruction from the portions of fabric found at the scene, the skirt would have come to the ankles on the basis of a 5' woman. From all the circumstances I think we might say that on the height standard alone it just could be "Billy".

This is another of the many police folders which appear to be incomplete but, at one point, a former work colleague of Gibson's (a Leonard Whyley)[72] advised that "Billy" had a gold tooth. This could have supported a claim of hers being the body in the tree although, based on the coroner's report, the killer would have had to remove the tooth after death, when the need to hide the body may have hindered logical thought. However, the police response to Hughes continues:

> The next consideration is the mouth. Unfortunately, "Billy" would have her mouth closed in the snap, so the picture does not help in this aspect of the matter, but you did mention a gold tooth, so I am enclosing a photograph of the jaw of the unidentified woman from which you will see from where the tooth had been extracted. I think it is about the position you mentioned. While on the question of teeth, do you think "Billy" had such an irregular set, as on the photograph? Of course it is possible and would account for a clever girl closing her mouth when having her photograph taken.

Williams also forwarded a photograph of the crepe-soled shoes to Hughes.

Concerns over "Billy" Gibson's safety emanated from the fact that she had not been seen for some years. Her husband[73] was identified by Hughes as Oswald Gibson, a Departmental Manager who had worked from 1936 at a local firm – Stewarts & Lloyds (S&L) – and had lived with her at an address given as Manor House, Hagley. Oswald Gibson had left S&L to take up a post in India in 1938, and it was not known whether

---

[72] This is the spelling used by colleague Leon Hughes, and within this narrative. Some records, however, show "Whylie".

[73] Although there did seem to be some uncertainty as whether the couple were legally married.

Some New Leads

"Billy" had travelled with him. Whyley and Hughes had been in regular correspondence with him; yet, despite requests as to his partner's health or whereabouts, Gibson – who had remained in India on war service – had not mentioned her once.

"Billy" Gibson was described as being attractive, fond of the company of men, highly strung and bad-tempered. She had been born "about 1912 to 1916", but little more of value is to be found within the file archive, and we again don't know whether the police were able to successfully eliminate her from their enquiries. At the end of the day, Leon Hughes did acknowledge that the chances of the body in the tree being "Billy's" were remote, although there do seem to have been grounds for investigating just what had happened to her. The war had ended by this time, but it may have been that there was limited appetite to investigate a respected army officer for a crime that may or may not have occurred nearly a decade earlier.

CHAPTER 6

Una Hainsworth, Jack Mossop and the Dutch Spy

In terms of investigation and reporting of the murder, 1953 would turn out to be pivotal. It was late in the year before anything unfolded, and even then, events began innocuously enough, with the first of two articles written by journalist Wilfred Byford-Jones in the Wolverhampton *Express & Star*. This was on 19 November. The events that followed, though, have seriously moulded public perceptions of the whole case.

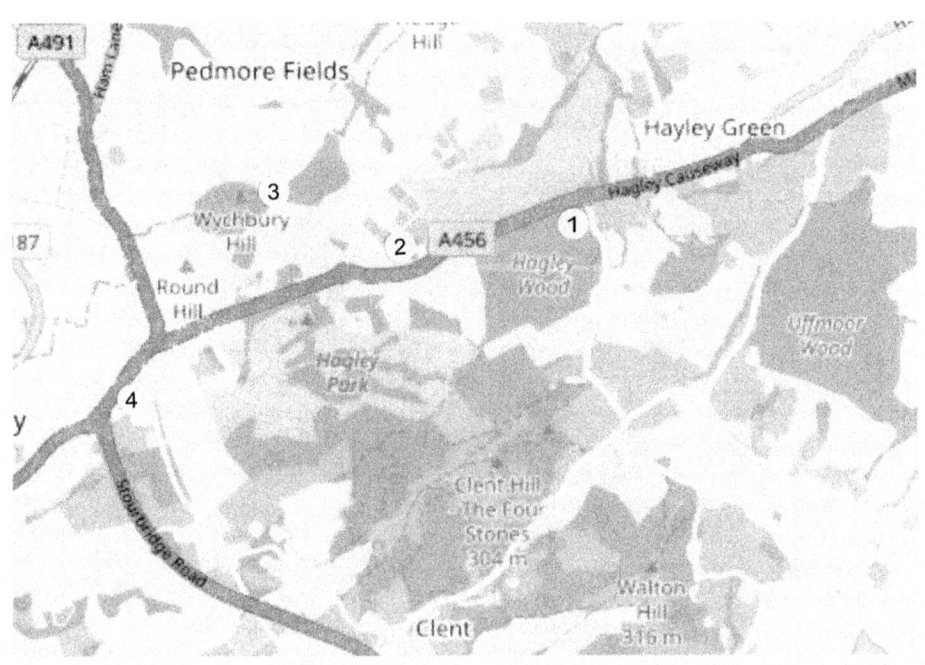

Hagley Wood and surrounding area.
Key: 1 – Deposition site, Hagley Wood; 2 – Gipsy's Tent (Badger's Sett) public house; 3 – Hagley Obelisk, Wychbury Hill; 4 – Lyttelton Arms public house, Bromsgrove Road. (openstreetmap.org/copyright)

Una Hainsworth, Jack Mossop and the Dutch Spy

At first glance, the articles appear to have been a space filler, bringing up an old unsolved murder which had elements bound to appeal to a new audience; and probably aimed primarily at stoking the letters page.[74] Writing under his *Quaestor* pen name, Byford-Jones's first article drew attention to the eerie qualities of Hagley Wood, rather melodramatically describing a visit there as follows:

> I felt that I was in hell itself. All around me were great squat wych elm trees ... like round-bellied devils with beards and shaggy hair.

It did, nevertheless, largely debunk the theories of black magic involvement. In his second piece (appearing on 20 November 1953), Byford-Jones again concluded that the witchcraft theories were too far-fetched to be given serious consideration, but also commented:

> As for the gipsy theory, whether the young woman is supposed to have been a gipsy who was ritualistically murdered with witchcraft or after a trial by her tribe, well, I do not accept it. It is true that there had been gipsies for years in the area, but every crime is laid at the door of Romanies.

Quaestor went on to say that whoever had written the wall messages and brought the names "Luebella" [*sic*] and "Bella" into the public consciousness must at least have known the surname of the victim / supposed victim. The *Express & Star* pleaded for members of the public to come forward, and even offered a cash reward of £100 to anyone who could assist in securing a conviction. There was a bumper crop of responses, many indeed from those championing the theories which supported witchcraft or Gipsy involvement. But, amongst the other letters from cranks and conspiracy theorists, one particular reply stood out. This was from a woman calling herself "Anna" of Claverley, who claimed to know not only the perpetrator, but also the circumstances of the murder. She wrote:

> Finish your articles re the Wych elm crime by all means. They are interesting to your readers, but you will never solve the mystery. The one

---

[74] This proved to be the case, enabling Byford-Jones to devote a further page to responses, within the edition of 23 November.

person who could give the answer is now beyond the jurisdiction of the earthly courts. The affair is closed and involves no witches, black magic or moonlight rites. Much as I hate having to use a nom de plume, I think you would appreciate it if you knew me. The only clues I can give you are that the person responsible for the crime died insane in 1942, and the victim was Dutch and arrived in England illegally about 1941. I have no wish to recall any more ... I am no hoaxer.

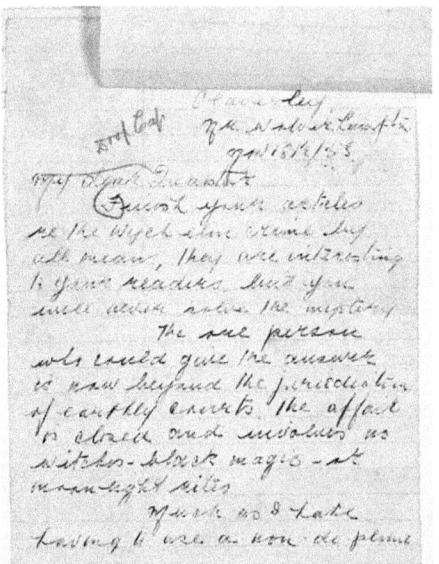

"Anna's" letter, with its last paragraph crossed through. (West Mercia Police)

The letter (a transcript of which appears at Appendix I) was forwarded by the editor of the newspaper to Sidney Inight, with a covering note explaining that the crossing through of the last paragraph was by the sub-editor, in preparing it for publication.

Apparently at the insistence of the Chief Constable, Lloyd Williams, *Quaestor* now made an appeal for "Anna" to make further contact, which she duly did.[75] Byford-Jones next arranged a meeting, to which he also persuaded the woman to allow the police to attend, and where she would divulge her true identity. At her suggestion, this meeting took place at the

---

[75] A transcript of her follow-up letter is at Appendix J.

Whittington Inn, an upmarket establishment on the A449, near Kinver.[76] In her letter, she went on to say: "at the 'Whittington' they have a back room (to) the left of the entrance called the 'Priest's Hole'". At this meeting, "Anna" identified herself as Una Hainsworth, a housewife now living at Kenilworth. She agreed to subsequently provide police with a more detailed statement.

The Whittington Inn. It remains as a classy hotel / restaurant, but is now known as the Manor House of Whittington.
(CC-BY-SA/2.0 - © Peter Evans - geograph.org.uk/p/4132814)

The story that unfolded was quite extraordinary. Una divulged that she had formerly been married to Jack Mossop, a worker in a local aircraft factory – a reserved occupation. Yet, despite what appeared to be good and solid employment, he frequently missed work, and it is clear that the young couple often struggled financially. But, at times – from 1940 – Jack seemed to have money to burn. He started to wear flashy and expensive clothes – sometimes an officer's uniform to which he was not

---

[76] Subsequently referred to in police records and elsewhere as "the Kinver Inn meeting".

entitled – and drinking to excess. This period of affluence seemed to have coincided with a friendship that he had struck up with a Dutchman by the name of van Ralt.[77] The Mossops' marriage had been going through a rocky patch, and Una couldn't cope with her husband's new lifestyle – particularly as she was not part of it. She questioned how this was being funded, and formed the view that van Ralt was somehow behind it, even though he appeared to have no regular job. She claimed to have met van Ralt on two occasions, and that he had a Rover car (which her husband had asked if he could drive). She surmised that he may have been a Nazi spy – and, accordingly, that he could have been paying her husband for intelligence relating to local factories involved in manufacturing aircraft parts and munitions.

The Lyttelton Arms today remains a charming country pub. At the time of the murder, it was on the main Kidderminster–Birmingham Road, although would have still been quite rural. The side road in the foreground is Hall Lane, leading to Hagley Hall (the Lyttelton family residence).

---

[77] Variations on this name were and have been used throughout the investigation and reporting.

Una Hainsworth, Jack Mossop and the Dutch Spy

The couple had separated at the end of 1941, but had continued to meet on an occasional basis. Una claimed that one of the last times that Jack visited her was in 1942, when he was in a highly distressed state. He was drunk and told an amazing story, relating that, one evening back in 1941, he had met up with van Ralt at the Lyttelton Arms at Clent. Van Ralt was with a woman, but ended up in an argument with her; he suggested that Mossop take them for a drive so that they could calm down. In the car, however, the argument continued to escalate, before the woman suddenly went quiet. Van Ralt admitted to Mossop that he thought that he had killed her and coerced Mossop – who was now in fear of his own life – into helping him dispose of the body. They drove around and found a likely spot, close to a wood. The next part of the story defies belief: having removed the body from the car, they found that the woman was not dead, just suffering from excessive intoxication. They panicked and stuffed her into a tree so that she might sober up. The following day, they returned to the wood to find that she now really was dead. Now Jack began to be afflicted by nightmares, having visions of the woman trapped in the tree, and divulged that he was close to a nervous breakdown. Anxious to unburden himself, he supplied some further detail to his estranged wife, including that "the Dutch piece"[78] may also have been a spy. But the police would not be able to follow up any of these details with Jack Mossop. For, after he had been admitted to St George's, Stafford (the county mental hospital) on 6 June 1942, his health had further deteriorated, and he had died soon after, on 15 August. The death certificate seemingly reflected that he had, indeed, died insane, recording the causes as being cerebral softening, myocardial degeneration, chronic nephritis and acute confusional insanity.

---

[78] For those who are not familiar with the origins of this turn of phrase, the term "piece" was widely used during the war – and for many years thereafter – and was a contraction of "piece of skirt" (vernacular for an attractive young woman).

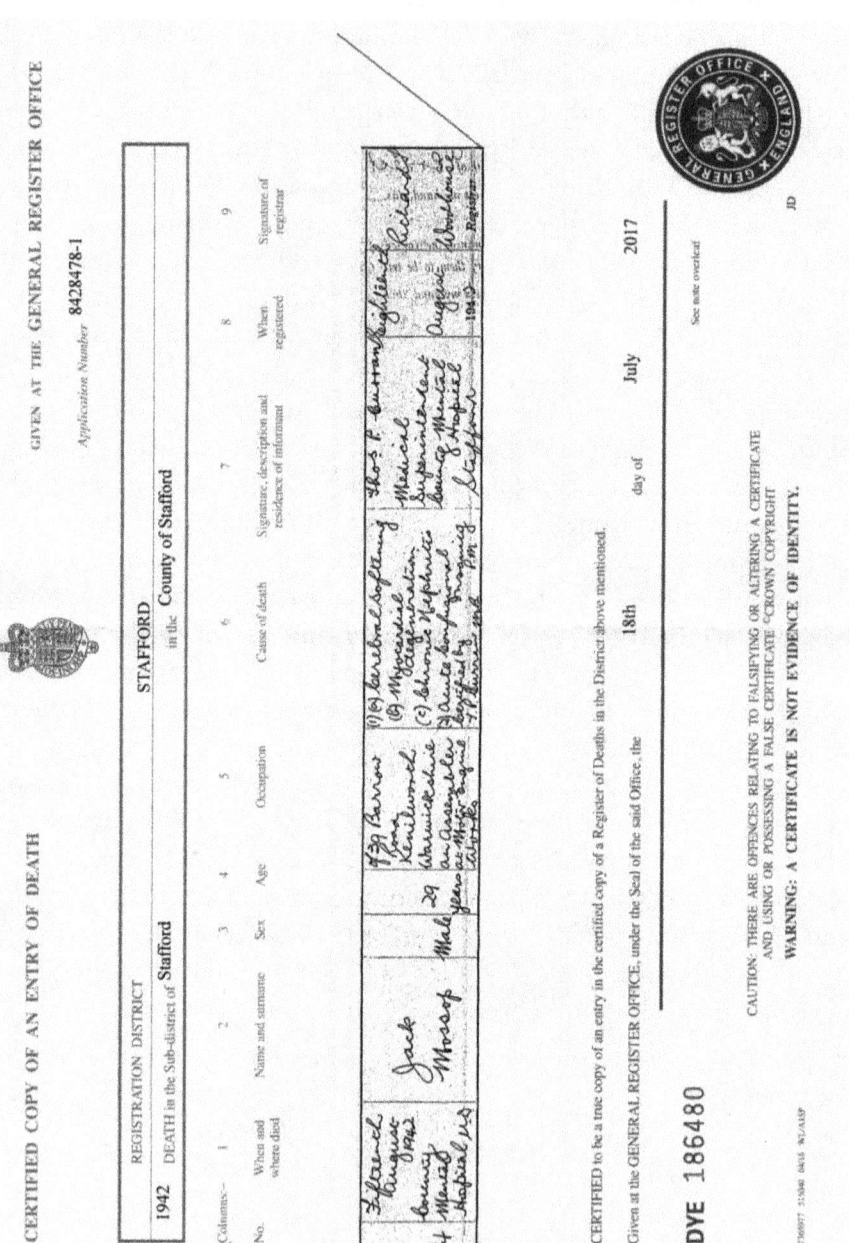

Jack Mossop's death certificate. (Crown copyright)

Una Hainsworth, Jack Mossop and the Dutch Spy

To the rather obvious question of why she had not come forward sooner, Una claimed that she had not seen any coverage of the discovery of the body at the time. It was only when reading the recent *Express & Star* article that she realised the possible implications of her former husband's behaviour and admissions. On any level, her tale was breathtaking, and the police were understandably extremely interested in it – managing to verify a number of salient details. Her evidence was purely circumstantial, yet – if she was truthfully relaying what her late husband had told her – there could have been little doubt that Mossop had been involved in (or at least a witness to) a murder. For, at the time that Jack Mossop allegedly made his confession to Una, nobody but those involved knew that there was a body secreted in Hagley Wood. Even at first glance, though, there are some obvious inconsistencies – not least that Una had (in her initial letter) described the person responsible for the deed to be "beyond earthly courts"; yet, she was now claiming that there was at least one other man in the car with her husband, and that he was more directly responsible for the woman's death.

The Kinver Inn meeting was followed up by a private meeting between Una Hainsworth and the police, on 28 December, at which she provided a signed statement. A transcript of this is at Appendix K, although this did not record everything that appeared within manuscript notes. One of the omissions was detail of a young Welsh woman identified by Una Hainsworth, named Lucy Stephens. According to Hainsworth, she disappeared from Brick Bridge Cottage (where the couple once lived), with her husband's money. Within this, it could be construed that Hainsworth was hinting that Stephens (by virtue of being known to Jack Mossop and having disappeared) may have been the murder victim – but this was not something either made clear, or followed up by the police.

Another issue which surfaced at one of these meetings but which did not make it into Una's formal statement is the possible involvement of a further individual, a man working in show business. There are suggestions (within other papers on police files) that he went by the name of Fruck but, from this time the police embarked on a line of enquiry within the case that involved an unusual and popular

Events and Their Reporting (Chronology)

ice-skating act known as Frick and Frack. The fact that this was now a police matter precluded *Quaestor* from disclosing too many details to his readership, and it would not be until January 1958 that he wrote an article headed *Kinver Inn Meeting sheds light on Mystery of Bella*.

CHAPTER 7

More Spies

It was certainly the case that, during wartime, the Midlands was heavily targeted by German bombers – for the understandable reason that there were so many factories there which were directly involved in the war effort. A prime target was the Armstrong Siddeley works, and another the site of the Spitfire aircraft works at Castle Bromwich. Any inside information would have been of great value to the enemy, potentially allowing better targeting of the bombing raids. The belief that the Home Guard had been instructed to be alert to agents parachuting into the Clent Hills and Hagley Wood during 1940–41 was widely held, and, to this day, rumours are still rife that German paratroopers did land in the north Worcestershire area. Although not borne out by official documents subsequently released, there were plenty of suggestions of a double agent having operated in the locality, and a lot of suspicion was attached to foreigners (as was the case throughout the country).

Karl Dickenhoff/Hans Caesar

In 1956, less than three years after Una Hainsworth had first come forward, Hungarian military historian and journalist, Ladislas Farago, published a book entitled *War of Wits: The Anatomy of Espionage and Intelligence*. Within this, he wrote:

> For every espionage exploit that becomes known, there must be dozens of cases which will remain secret for ever. Among these, indeed, are the true spies of espionage, in which the identity of the agent is never exposed, not even deduced from the sometimes monumental clues he leaves behind in the frequently historic consequences of his successful mission ... Throughout both world wars, the British had a high-ranking

officer of their secret services planted within the German General Staff. But only a handful of initiated persons knew the identity of the spy ... While Britain succeeded in unmasking most of the German agents of WWII, one truly effective German spy managed to evade the net. This man succeeded in outwitting Britain's entire counter-espionage machinery for seven years, from 1937, when he entered Britain allegedly from Canada, to 1944, when his trail eventually vanished. During those seven years, this phantom spy supplied the German Secret Service with a remarkable collection of intelligence.

Farago provided six examples of this "phantom spy's" exploits, which resulted in numerous classified and top-secret documents being passed to the Nazi regime. These included information relating to the Scapa Flow naval base (and which allegedly led to the sinking of the *Royal Oak* battleship, with the loss of more than 800 lives). But another was a complete report on the dispersal of British industries and on the organisation of so-called shadow factories concentrated around Birmingham and Coventry. The spy was supposedly later credited with the guiding of the German bombers to these "crucial targets". Farago went on to conclude that:

> Even today [1956] no one professes to know the answers to these questions. Some say that all these scoops were scored by a single operator, probably one of the greatest spies who ever lived. Others presume that there were, in fact, three different men behind those coups, none of whom was ever caught. Still others insist that they were the work of a brilliant network of Germany's ace operators led by a single genius who not only understood how to direct his men but also how to protect them from the spy-catchers ... It may be that this elusive Scarlet Pimpernel was someone who MI5 and Scotland Yard did meet, but only as a corpse, in a deserted air-raid shelter in Cambridge, with a bullet in his head and a German revolver at his side, apparently a suicide. From the papers in his pocket he was identified as a native of Holland, Jan Willem Ter Braak, but it was obvious that this was an alias. Later the body was recognised by a landlady who reported one of her boarders missing. In Ter Braak's abandoned room, the spy-catchers found forged documents and a powerful German made radio transmitter ... However, it is more likely that the phantom spy was a German–Canadian who

called himself Karl Dickenhoff. He lived quietly in a villa in Edgbaston. His real name was Hans Caesar. His is a weird story, somewhat in the Conan Doyle tradition. Caesar is said to be still alive and in England, the demented, amnesia-stricken inmate of an asylum. Nobody will say whether he is really unbalanced or merely simulates insanity to escape the consequences of his wartime activities.

Variation on a Theme

The spying angle was later (in 1968) picked up by journalist Donald McCormick. McCormick had worked for Naval Intelligence during the Second World War before joining the foreign desk of the *Sunday Times*, where he famously, at one time, worked with Ian Fleming. Intriguingly, not content with merely developing the spying theme, McCormick managed to conflate the espionage link with the previous stories of witchcraft. It is for that reason that his book was entitled *Murder by Witchcraft*.[79] It drew quite heavily on Margaret Murray's work, but was full of ambiguities and is quite difficult to follow at times. Nevertheless, he made the further claim of having seen previously unrevealed wartime Abwehr (German intelligence organisation)[80] papers, which referenced Verbindungsstab[81] records that identified an agent by the name of Lehrer. These "confirmed" that a mission had been planned to set down Lehrer and a wireless operator in south Wales, to establish a communications network within the UK. Further, McCormick also claimed that the Abwehr records show that, in March and April 1941, five agents from Holland were sent to England. Two of these were captured, two more sent by boat (their fate is not clear) and the fifth – a woman – was parachuted from a plane in the Midlands area (specifically between Birmingham and Kidderminster) during an air raid. This spy was codenamed Clara, and McCormick suggested that this could be the real victim of the tree murder.

---

[79] Confusingly, McCormick also wrote under the name of Richard Deacon, and one edition of this book bears that name.
[80] More specifically, these records were mostly of Abwehr III, which had responsibility for penetrating the Allied agents' networks in occupied countries.
[81] An organisation created by Rudolf Hess, who was contemptuous of the Abwehr.

Events and Their Reporting (Chronology)

McCormick related that he identified three people from Abwehr records who might be able to shed light on the identity of Clara. He managed to track down one of these, Franz Rathgeb, who had previously (pre-war) been in the German steel industry – work which frequently took him to the Midlands. Rathgeb was now living in Paraguay, under an alias. Rather predictably – since he was trying to escape his past – he was reluctant to talk at first, but McCormick claims to have won his trust and that, eventually, he admitted to knowing Lehrer, and confirmed that the latter was a spy. Moreover, Rathgeb advised that Lehrer had a Dutch[82] mistress who was not only fluent in English, but spoke it with a Birmingham accent. This was on account of her having lived in Birmingham for five years during the 1930s, when working in a factory – at which time she had embarked on an affair with a man from Stourbridge, which is only about 5 miles from Hagley Wood. She was attractive, of below average height, and had slightly irregular teeth. Rathgeb could not recall her name, but knew that she had a photographic memory and detailed knowledge of most of the main Midlands' factories, together with their evacuation plans. Rathgeb also allegedly agreed that Lehrer's mistress and Clara could well have been one and the same. McCormick briefly considers the possibility that, if Lehrer's mistress had parachuted into the area, it may have been to re-establish contact with her former lover in Stourbridge; but then (understandably!) rejects the notion. He goes on to relate that Rathgeb had told him that the woman was a firm believer in astrology and horoscopes – and raised the possibility that she may have been rounded up as part of *Aktion Hess*.[83]

As McCormick's investigations progressed, Franz Rathgeb suggested that he should contact a woman named Cremer[84] in Amsterdam. Frau Cremer was interviewed and, whilst not recalling a woman by the name

---

[82] Rathgeb acknowledged that she could, alternatively, have been German, but that a Dutch identity better suited her espionage purposes.

[83] *Aktion Hess* was Hitler's reaction to his deputy's defection, and involved, inter alia, rounding up over 600 astrologers; McCormick suggests that there could be a link to Bella's death.

[84] McCormick does not indicate how Cremer was involved. Presumably she would have been part of the same spy ring as Lehrer and Rathgeb.

of Clara, "felt sure" that the description given for Lehrer's mistress fitted that of a woman named Dronkers – a relative of Johannes Marinus Dronkers, a Dutch national who had been executed by the British as a spy, at Wandsworth in December 1942. According to Cremer, this woman may have been a double agent. She:

> always posed as a friend of the Dutch Resistance, but there were some who had their doubts about her, and remarked on her frequent trips into Germany. We rather suspected she might be playing a double game. But it was never proved who she was working for.

Frau Dronkers was also, according to Cremer, both highly superstitious and a serious student of astrology. McCormick further developed the theory that Frau Dronkers and her colleagues were aided and guided by an agent firmly embedded in the Midlands. This was none other than the German–Canadian, Karl Dickenhoff (aka Hans Caesar), previously identified by Ladislas Farago.

Clara Bauerle

Although McCormick claimed to have seen some MI5 files, he presumably hadn't come across any in respect of Josef Jakobs, a Luxembourg-born German agent.[85] With the official declassification of wartime files, those relating to Jakobs came into the public domain and offered a potentially fascinating adjunct to McCormick's theory. Jakobs had been parachuted into Cambridgeshire in 1941, and been arrested by the Home Guard very shortly after (having broken his ankle on landing). At the time of his arrest, he was carrying a photo of a woman who, he claimed, was his lover. She was named by Jakobs as German cabaret singer and movie actress, Clara Bauerle.[86]

---

[85] Some sources erroneously state that he was Czech born. Inevitably, he met his death at the hands of a firing squad in August 1941, and earned a footnote in history by being the last prisoner to be executed at the Tower of London.

[86] Born Hedwig Karla Baurle.

Josef Jakobs (1898–1941), pictured in 1940 (courtesy Gigi Jakobs); and a publicity shot of Clara Bauerle.

The files show that, under interrogation, Jakobs disclosed that he had first met Bauerle in the Café Dreyer in Hamburg, when she was singing with the Ette Orchestra. They had become lovers, and Jakobs claimed that she, too, had been recruited as a secret agent, and was also due to parachute into England, but specifically in the Midlands. This, however, was to have been after Jakobs had established radio contact, and his capture meant that her mission would probably have been aborted. MI5 established that Clara Bauerle had been born in Stuttgart in 1906, making her 35 years of age in 1941. And, not only was she a cabaret artist, but she had spent two years in the music halls of the Midlands prior to the outbreak of war, so was familiar with the area. During this time, it seems that she had even managed to acquire a local accent. The case for her being "Bella" was much later (within a piece published in 2013) developed by *The Independent* newspaper journalist Allison Vale. Her article included the following:

More Spies

It isn't difficult to see how the name Clara Bauerle might have been more easily remembered as "Clarabella" by English music hall audiences. And "Anna" [Una Hainsworth] would later allege a connection between "Bella", espionage and music hall, in her letter to *Quaestor* in 1953 ... The timings of these disparate strands of the story are remarkably convergent. Jakobs said that Clara had been due to parachute into the Midlands in the spring of 1941.

Further, reports stated that there were no gramophone recordings, live performances or movie appearances bearing Bauerle's name after this date. Indeed, her singing career seems to have come to an abrupt end. The police investigation into the Hagley Wood murder had been formally closed at this point, but many were now asking the question: could this have been McCormick's Agent Clara? The new theory ran that, rather than aborting her mission, she was parachuted into the West Midlands in early 1941 – but was either captured and executed soon after, or landed in the tree and died of her injuries.

CHAPTER 8

From Beyond The Grave

Although police and public attention had been diverted by the spying stories that circulated in the wake of Una Hainsworth's revelations, *Quaestor's* newspaper articles also resulted in even more members of the public coming forward with their own theories and claims. Inevitably, these included self-proclaimed psychics who promised that they could help the police. At this time, there had been some reported instances of psychics being useful to police in unsolved murder enquiries. Unfortunately, most of those that came forward in this case seemed to suffer from delusions and mental health problems. This does not necessarily mean that they were distorting their perceptions of the truth, but the interest in the case meant that the media was all too ready to give them the oxygen of publicity. The police interviewed them and correspondence was retained on files; there is no evidence, however, that they afforded them any serious consideration.

Zita Boyden

From late 1953, Zita Boyden emerged as a serial letter writer, bombarding Tommy Williams with a succession of ramblings which purported to offer help in solving the crime. She claimed to have been directed by a spirit guide named Jacques, and there are no less than nine of her letters on police files. Most bear her home address of 58A Compton Road, Wolverhampton, although one has a different address: 21 Oaks Crescent (also Wolverhampton). In her correspondence, Boyden also claimed that she had recently helped a number of other forces – including Scotland Yard, Halifax Police, Carmarthenshire Police and Richmond Police – in resolving previously unsolved cases. These included the towpath murders, which took place alongside the River Thames in May 1953. She would also later assert that she had seen the "dumb boy David Anderton in a stream". This is a reference to an eight-year-old boy who went missing from his Manchester home on Christmas Day and was found dead some three days later.

According to Boyden – who styled herself "Madame Zed" – "Bella" was:

> [a] country type, slow spoken, fresh coloured [sic], [with] brown or chestnut hair. She had small, fat fingers with pointed ends and was dressed in handed-down clothes from her place of work.

This place of work was apparently an institute or home which probably looked after children: "I believe a Catholic place, as a general help". The building where she worked had good, solid oak polished floors and was not carpeted. "Bella" had died "with something wrong with her throat or maybe strangulation". She had been "hauled into the tree by means of a rope … the rope was not tied with knots but was expertly looped so that once the victim was released from being hauled the rope could easily be pulled away".

Boyden would add more detail in subsequent correspondence. This would include that "Bella" was a Dutch–Canadian woman who was 5' in height; that her hair – contradictorily – was "straight and curly (permed)"; that she had "a wide, happy, toothy smile"; and that her workplace was (more specifically) probably a home for boys – as Jacques had "seen" socks on the washing line. Further "revelations" were that "Bella" used an old-fashioned iron for her laundry and, in presumably earlier times, had pushed a cream-coloured pram with a black or navy-blue canopy. "Bella" had allegedly been murdered on account of her "not being married, but wanting to be".

A theme running through Boyden's letters is a Roman Catholic dynamic. In addition to extracts already quoted, in one of her letters she states that she sensed a "Catholic atmosphere". She mentions a house in Churchill, a village near Kidderminster, where the resident (a Mrs Williams) allegedly saw the ghosts of dead monks. She suggests that the home may have been used as a reception centre during the war, and the inference is that this may have been where "Bella" worked. Advocating that the police should investigate local Catholic homes and institutions, it becomes clear from reading all her letters that Boyden was a lapsed Catholic who suffered guilt pangs over what she described as her own "villainy in leaving the Church". This affected her deeply, and no doubt fuelled her pronouncements in no small part.

Names which are thrown into Boyden's letters, almost at random, are Hipkins (or Hipkiss), Louis Mellor and Queen Juliana (presumably the woman who was Queen of Holland at the time). In one letter she puts forward the name of John Worthington, a Liverpudlian. He had "very forward projecting teeth" and was the father of an unspecified number of daughters, one of whom (Georgina) now lived with him in the USA.[87] He also allegedly had a son named Francis (known as Franc or Franz) who, confusingly, Boyden describes at other times as being a Dutch civilian and who may have used a different surname (Christener). According to this version, this was the man who had put "Bella" in the tree. Tall and blond, with blue eyes, fresh skin and a straight nose with a tip to the end ("like a boxer's"), he habitually wore a leather jacket with sheepskin collar. By profession, he was possibly "a traffic cop – at any rate one who rode a motorbike and was dressed in dark blue uniform with a badge". He had suffered from shock during the war, and then settled in the Midlands. Boyden suggests that he may have died insane.

Variations (her letters display many inconsistencies) include either a suspect or key player wearing a Canadian army uniform; and another Worthington (Harry) having an involvement. Places mentioned included the town of Haarlem in Holland, the Wayside Inn (a pub at Alcester, near Wolverhampton),[88] County Place (an unknown reference) and a number of others on a hand-drawn map of a part of Wolverhampton.[89] Boyden further provided details of "Bella's" child, which she had gleaned through a picture shown to her by her psychic friend. This was allegedly a girl of about 12 years of age (this, presumably, at the time of the murder). She was "a bonny child resembling her father", "solid, perhaps with straight hair, stout tied with ribbon", and with a broad, flattish nose and blue eyes.[90] Boyden suggested that she, too, may have

---

[87] This is the most likely interpretation of her story. Boyden's letters are difficult to follow and "Georgina" could have been another relation, or even his wife.
[88] Not a pub that the authors have been able to trace.
[89] Specifically, Bath Road and 74 Lord Street (both just outside the city centre).
[90] This may even have been the "Georgina" now supposedly living in America with John Worthington.

been in a home or institution – having been "sectioned" at around the time that war had broken out.

A note within the margins of one of Boyden's early letters indicates that WPC Florence Hill accompanied a senior officer (almost certainly Tommy Williams) to Boyden's home in the first instance – presumably because they were running out of options. There is nothing documented as to why they decided to take this course of action, nor of the outcome. There is no indication that they checked Boyden's claims (regarding previous assistance) with other police forces. As the correspondence continued, Boyden grew more and more confused and eccentric, with one letter including the comment: "I am printing [this] to stop someone else from pushing my pen". She would also amend her stories to accommodate new information as other people came forward. The police soon seem to have dismissed her in terms of a source of potential information, whilst continuing to treat her (as they did Victor Crumpton) with some commendable compassion.

George Elwell

Despite already having had to deal with Zita Boyden's eccentricities, the police still professed to be open-minded when, in January 1954, another self-publicist and self-proclaimed psychic put himself forward. This was George Elwell, a British Railways worker who had visited the Hagley Wood site and made a recording of himself supposedly in a trance. He claimed to have ascertained that the victim was a Leeds woman by the name of Annie Bradley, and that her murderer was a tall, moustachioed serviceman. Unsurprisingly, the police could find no trace of any missing woman by the name of Annie Bradley, but there was a consequence which demonstrates the heartache that such individuals can cause. As the result of renewed publicity, an Irish family named Bradley became concerned that the murder victim may have been their long-lost daughter. Tommy Williams was able to provide reassurance that this was very unlikely to have been the case, but not before the family had suffered much anxiety. It was the case, however, that one of the travelling families interviewed by the police in relation to their Mary Lee enquiries was named Bradley, but this was unlikely to have been anything more than coincidence.

Events and Their Reporting (Chronology)

It is probably of no great surprise that, following Elwell's revelations, Zita Boyden came forward again. Just three days after George Elwell had "identified" the victim as Annie Bradley, Boyden ascribes another identity to the victim – that of "Anna" from "The Leads", a street in Bradley (and who she claimed may have been related to her killer). Bradley is a village that falls within Wolverhampton's Bilston ward, but there is no evidence of any street of this name.

CHAPTER 9

Later Developments

In addition to spawning fresh spying theories, the *Anna of Claverley* letters undoubtedly changed the way that most of the public (but not necessarily the police) perceived the whole case. Thereafter, anything related to her disclosures became newsworthy, and provided a rich seam for any journalist – whether working within the written or visual media – who wished to revisit it. This has remained the case, even after formal closure of the police investigation.

Claims that the case had been solved

More immediately, another potentially key event in the case occurred in 1956. Nearly seven years had passed since the *Hull Daily Mail* had run their story of an imminent breakthrough, when a new bombshell was dropped within an ITV broadcast. Television was now becoming a more important and influential medium, and the programme in question was screened in May of that year. A pathologist who claimed to have had the task of piecing together the skeletal remains of "Bella", and who was referred to throughout as "Professor" (he was not formally named – due, it was explained, to an instruction from the British Medical Council) said:

> I determined she had red hair and rather prominent buck teeth and that the twin incisors crossed at the front. I gave this information to the police, but unfortunately the description fitted nearly 200 women who had been reported missing in the last few years. But after extensive inquiries by the superintendent, he was able to identify her. It was a classic piece of detection.

This was puzzling, on so many levels. Unfortunately, there is no known surviving copy or full transcript of the broadcast. But there were only two people who had been involved with the re-assembling of the victim's skeleton: Professor Webster, and his assistant, John Lund.[91] Those who watched the transmission are adamant that it was Webster – who had retired from his post as Director of the Birmingham laboratory the previous year – who was featured. The *Wolverhampton Express & Star* subsequently posed the rhetorical question: "Who is the professor?", but also phoned Webster at home the following day, for a comment! Webster's enigmatic response was: "I know nothing about any broadcast. I have nothing to say about it at all." A further article the next day contained a statement from a senior police official denying that "Bella" had been identified. This police officer is unknown, but was probably not Williams, as he was formally invited to comment by the press, but would only say that: "Bella's hair certainly was not red".

It has been suggested that the broadcast may have been orchestrated by Williams, in an attempt to keep the case in the public eye, but we can only guess as to the motive had the broadcast received covert police blessing.

Retrospective evidence / witnesses

Increasingly, the media would find people who had not come forward at the time, or relatives "persuaded" to share secrets that had been passed down to them over the years.

William Douglas-Osborn's account

William Douglas-Osborn was the squadron leader who, by dint of his special constable status, had had the unenviable job of guarding the crime scene in Hagley Wood before the body of "Bella" was recovered. Post-war, his return from Europe was delayed, and he found himself in Holland awaiting onward passage. Very much after the event, his son Peter made some fascinating claims about this period of his life. By an extraordinary twist of fate, his father was apparently befriended by a group of Canadian soldiers, who had been charged with reviewing and sorting a cache of German Secret Service records, and also ascertaining

---

[91] Lund went on to have a very distinguished career in the field of microbiology and died only in 2015, at the age of 102. He did not, however, become a professor.

if these would shed any light on the fate of British Special Operations Executive (SOE) staff.[92] Douglas-Osborn told them about "Bella", and they advised him that their work had identified an active spy ring in the Midlands. Further, one of the documents they had seen purportedly described a woman parachuted into the area in 1941, and whose appearance matched that of "Bella". Peter Douglas-Osborn also went on to say that, when he had been growing up, his father had often taken him for walks in Hagley Wood. During these walks, his father not only pointed out the site of the tree, but had been happy to talk of the events surrounding it. When Peter reached adulthood, however, his father refused to talk about any aspect of the incident.

Warwick Plant

If the informant can be believed, one of the most remarkable of the many strange twists in the whole case came in the late 1990s, when a journalist put researcher Joyce Coley in touch with an ex-serviceman. His name was Warwick Plant, and he claimed that it was whilst on home leave from the RAF that his sister showed him an article on the "Bella" investigation. This apparently appeared on the front page of the *Daily Sketch*,[93] and included a photograph of one of the crepe-soled shoes, which they both recognised as being of the pair that their mother had gifted to a displaced woman whom she had befriended. This woman was known by the name of Bella. Plant's sister[94] then went to the police and the newspaper, but neither showed any interest.[95]

Warwick Daniel Aston Plant was born in 1912, and had lived in Brierly Hill all his life – up until his call-up to the RAF. His parents had run the rather upmarket Three Crowns public house[96] in Brierly Hill High Street, as had his grandparents before them. Plant himself had decided that the pub / hotel trade was not for him, and instead found employment with a firm of accountants at nearby Dudley. He was in the

---

[92] These documents had allegedly been held in an office in the Hague, next door to the house that had been the one-time home of the spy Mata Hari.
[93] A national newspaper at the time, and which operated until 1971.
[94] Doris Aston Porter, b 1906.
[95] It must also be stressed that there is no record of any such visit within police files.
[96] Erroneously referred to as the Crown by some sources.

Events and Their Reporting (Chronology)

habit of returning home to the Three Crowns for his lunch, and it was here one lunchtime that events started to unfold. On this particular occasion, he turned up to find that the bar was quiet, with the resident pianist having taken her own lunch break. Plant's mother was talking to a customer, whilst a "small woman in poor clothes" waited patiently to talk to her. She asked if she might be allowed to sing, and seeing the piano in the room said that (in the absence of the pianist), she could also play the instrument. She was apparently not looking for payment, but Mrs Plant was happy for her to keep whatever money was taken by collection from customers.

The Three Crowns, Brierly Hill. Due to the prominence afforded by the "Bella" reporting, it is still known to some locals as "Warwick's". (CC-BY-SA/2.0 - © Brian Clift - geograph.org.uk/p/1100339)

So impressed was the landlady by this woman's singing that she was asked to return, and subsequently performed there twice a week. She was a "natural", and popular with the customers. As news of her talent spread, she was also engaged to sing at the Mitre, in Stourbridge. Over time, Bella explained to Mrs Plant that she had been a professional singer and part of a concert party that was touring Europe when war broke out; the war had caused the group to disband, and she had fallen on hard times. In the Midlands, she had struggled to find suitable accommodation, and ended up in cheap lodgings in Birmingham Street, then a poor area of Stourbridge. The two women became close, and Bella would further confide that her landlord could be violent when drunk.[97] If her proper name was divulged, there is no record of this; "Bella" was apparently a nickname given by her father on account of her fondness for singing.

The key events cannot be dated with anything approaching accuracy, but Warwick Plant recalled a day of bad weather, when Bella arrived soaked to the skin and very cold. Mrs Plant ushered her into the kitchen to dry out, and noticed that part of the problem was that Bella had holes in the soles of her shoes. She accordingly gave the woman a pair of her own shoes. These were crepe-soled, but had rarely been worn on account of Mrs Plant not particularly liking them. Plant remembered these as being two-tone, in tan and cream, and Bella was delighted with them. On a subsequent occasion, Bella turned up to sing with a black eye and facial bruising. She explained that her landlord had beaten her up whilst drunk; although none of the Plant family would have been aware, this was the last time that they would see her. Mrs Plant was soon convinced that something had happened to her, as the bond that they had formed would have mitigated against her walking away with no explanation. So concerned was she that she despatched Warwick to the Mitre on more than one occasion, to find out if Bella had been there. Each time, he reported back that her absence had been similarly noted. During these visits, Plant had even seen her landlord, but had been too intimidated to confront him.

---

[97] There is a clear implication that the relationship may have been more than just that of landlord and tenant – possibly lovers, or pimp and prostitute.

Events and Their Reporting (Chronology)

The Mitre, Stourbridge, in 2016. (CC-BY-SA/2.0 - © Bill Boaden - geograph.org.uk/p/4781886)

There is another aspect of Warwick Plant's account which is of great interest, stemming from the fact that, although based at Dudley, his accountancy firm had a branch at Bromsgrove. He was occasionally required to visit this office and, on one such occasion, when travelling by bus, claimed to have seen Bella working in a field adjacent to Hagley Wood. She was with a man; whether Warwick was able to identify him is not recorded – nor, inevitably, is the timing of the incident (although it seems likely that it would have pre-dated Bella's last appearance at the pub).

A new newspaper

The launch of a new local newspaper – the *Black Country Bugle* – in 1972, some 30 years after the murder should, on the face of it, have very little bearing on its resolution. Nevertheless, there were three factors which conspired to suggest otherwise.

Firstly, by this time, Wilfred Byford-Jones had long departed the local journalism scene, and the Wolverhampton *Express & Star* no longer seemed keen to revisit the case on such a regular basis. Secondly, the *Bugle* was based in Halesowen, a town which, for numerous reasons, has become central to the case. But perhaps most significant was that its editor, Harry Taylor,[98] had an interest in the case that was close to obsessional. Taylor now had a vehicle to pursue his own agenda, and a fairly clear field in which to operate. Accordingly, he wrote a long article

---

[98] Also presenting himself as the *Bugle*'s crime "consultant".

reprising the main facts of the case, which was published in September 1973. Just as the *Express & Star* articles nearly 20 years before, this produced a bumper postbag and resulted in some further interviews with individuals claiming to have something new to offer.

The most interesting of the meetings undertaken by Taylor were with former police inspector Richard Skerratt, who had been one of the first on the scene when the body had been discovered, and a David Partridge. Skerratt gave some information regarding the shoe enquiries which wasn't fully consistent with previous reports, but that doesn't appear particularly significant. Similarly, differences between his account of the incident in July 1941 when he and Jack Pound investigated screams emanating from Hagley Wood and the official version (he suggests that only one individual had reported the incident rather than two) don't seem to have a great deal of relevance. What is potentially useful, however, is his assertion that Pound had felt that the killer was from the services ("I reckon as the chap we'm [sic] looking for is now helping to drive Rommel out of North Africa"). This view had not previously made it into either the police or public domain. David Partridge was a contractor engaged in tree felling in Hagley Wood at the time that the body was discovered, and claimed to have found the tree which had entombed "Bella". This contradicted the perceived wisdom that the tree had been demolished in the process of extracting the body. Partridge contended that only a portion of it had been removed, and was pictured standing next to what he claimed was the tree in question.

The following month, two former Home Guards came forward with "new" information. The first of these was Geoffrey Grove, who had been an NCO within the Cradley unit in 1941. He claimed that it had been common knowledge that witches' covens had been regularly held in Hagley Wood and, secondly, that two of his colleagues had discovered two German parachutes, hidden at Colman Hill (Belle Vale). He reported that his colleagues had taken them home (silk parachutes were always in demand for use in the repair and making of clothes), but that they had been discovered by police and confiscated; and stated that the Home Guard "knew" that the parachutes had been used by two enemy agents, one of whom "was Bella".

The second Home Guard soldier to come forward with information was Harry Basterfield, yet another native of Halesowen. He actually turned up in person at the newspaper offices and recalled that, in 1941, Home Office patrols had been stepped up as a result of intelligence indicating a potential parachute drop into Hagley Wood. One evening, Basterfield was part of a four-man team which was at the end of Hagley Wood Lane, when they heard the persistent sound of a car horn. Driving back up the lane, they found a parked car with two occupants: a male and a female. The driver was wearing an RAF uniform, and allegedly produced appropriate identification, whilst the female was under a blanket. Reading between the lines, it seems that the Home Guard officers felt that they had interrupted a lovers' tryst and, to counter the embarrassment of all involved, swiftly left without speaking to the female or asking her for identification.[99] The Home Guard advised the driver that a clearance order was in place, and told him to drive off. When the patrol returned half an hour later the car had, indeed, gone. The article stated Basterfield's assertion that the car had been parked only 200 yards from where "Bella's" body had been found; in answer to the question as to why he had not come forward sooner, Basterfield claimed that he had left the area soon after and been unaware of the discovery of the body – only connecting the two incidents when he had read the *Bugle* article.

In a development strangely echoing previous events, the *Bugle* now received an anonymous letter – seemingly posted from Toronto – asking a series of questions, some of which were rhetorical:

> Who put Bella in the Wych Elm? Hasn't the answer been known to those that matter for many years?
>
> Didn't he die a year before she was found?
>
> When the answer was discovered, wasn't it allowed to rest out of kindness to those, dead and alive, who were involved for the most part unwillingly in a situation that was not of their making?
>
> Aren't these the questions that you should ask?
>
> What was the connection between Hagley Wood, Germany, Canada and Holland?

---

[99] In this scenario, one wonders if even the driver would have been asked to show his ID card.

Later Developments

Who were the pro-Nazi sympathisers in Birmingham, Wolverhampton and Stourbridge before and during the war?

Who knew the Dutch girl living under the name of Dronkers in Birmingham before the war?

Who knew the Dutch girl's man friend in Stourbridge?

Who was the Dutch girl known as Clara?

Did Clara work for Abwehr?

Did Clara drop in on her old friends in 1941?

Did Clara visit anyone in Stourbridge?

Who died insane in 1942?

Was Karl Dickenhoff really a Canadian?

What did he do while he was living in Edgbaston?

What happened to the dead woman's child and who was the father?

There are those on both sides of the Atlantic and in both hemispheres who you could ask these questions but why?

The writer finishes by stating that: "there is an eternal justice beyond earthly laws".

Still following in the footsteps of Byford-Jones, Harry Taylor returned to the matter in June 1978, when a further article appeared in the *Black Country Bugle*. This was fairly formulaic – reprising some older interviews whilst building in an element of "new" information. In addition, there was a tasteless and gratuitous recreation of the murder scene, with staged photographs using a plastic skeleton borrowed for the purpose from Halesowen Fire Station. The new element was provided by a shoe repairer, Leonard Cogzell. Cogzell claimed to have watched a TV programme screened around 1970 which had shown the shoes allegedly found in Hagley Wood. He recalled that one of these had a cut in the upper, which had been stitched. He (as some of the youths who had discovered the body) lived at Lye, near to a sheet metal factory that made buckets and baths. The metals used here frequently cut into the shoes of the factory workers who, rather than throw them away, would choose to have them stitched by a local cobbler. Stitching varied from cobbler to cobbler, and provided almost a fingerprint to those in the trade; Cogzell thought he recognised the stitching as that of fellow tradesman "Billy" Field, and said that, on that basis, it would have dated from 1933. If he could see the shoe in question, he might be able to confirm this, and provide a vital clue.

Cogzell further claimed that he had tried to follow this up with the police but got nowhere – hence his decision to involve the newspaper. The *Bugle* now got in touch with Birmingham University's Forensic Department, which had taken over custody of items relating to the case. Cogzell (and probably a representative of the *Bugle*) met with a Dr B. T. Davies of the University's Medical School to examine the shoes, but declared that these were not those shown on television. He was photographed examining the shoes, and further claimed that Davies was obstructive. Unfortunately, media at this time did not operate as now (with ready access to recent broadcasts), and the *Bugle* was reduced to asking its readers to recall details of the television broadcast – with no success.

Again reflecting earlier events, this same article generated further letters – one of which bore a Devon postmark. Part of it read:

> It was 25 September 1973 when my [previous] letter was mailed to you from Toronto. Her death was not self-inflicted. The broken bone in her neck proves the way she died ... The owners of the parachutes found in the Bath Meadow by the man who looked after Mr Holden's horses in 1941 [sic]. Knew all the answers. Please let it rest. The authorities did.

If this is to be taken at face value, it is certainly of interest. Bath Meadow is close to the Colman Flats at Belle Vale referenced by Harry Basterfield (as the site where the parachutes of "Bella" and her colleague were allegedly found) and also to the site of at least one of the "Bella" messages.

Harry Taylor would later (in 1987) pen a book: *Black Country Ghosts & Mysteries (including that baffling wartime riddle WHO PUT BELLA IN THE WYCH ELM)*, under the pen name Aristotle Tump.

Later Developments

The squire of Gatacre Hall

Gatacre Hall,[100] just to the south of Claverley, crops up from time to time in relation to the "Bella" mystery. There are some oblique references elsewhere, although it is only within Joyce Coley's 2007 booklet[101] that it receives much prominence. Unfortunately, Coley's narrative is another that is sometimes confusing and hard to follow – and this is certainly so where Gatacre Hall is concerned. The story is that related to her by Judith O'Donovan (a woman who had been brought up in the area and knew much about some of the characters involved in the case).[102]

The Gatacres are an old "recusant" Shropshire family, which took their surname from the lands they owned. The individual of relevance was believed to be the second son of the previous squire, and had not anticipated inheriting the title. He settled in Canada where he married a local woman but, when his elder brother was killed in the First World War, returned to take over Gatacre Hall. The place was by then fairly rundown, with death duties having taken their toll. The new squire did not endear himself to the locals, spending what money he had on drinking and womanising rather than on maintaining the house. With these two hobbies, it was probably inevitable that he moved in some of the same circles as Jack Mossop, and the two supposedly became close. It was also predictable that his wife would be unimpressed by his behaviour and, after their young child had died, she left and returned to Canada. It was rumoured that the squire had fathered another child out of wedlock and, one morning in 1941, he also left – disappearing after breakfast without taking any possessions and leaving the place unlocked.[103] Gatacre House and Park were then taken over for use as an American Forces' base. Many years later, the squire returned and married another local woman (from Clent). Running throughout this account is an implication that the squire's estranged wife, rather than having fled to Canada, may have been the unidentified murder victim.

---

[100] It seems that this was the original spelling, although at some point this changed to "Gateacre" before reverting.
[101] *Bella: An Unsolved Murder.*
[102] Judith's father was seemingly a cousin of Jack Mossop.
[103] Sources have indicated that he in fact went back to Canada (whether or not to attempt a reconciliation with his wife is not stated).

Events and Their Reporting (Chronology)

Postcard of Gatacre Hall, 1910 (britishlistedbuildings.co.uk).(CC-BY-SA/2.0)

TV coverage

As television became more ubiquitous, the longer the case remained unsolved and the more that it received the oxygen of publicity, the more it appealed to producers. Accordingly, it has spawned a number of TV programmes, some of which have been more professional and objective than others. A prominent broadcast was an episode of the ITV Central Television *Crime Stalker* series, presented by John Stalker, and transmitted in September 1994. In September 2005, BBC West Midlands screened a documentary as part of the *Inside Out* series, although little is known of the episode devoted to the Hagley tree murder. A BBC Radio 4 broadcast from 2014 – *Who put Bella in the Wych Elm?* – was part of a series (*Punt PI*) offering a light-hearted and quite tongue-in-cheek analysis of unsolved crimes. It featured a range of interviewees and some expert witnesses with no obvious axe to grind. These included Professor Ronald Hutton and James Hayward. They respectively stated unequivocally that the facts as presented demonstrate no obvious link to the occult; and that historians were "pretty confident" that there were no spies unaccounted for in the Midlands during the Second World War. Within this programme, Peter Douglas-Osborn acknowledged that, if there were a cover-up, it was not for reasons relating to national security.

Of all the still-accessible broadcasts, however, it is the 2018 UKTV *Nazi Murder Mysteries* episode that has attracted the most publicity. It contains an interview with biologist John Lund's son, Richard, and another with historian Nigel Jones, who re-states the view of military experts that there were no spies unaccounted for during the Second World War. Further, Peter Douglas-Osborn reiterates that his father refused to discuss his experiences, although not stating this time that he was, initially, very keen to do so.[104]

New Nazi papers emerge

In April 2005, another twist was added, after a sheaf of papers from the 1940s and which had been found in a deserted Nazi post in Belgium, went to auction. Amongst these was a document suggesting that, despite being defeated in the Battle of Britain, Hitler still had designs on invading Britain in 1941. Further, these showed that the Third Reich were considering the Shropshire towns of Bridgnorth and Ludlow as possible British Headquarters in the event of a successful campaign. There were those who pointed to this as confirmation that the Midlands were crucial to Hitler's ambitions, and that this reinforced the likelihood of spies having operated in the area.

The end of the road?

The police formally closed the case in 2005. This process followed formal protocols of the time, and was probably largely completed by administrative staff. A transcript of the Closure Report appears at Appendix B.

The fact that the police had declared the case closed has not precluded further research into the surrounding events, or fresh evidence coming to light; and the release of police documents to the public in 2016 has provided opportunities for further research as well as generating some fresh and ongoing interest. In this respect, the recent media broadcasts have already been alluded to, as has the work of the late Joyce Coley. But others have undertaken fuller, more detailed and objective research.

---

[104] It is acknowledged that this may be down to the programme edit.

Events and Their Reporting (Chronology)

Alex and Peter Merrill

More recently, father and son team Peter and Alex Merrill have used what is new to supplement existing knowledge and produce a new and highly useful analysis of the case. There were three particularly useful strands of work that they undertook. The first of these was to commission Face Lab at Liverpool John Moores University to produce a facial depiction of the victim from the original forensic photographs of the skull. This was a major piece of scientific work – believed to be the first time that such a reconstruction had been undertaken from just photographs. Whilst obvious caveats apply, this meant that, an image of the victim could finally be viewed.

The Merrills also managed to speak to Joyce Coley, who expanded on her earlier research which had found that many locals were aware that a family group had left a number of their caravans on the edge of Hagley Wood whilst working on the harvest at a nearby farm. The purpose of this action was supposedly because their traditional winter "pitch" (the Jameses' farm) had closed, and they wanted to secure an alternative campsite for the coming months. The action of Felix Tate in moving a party of Travellers on from his premises had also put pressure on suitable camping sites. No names had been put forward at the time, but Coley told the Merrills that, after the publication of her booklet, people had come forward and told her that the story that had been passed down stated that the original Travellers who had staked a claim to the pitch in question were the Lee family; and that it was members of the Smith family that had tried to oust them. There had been a violent confrontation, during which a woman received fatal injuries. She also indicated that a credible source had told her that the body had been moved, and that the tree was only a secondary deposition site.

The third piece of the Merrills' research referenced above also built on the knowledge imparted by Coley. In the absence of official records from the early 1940s (i.e. the war years), they turned to the 1939 Register in an attempt to identify Traveller movements. Compiled in September that year (at the outbreak of war), its principal purpose was to facilitate the production of identity documents and ration cards. It was not restricted to households, but included those living in caravans and tents. Whereas Travellers may have had little interest in run-of-the-mill census returns, they were aware of the value of both identity and ration cards (as the Forrest family would later demonstrate), and so more willing to register.

Whilst the 1939 Register shows nothing of particular and obvious relevance to the case in and around Hagley, extracts from Bromyard – some 30 miles from Hagley Wood and 13 from Hereford – reviewed by the Merrills are more illuminating. Bromyard, which is close to the Worcester Road, had a number of established Traveller camps, used at various times of the year by those families on the fruit- and hop-picking circuit. These included branches of the Lee, Smith and Loveridge families. Although the Lees and Smiths were large Traveller families, this was undoubtedly the same group that regularly stayed in the Hagley area – confirmed by the presence of "Charlie Boy" Lee (who, as established, was probably Mary Wenman's father). Amongst all the other names recorded at Bromyard sites at this time, the Merrills identify nine women who fitted Professor Webster's wider age parameters of the Hagley Wood murder victim. Three of these fitted Webster's more precise age estimate. These were: Rose Watton (shown as a farm labourer); Sarah Evans (housemaid); and Isabella (Bella) Evans (a hawker). Webster's report had stated that the victim would have been "around 35" at the time of her demise, and one of these three – Isabella Evans – would have been 35 in 1941.[105]

---

[105] Born 19 February 1906.

PART II
Analysis

CHAPTER 10

Officialdom – The Forensics and Police Enquiries

Over the years, the way that the investigation of this case was undertaken has attracted a lot of attention from various quarters. It is undeniably true that a number of files are incomplete or have gone missing, and it is easy to be critical of the actions of the police. However, it is unfair to judge actions undertaken 80 years ago by modern standards, and allowance has to be made for the constraints imposed by war. Further, numerous re-organisations of the various forces involved hardly helped the situation. Unfortunately, their failure to follow some leads, allied to gaps in records, has allowed some commentators to put forward (often outrageous) conspiracy theories and make claims of a police cover-up – which, for the most part, don't appear to be justified.

Forensics

Professor James Webster

Although much criticism has been directed at the police, they were hardly aided in their labours by the quality of James Webster's work. If the Home Office's flagship forensic science laboratory was supposed to make the policemen's lot a happier one, then the latter must have been most disappointed by Webster's input.

Webster was initially a police surgeon before becoming a pathologist. He rose to become Director of the Birmingham Forensic Laboratory, and later Professor of Forensic Medicine at Birmingham University. Described in rather lazy and clichéd terms by some newspapers as a "real-life Sherlock Holmes", many of their articles rather concentrated on his eccentricities. In this regard, he was something of a gift to the media: a large, imposing Scotsman, he had a glass eye and wore a monocle in the other; caring little for sartorial elegance, he favoured an old and shabby Harris tweed jacket and baggy trousers, whilst invariably wearing his tie at half-mast. On one well-reported occasion, he wore a pair of carpet slippers when attending an inquest. Aware of the coverage that he was attracting, he countered that his dishevelled appearance was down to long hours spent in the field, which often meant that he was unable to return home and freshen up / change before attending court cases or inquests. Eccentricity does not, of course, equate to incompetence and, in the early part of his career, some journalists compared Webster's work to that of the eminent Sir Bernard Spilsbury. For a time, he was considered to be one of the most respected pathologists of his day.

The passage of time, however, and analysis of his performance in other cases has resulted in Webster's reputation being re-evaluated.[106] The Merrills[107] have also undertaken some quite detailed research into some of Webster's cases – a surprising number of which remained unsolved – and concluded that his reputation may have been significantly overstated.[108] With the application of hindsight, Webster comes across as having been extremely suggestible, and the fact that he was made to take early retirement from his public post against his will at the age of just 57, is of note. Webster certainly didn't enjoy good health, having sustained heart attacks and suffering from severe arthritis in addition to numerous other ailments; yet he still fought against the decision. Webster was a confirmed workaholic, but there were reasons other than health why the Home Office may have been glad to see the back of him. Increasingly, there had been friction between the forensic science laboratories and the Home Office, who didn't believe that that any Laboratory official should give evidence for the defence in a case where another employee was acting for the prosecution. An edict was issued underlining this, yet in at least two cases, Webster would go against this (acting for the defence both

---

[106] Not least, the 2019 BBC programme *Murder, Mystery and My Family* (series 2, episode 6) has cast doubt over Webster's analysis in the murder trial of Harold Merry, who was convicted of killing his lover (Joyce Dixon) in Birmingham, in 1942.

[107] *Who Put Bella in the Wych Elm? Volume 2 A Crime Shrouded in Mystery.*

[108] This is potentially a massive understatement!

Officialdom – The Forensics and Police Enquiries

times). Nor were these isolated examples of his disdain for authority: Webster increasingly became a thorn in the side of the Home Office.

The Merrills have identified a close link between Professor Webster and Mervyn Phippen Pugh. Better known just by his initials "M.P.", Pugh's official position was Agent for the Director of Public Prosecutions. Although precise roles have changed slightly over the years, this wider position was largely like that of today: it was Pugh (who served in this capacity for 34 years) who was responsible for reviewing police evidence and deciding whether a case should proceed to prosecution. He was fiercely defensive of his record, and thus ensured that only those cases where there was almost certainty of success should go ahead. Consequently, there were commentators who suggested that there were cases which the police felt they had effectively solved, but which never made it to prosecution. Possibly through their regular working contact, both Pugh and Webster had developed a shared hatred of capital punishment, and this has also been put forward to explain a reluctance to pursue cases. Their antipathy, however, was based upon concerns over miscarriages of justice, and of innocent persons being hanged. There can be no suggestion that, in this case, the lack of a prosecution was down to concerns that an innocent man had been framed.

In terms of this particular case, some of Webster's assertions would have been most unhelpful to the police. The characteristics of the victim would have been fundamental to the subsequent investigation yet, even in terms of her height, Webster was vague. His figures here were based upon the Karl Pearson theory, which was still quite in its infancy. This methodology involves taking the length of key bones to determine the likely height of a body; but it remains disappointing that, when all the major bones had been recovered, Webster could not come up with a more precise estimate of height which would not be later questioned. The fact that he would initially put this at 5' and then reduce the figure to between 4' 9½" and 4' 10", seems to be greatly at odds with later beliefs (Tommy advising that she could have been as tall as 5' 8"). The fact that police were then having to work on the basis of the victim being somewhere between 4' 8" and 5' 8", would have eliminated less than 10 per cent of the female population!

Having made his initial pronouncement, Webster did not then identify

Analysis

that shoes of size 5½ would have been considered large even for a woman a foot taller. Another aspect of Webster's work that causes concern is his opinion over the time that death occurred. This is often key to solving a murder and, notwithstanding technological advances, his placing reliance upon plant growth is a concern. What Webster seems to be saying is that the condition of the bones led him to believe that the body would have been there from around October 1941 (i.e. 18 months before it was found) whilst the growth through the clothing suggested a period about six months longer (dating to April 1941). Yet, to the layman, 18 months seems to be a relatively short time for all flesh to have disappeared from the bones; and two years a relatively short time for plants to grow completely through garments (even if of very poor quality) in a dark place. Further, Webster wouldn't fully commit himself on the issue of whether the body may have been moved from an earlier deposition site. In his defence, Webster did express his own concerns at the artist's sketch – portraying a quite glamorous woman with a waspish waist. This image was at odds with Webster's contention that the victim had been neglectful in her appearance, and may have been counterproductive. This could have prevented members of the public contacting police with the names of missing people, as their circumstances would not have fitted perceptions.

The Closure Report does acknowledge that advances in forensic science might make other of the original findings worthy of re-evaluation, and this may apply to the missing part of the victim's hyoid bone. No great relevance was attached to this at the time, but modern science now identifies a broken hyoid bone as an indication of strangulation – and often associated with domestic assault or unpremeditated killing. Just about the only cause of death that can be ruled out, from Webster's report, is blunt trauma – as he is categoric that there were no marks of injury on the skull.

The interment site

From the outset, there was so little on which we can place reliance. We cannot even be sure that the much-copied photograph reproduced within the *Express & Star*, with the caption "Body was found here", which has become the iconic representation of the site, is of the tree in question. The first time that this particular photograph appears in print is within that newspaper's article of 20 November 1953. Whilst a copy bearing the same annotation ("tree – now cut down") and containing the arrow supposedly showing where the body was found appears on police files, the sequential file number of a similar photo suggests that the former may not be one of the original shots. There is thus the possibility that it is of a different – but similar – tree, and even taken at a later time.

The need to take detailed photographs before a crime scene is disturbed had been established by police protocol in the 1930s, so would have been well known to all police officers on the case. Within the case Closure Report, DI Nicholls states that a forensic archaeologist:

> ... may have been able to assist had there been any photographs of the scene recorded. At this stage I am unable to identify whether this was the case. Most certainly there is no record of such on the file.

This is baffling as, in accordance with the protocols, a photographic booklet (dated 19–20 April) was produced. Many of the photographs do appear to have gone missing, although 19 of the original 45 survived within the police documents made available to the public in 2016. Whilst the majority of these depict bones and part of the skull and skeleton, a few do show the deposition site. Granted, these are not of great quality and do not address a lot of the outstanding questions – but it is not true to say that they do not exist (unless, of course, they had gone missing at this time and were later located / retrieved from other files). Alternatively, it might just reflect that very little attention was paid to the compilation of the Closure Report.

The issue of how the killer(s) chose the tree in which to dispose of the body is an intriguing one. At the regional police conference, Professor Webster said that: "the wood is well known to many people and the tree in which the body was hidden was the best and indeed the only place where a body could be hidden in the wood. The use of such a place of concealment would appear to indicate local knowledge." This may have reflected the general view, but Webster was unlikely to have been in a position to know that this was the case: whilst he had disinterred the body, there is no suggestion that he had undertaken a detailed inspection of the rest of the wood, so he must have been relying on hearsay or guesswork. Similarly, whilst Professor Murray would later state that there were "many other hollows where the body could have been more easily hidden", she was in a minority of one, and in no position to make such a pronouncement; she seemed happy to bend any facts to suit her arguments. More significantly, Walter Willetts, the timber merchant from Hasbury – who did have detailed knowledge of Hagley Wood – told Tommy Williams that: "the person who put the body in this particular tree must have had a good knowledge of the Wood or else was extremely fortunate". Ignoring the possibility that Willetts may have had an interest in the case, this seems a fair assessment: whilst logical to assume that the killer was familiar with the wood, lack of such knowledge would not eliminate a suspect. If it was the case that the killer knew of the tree's properties, then it might indicate that the murder had been premeditated – the victim being lured to the spot so that the killer could quickly dispose of her body. If not, then the killer may have had to quickly transport the body to the wood – or initially hide it elsewhere, until rigor mortis had passed. Certainly, in the annals of crime, it is not that unusual for a killer to take a victim to a location with which he is familiar. In 2006, for example, Michael Gifford-Hull was convicted of murdering his wife after her body was found in woodland near Winchester. The spot in question was where Gifford-Hull had had numerous trysts with prostitutes. It is not outrageously speculative to suggest a parallel here.

If the victim had been transported (whether dead, unconscious or awake) by vehicle, the most obvious point of entry to the wood would have been from Hagley Wood Lane which, as established, was in places no more than 35–40 yards from the deposition site. It is similarly possible that the perpetrator(s) had the intention of dumping the body in the wood, and just happened upon the convenient hiding place. One has to consider how even locals would have known of the hollow bole and the answer may be just the same: by accident, perhaps because their presence had scared a bird or animal from the inside of the tree. Even if a local person was aware of its properties, there's not many individuals who would discover a hollow tree and make a mental note that it would be a good place to hide a body. One of the more intriguing theories that has been put forward (in relation to the possible involvement of Jack Mossop) is that the tree may have been used by him, or another black marketeer, as a place for concealing contraband goods. But, on any level, this is just wild conjecture.

Both Webster and Lund clearly made the assumption that the clothes and shoes did belong to the victim. This may have been a reasonable deduction, but it must be considered that, if the site was known to be a hiding place, it may have been used as such by others not linked to the crime, or even previously by the killer(s). It may also be the case that, at one time, the hollow nature of the tree (prior to the opening being obscured by further growth) would have been much more obvious. The police photographs show a shoe sitting above the leaf litter and other debris at the bottom of the tree, but the other shoe was outside it. Whilst it would be understandable for bones to have been removed by animals, it is less likely for a shoe to have been taken in this way. Further, had it become detached whilst the body was being placed in the tree, the killer would have run the risk of having his crime discovered – the site being only a short distance from the lane. It could be that the youths who discovered the remains had much disturbed the scene (perhaps in a panic), and inadvertently removed the second shoe from the tree. But it is also possible that both the shoes and the clothing were deposited at different times from the body, which would further cast doubts over Webster's timings. Indeed, although there is lack of clarity within reports, the implication that tree roots and other foliage could have grown through clothing in this period is suggestive of different times of deposition.

It is difficult to tell from the surviving photographs just how accessible the tree bole was, and those photographs (if of the tree in question) suggest that branches and foliage may have significantly obstructed it – depending on the time of year. In dismissing the notion of suicide, Professor Webster deduces that the woman would have sustained injuries if climbing in herself. It might be inferred from this, and the height of the tree, that it would have been very difficult for someone to have placed even a small body into the top of the tree if working alone. Stuffing a body into an aperture just 3' 6" above the ground unaided, however, may have been a practicable possibility, given the detail provided by Webster. Against this, the diameter of the tree being just 17" in places, there would have been very little scope to compress the body, so her head and shoulders may have needed to have been forced in.

Analysis

Also of possible relevance is that the body, wedged into the tree in an upright position, must have been inserted into the tree feet-first. This could suggest that either an individual had premeditated the murder and placed something within the wood to assist (Webster, himself, required a stepladder to view the body *in situ*), or that more than one person was involved in secreting the body. It would certainly have been easier to put the body in head-first; the fact that the body was seemingly placed "right way up" might be indicative of the killer(s) having had some respect for the victim. Of course, if the murderer was mentally impaired, any attempt at rational explanation is doomed to failure. In view of some of the suspects that would later emerge, this may be relevant.

The police photos of the bones and skeleton do not really add a lot in terms of identifying how the body was secreted, because of the fact that they may have been disturbed by the youths who had made the discovery. There is little to be read into the fact that some bones were missing: given the remote woodland location and presence of wildlife, it would have been more surprising had the skeletal remains stayed complete and in one place. Notwithstanding, it is of great interest in view of later claims that there is no reference within official documents to the severing of a hand, or to the hand being found away from the tree. Something as significant as this would surely have been included in Webster's report had it been the case. Although the severed hand has become one of the accepted "facts" around the case, it would seem likely that it was a deception perpetrated by a journalist or other commentator. Given that there would have been very little natural light left in the wood at this time of day and year, it is also likely that the search of the site was not undertaken until 21 April 1943 (the day after the body was extracted). Accordingly, either a vigil must have been maintained for another night (of which there is no record), or the scene was left unguarded – allowing for further contamination or disturbance.

The timings of some key events and sightings would support a theory that the body may have been placed in the tree significantly after death. Whilst Webster's report strongly implies that the body was intact (rather than just a mass of bones) when placed inside the tree, this cannot be taken as read. Nevertheless, the action of animals in stripping flesh from

Officialdom – The Forensics and Police Enquiries

the bones could have resulted in a much faster rate of decomposition than Webster's timings considered.[109]

The shoes and clothing

If it is considered that the clothing and shoes did belong to the victim, and that this was the only deposition site, then the body could not have been in the tree for much more than 28 months (regardless of Webster's estimates). This is because police enquiries had identified that the type of shoes involved were not manufactured until around June 1940 and had been subject to at least six months' hard wear. It is interesting to note that, during extensive police investigations into the source of these shoes, dealers seemed to be more perceptive than James Webster. One outlet, indeed, advised that there was very little demand for shoes of such a large size.[110] Whilst it could be argued that Webster may have significantly miscalculated the victim's height, a more likely explanation would be that the shoes were not bought for her, although there is no suggestion that any padding was found inside the shoes (which could be expected if the wearer had much smaller feet).

If Webster had not thought it odd that such a short woman would wear such large shoes, John Lund[111] at least noted that the dress found would have extended to the ground on a person of 5' or less. Whilst Tommy Williams expressed the view that part of the clothing could have been a nightdress worn under the victim's other clothing – thus suggesting that she may have been taking cover during an air raid – this does not appear to fit with Lund's analysis. Much has since been made of the fact that there were no labels attached to the clothes, with the

---

[109] Assuming entry through holes at ground level.

[110] It must be borne in mind that the average size of women's feet has increased, in excess of average height, in the intervening period. Even as recently as 2000, the average woman's shoe size has been stated as being only 4½. However, this is slightly contradicted by Alan Barnes, Secretary of the Northampton Boot and Shoe Manufacturers Association, who told Tommy Williams that he would expect somebody of 5' in height to take a shoe of size 4–4½. It should be noted that this particular shoe was also manufactured in sizes up to 7.

[111] John Lund was interviewed for the *Punt PI* radio broadcast and was an incredibly lucid interviewee for a man of 101. However, his evidence in respect of the clothing is a little contradictory.

suggestion that they may have been cut out. The *Birmingham Daily Gazette*[112] reported that the "dress material adhering to the bones [was] so rotted that neither colour nor texture is distinguishable".[113] Although the source of their information is unknown, this and other similar comments are quite at odds with the official findings in relation to colour, the contention that the length of the dress could be ascertained, and that the labels **had** been cut out. There is some justification (as later put forward) for suggesting that, if the labels had been deliberately removed, this could be indicative of the wearer being a foreign agent. Guidance to British spies did include the need to remove clothing labels, and it might be reasonable to expect reciprocal behaviour. Nonetheless, German Second World War spies were often poorly trained, and some that were captured still had labels in their clothes. Statistically, the poor quality of the clothes themselves indicates a greater likelihood that they had been purchased at a market.

The police investigation

Over time, many stories and theories – few of which are supported by hard and surviving evidence – have grown up around what was found in Hagley Wood. These include that both a woman's identity card and a green bottle were identified in the vicinity of the interment site. These were allegedly considered at the time to be of significance, yet there is no mention of either within Webster's report.

Some commentators have suggested that the police initially considered that the discovery of the identity card meant that the case would be quickly solved. This particular thread has it that the police traced the card to a woman who was alive and well, but who claimed that she was unaware that she had lost it and had never even heard of Hagley Wood! It is likely that, at a later time, the prurient press was keen to explore the angle that she may have been involved in a clandestine assignation in Hagley Wood, and the story gained so much prominence

---

[112] Issue dated 24 April 1943. The *Gazette*'s claim is not shared elsewhere, and does not appear within official reports.

[113] The assertion that the material was adhering to the bones seems to be a case of journalistic licence.

Officialdom – The Forensics and Police Enquiries

that it was even referenced in letters written by members of the public to the police and media. Yet it would appear that this is one more matter that has become confused over time, and relates to the finding of a handbag belonging to a Dr Markham near the murder site some 18 months later (in November 1944).[114] There is no possibility that Dr Markham was in any way related to the body in the tree: her handbag had been reported as stolen in 1939, and the thief had presumably thrown it away in a remote place that nevertheless had road access. It could just be that the timing of its disposal was an attempt to fool the police, or waste police time, but it was more likely that it had lain there for five years.[115] This raises further questions as to how thorough the original police search of Hagley Wood had been, and the site chosen further indicates just how accessible it was from the nearby road. It is disappointing that there is no further mention of the green bottle allegedly found at the scene of the crime. Later reports suggest that the police felt this could have also been important at the time, but it is hard to know what to make of it. It may well be that those initially involved felt that it did not relate to the crime, but any record presumably disappeared with the numerous files that subsequently went missing – if it did indeed ever exist.[116]

From the outset, the police faced some extreme challenges in solving the case. Although most murder enquiries at least have the name and the background of the victim to work from, in this instance even these details were denied them. Trying to match a victim to a list of missing persons can be challenging at the best of times but, in wartime, problems are compounded: so many people become displaced or disappear to avoid

---

[114] It seems likely that the original story was one of the many leaps of faith first made by the author Donald McCormick, and has subsequently been quoted as fact.

[115] Although the press may have speculated as to why Dr Markham was parked in Hagley Wood Lane, a logical possibility is that she had been called to offer medical aid to an individual, indicating that there may have been a travelling community camped here pre-war.

[116] It appears likely that the reference to a green bottle may have come from a comment made by Bob Farmer (one of the youths who discovered the body) many years later, but there is no contemporaneous confirmation / corroboration that the author has been able to trace.

Analysis

conscription or for other reasons, often taking partners with them. The few clues that the police had to work from were not strong. Further, police resources were also stretched by the demands of war. Added to this, the nearby Bromsgrove Lunatic Asylum had been taken over during the Second World War to become one of the country's largest emergency hospitals, treating everyone from air-raid victims to those seriously injured on the front line. Many patients had been badly disfigured and were encouraged to mingle with the community as part of their rehabilitation. This all meant that there was no shortage of strangers in the vicinity. Few would be required to account for their whereabouts, or be challenged as to their actions.

Hard evidence

One of the few pieces of documented evidence available to police at the time of discovery of the body that appeared to be possibly relevant, was the July 1941 report of screams emanating from Hagley Wood. Accordingly, this report demands closer scrutiny. A number of sources have sought to discredit it – possibly for the reason that it might contradict the view that "Bella" was already dead by the time she was deposited in the wood. One of the counter-arguments is that the sounds of foxes may have been mistaken for human screams and, as country dwellers will confirm, the mating noises of foxes can be unnerving and sound very much like a human in distress. But it has to be borne in mind that the area was very rural then; and the two men who reported the incident were not city dwellers, but locals who were used to the sounds of the country. They were apparently reliable professional men (one of them a teacher) who – some 21 months before discovery of the body – had no obvious ulterior motive for trying to deceive the police. There is no evidence that police were regularly called out to investigate animal sounds emanating from the wood, whilst this particular incident was documented in their files. Although on searching the wood nothing was found, this was hardly surprising: the search was conducted at night with little clue as to which part of the wood in which to look; and, if a killer had deposited a body in a tree just 35 yards from Hagley Wood Lane, he would have been long gone by the time the search commenced. There is no mention in the police report of Gipsies or Travellers camping in the area, and the official line was that there was no such activity in the wood – but anecdotal evidence strongly suggests otherwise.[117] This begs the question of whether the search identified the families camping nearby and, if so, whether a conscious decision was taken not to interview them. There was plenty of precedence for police forces choosing not get too involved with the workings of the travelling community.[118]

What is interesting is that this report of screams is one of the few early leads which exactly fits the timeline as established by Professor Webster. This, of course, remains peripheral, but is better than much evidence presented elsewhere; and there must remain the possibility that this was the night that "Bella" died. It would also be consistent with John Lund's conclusion that the woman was wearing summer clothes. And it can be argued that this doesn't necessarily detract from the argument that "Bella's" body may have been brought to the wood for disposal. If we are talking about a spontaneous (rather than premeditated) killing, the perpetrator may have thought that he had killed the woman (through, for example, strangulation). If she had instead been unconscious, it is conceivable that she may have regained consciousness as she was being carried into the wood / thrust into the tree, and that the terrible realisation of her fate was responsible for the scream that the two individuals heard. Such a scenario would undoubtedly have caused panic in the mind of the killer, perhaps prompting him to finish the job. Equally, the screams could of course, have resulted from other liaisons within the wood which did not have fatal consequences.

The police files

The police files released in 2016 are unquestioningly disappointing: there is a lot of duplication (arguably reflecting police protocols of the time); and some folders are empty – with two possibly not even released to the archive. It is an interesting question whether these may originally have contained documents; their contents gone missing in transit; been deliberately removed; or were overlooked by the team responsible for scanning documents prior to their release into the more public domain.

---

[117] There were even Home Guards camping in the wood when on exercises during this period.

[118] See also Chapter 11.

Analysis

One of the many significant problems that the police faced in investigating the Hagley Wood murder was that enquiries spanned more than one force, and communications between each of those involved were not always good. In particular, the forces in whose jurisdiction some of the wall messages were found were not always quick to notify their colleagues in Worcestershire CID. The most obvious example of this may have been in relation to the alleged apprehension of the message-writer by PC Horrobin. At the time, Old Hill was administratively within the county of Staffordshire (not transferring to Worcestershire until 1966), and it seems quite possible that a failure by the Staffordshire Constabulary to pass on information to the Worcestershire CID severely impacted upon this part of the investigation. Similarly, whilst police records demonstrate that other forces were circulated with photographs of the jaw and distinctive dentition of the victim on at least two occasions, there can be no guarantee that all forces pursued the matter with diligence.

Among files known to have been lost were those containing statements taken from officials and volunteers who made the initial sift of the area around the witch hazel tree. It is hard to imagine that these would have revealed too much, though: given that some of the searchers were adolescents (Boy Scouts), it is hard to apply the same standards of evidence and accountability that would be the norm in a modern murder investigation. Clearly, nobody would suggest today that the search of a murder site should involve youths – but such was the reality of wartime constraints. In the investigation of the aforementioned wartime murder of Florrie Porter in nearby Lickey End (Bromsgrove), schoolchildren were drafted in to search for the murder weapon. More generally, without reference to the files of other long-running cases of the period, it is difficult to make valid comparisons. Nevertheless, a more thorough investigation of the site would probably have identified Dr Markham's handbag.

What is of greater concern is that there is also little surviving documentation covering the period between the issuing of the forensic report and investigations resulting from the discovery of the wall messages. By then, nearly a year had elapsed. Accordingly, there is little to identify just how thoroughly the police initially investigated the case, or to indicate what priority it was afforded at this time. Although railwayman Arthur Edgington was never a serious suspect in this case, the fact that the police record that there was some similarity between the writing in the anonymous letter accusing him with an earlier letter is of interest here. For the earlier letter is not on the file, and this once again suggests that there may have been further letters received from the public soon after the discovery of the body, but which have not survived.

It would seem likely that all these early case papers – if not deliberately destroyed – were lost at the same time or times, possibly when transferred between forces. As a result, it is difficult to know what to make of the subsequent police claim that they investigated 3,000 missing person reports. Even in the absence of complete files, though, this would appear to have been a huge exaggeration. The related claim that this included all cases within 1,000 square miles may also sound impressive, but is a fairly meaningless soundbite: it applies only to those within an 18-mile radius. In similar vein, the police assertion that they tracked down all but half a dozen of the 6,000 pairs of shoes is rather disingenuous, as very few had been of size 5½, and the majority could thus be (and were) immediately dismissed. Tommy Williams own notes also show that some short cuts were taken. He freely accepts the boot repairer Leonard Pass's assertion that the purchasers of the crepe-soled shoes on his invoices were all still alive, without any independent verification. A newspaper article[119] would later claim that Webster's description of the victim matched that of nearly 200 missing women, but this is also unverifiable – as is any information on how these leads may have been pursued.

Some documents – dating back as far as the 1920s and including traffic point duty reports – that were copied to file are clearly unrelated to the case. This reflects in part that, in a bid to save money, use was made of the reverse side of earlier and redundant case papers. There are also documents which are quite obviously misfiled, and a reasonable inference is that some missing "Bella" papers probably appear on files relating to other investigations. Not infrequently, there are documents marked "continued" or with a sequential number, but with the preceding

---

[119] *Wolverhampton Express & Star*, 23/05/1956.

or following sheets absent. Some rather strange content includes an article from *Tit-Bits* magazine which is a piece of fiction about a killer who is brought to book by his conscience.[120] In addition to the gaps and duplication of documents within files, some of the categorisation also leaves much to be desired. It is apparent, however, that at least some of this is down to those subsequently tasked with copying papers and transferring them to electronic media. It is also quite possible that some file reorganisation took place over the years, and that the original structure was somewhat different.

Hindlip Hall – the imposing Worcestershire CID offices where Tommy Williams and his team were based from 1947. Built in 1820, the building passed through the hands of several titled families before it (and the surrounding estate) was sold to Worcestershire County Council. From 1967, it has been the HQ of the West Mercia force.
(CC-BY-SA/2.0 - © Trevor Rickard - geograph.org.uk/p/2918761)

---

[120] There is reference in police records to a similar article from a magazine by the name *Armchair Detective* (this is previously the magazine more correctly referred to elsewhere as *Armchair Science*). This was provided by witness John Jones, who had also annotated it with his own thoughts. It may just be that this is the same syndicated article, which purports to examine the working of the criminal mind.

Officialdom – The Forensics and Police Enquiries

Much has been made of the fact that there are no documents on file recording dialogue between the police and MI5. Yet, we only have the word of Wilfred Byford-Jones and other third parties that the police even notified or consulted MI5, and these sources can be easily discredited. The inference from this is that the police felt there was little or nothing in the spying allegations to warrant their involvement. The files do also throw up some obvious contradictions and errors, though. One example is that relating to possible victim "Billy" Gibson, with an officer putting in writing (in a letter to the informant) that the victim's shoes "were said to be very cheap".[121] This was a complete misinterpretation of the facts and displays a disappointing level of knowledge about a key element of the case. And one of the most puzzling aspects of the investigation is the categorisation of Jack and Una Mossop's son Julian (probably only about eight years old at the time of the murder) as a suspect. Although it might again be argued that this could have been due to an administrative error, police did continue to monitor and record his whereabouts in relation to this case until the 1950s.

Another observation is that some of the wording within statements provided by the travelling community seems very formal – rather reflecting police terminology – and parts of statements given by individuals are quite similar. This is a little disturbing in view of the fact that many of the Travellers interviewed were illiterate (this is not a sweeping generalisation: a large proportion of the statements that were taken were signed only with a cross). This is not to suggest that individual police officers were deliberately falsifying statements, but might point to short cuts being taken, and genuine assumptions being strengthened.

With the benefit of hindsight, there were some aspects of the inquiry which could have been much better handled, as well as some seemingly obvious errors and missed opportunities. These include failure to:

- fully investigate Bill Fletcher and Eddie Shearwood's motives after they had been overheard discussing the case;
- establish the true identity of Kenneth Patten's "partner";

---

[121] Tommy Williams in correspondence with Leon Hughes.

Analysis

- follow-up Vivienne Coss's claim (and, in particular, the failure to interview the dairy owner, Mr Parsons);
- satisfactorily close out enquiries in relation to Bella James;
- identify or record the further complex family relationships of those living in houses opposite the Rose & Crown;
- more thoroughly consider the actions of Horace Edmonds;
- properly investigate the different addresses given for the Lavin family, as well as the recording of an address for a Ms O'Grady (by the Manchester force) which was apparently inhabited by the Lavins; and
- pursue details of Jack Lavin's employment in May 1941.

These issues are further discussed in subsequent chapters.

Against this and, in the interests of balance, some of the detective work was impressive. The police were sometimes meticulous in following up the few definite leads that they had, particularly, for example, in relation to tracing some of the Traveller witnesses and in their detailed enquiries into both the horse slaughterers and some aspects of the shoe investigations. There was considerable continuity of staffing throughout the case, which included Tommy Williams remaining in post for well over 25 years – although this reflected employment and social trends rather than any conscious strategy on the part of the Worcestershire force. Spanning the years in question, officers knew their patch and tended not to move between forces.

Local knowledge can, however, be both a blessing and a curse. There are a number of examples within the files of the police closing down a particular line of enquiry on the grounds that a witness was known – and felt to be reputable – but where a more objective view should have been taken. This applies in particular to the treatment of Walter Willetts, who was possibly implicated within some of the graffiti messages; it can be argued that Williams' friendship with the Willetts family and others may have clouded his judgement. Unless Williams was already satisfied that the messages in question were hoaxes, this was surely, at best, a missed opportunity; at worst, a failure to interrogate a possible suspect. Another individual eliminated by police largely on knowledge of his character (and thus being "satisfied" that he had no involvement) was Horace

Officialdom – The Forensics and Police Enquiries

Edmonds. These aspects are considered further within Chapter 12.

The police have also been criticised in some quarters for not properly following up the leads relating to the reported Home Guard sighting or Warwick Plant's claims, yet it seems that these were incidents never formally reported to them. Even if some of those other "witnesses" who came forward years after the event were genuine, it is easy for recollections to change over time to better fit the many facts that had been reported in the press. None of this would have aided the police much in their work. It may also be the case that, forming the early view that the victim was a woman of low repute who had not been missed, the police would not have given this investigation the highest priority. This would have reflected the attitudes prevalent within society at this time. At no time do police files suggest that an identified soldier may have been considered as the perpetrator, and it was only in 1973 (via the *Black Country Bugle* article) that Richard Skerratt claimed that PC Jack Pound had aired the view that a serviceman subsequently based in North Africa may have been responsible.

Media involvement and claims that the case had been solved

At this time, it was not routine for police to seek the assistance of the media in solving major crimes. It was Insp Bache who persuaded Tommy that "a little amount of publicity with the assistance of the newspaper people" would be a useful way forward. Within an internal memo dated 4 August 1944, Williams acknowledges that the *Wolverhampton Express & Star* "has promised to assist us by publishing a request for this person [*sic*][122] to come forward if he has any information of value which would assist in this enquiry". A linked article appeared in that newspaper on 7 August, although it did not carry a direct appeal, and it had no byline. One has to wonder whether, in the fullness of time, Tommy Williams came to regret the decision to involve the press.

Also in terms of evaluating the various claims that the case had been solved, it is worth noting that Williams wrote to Mrs Mary Bradley in January 1954 of her missing daughter, reiterating that: "the woman who was placed in the tree has never been identified". Despite the lack of evidence, rumours persist that the police had secretly solved the case;

---

[122] In relation to the writing of the wall messages.

even the family of one man who had been in the force at the time believed (from him) that this was so. Once again, it is difficult at a distance to know what to read into this. The most likely interpretation is that the media versions have passed into the realm of general consciousness. But, if certain police officers did believe that they knew the identity of any of the protagonists, the likelihood was that they felt that they had got to the bottom of the Hagley Road references within the chalk messages. The July 2005 police Closure Report certainly adds very little of value here. It is purely a summation of the main papers on the file, and does not explore any of the loose ends, look at underlying issues or seek to identify further suspects. It is in no way a cold case review and appears to have been prepared by administrative staff rather than by CID officers who had re-examined the evidence. It contains numerous errors of detail in relation to key issues – such as the roles played by Bill Fletcher and Private Haywood – which undermine its credibility. Within it, DCI Nicholls also states that, by more modern standards, "to make the link to murder is questionable". This may be suggesting that manslaughter would be a likely defence in more modern times, but some have interpreted it as entertaining the possibility of suicide. Although overall suicide rates tend to decrease during wartime, individual cases of hardship pushed many over the edge in the Second World War, and the case has identified numerous individuals with mental health issues. It is, however, very difficult to conceive of a suicide being carried out in this way. A further, if unlikely, deduction is that the woman could have died of natural causes and her body just dumped – something not given consideration at the time.

A cover-up?

In a case which has attracted so much publicity from different quarters, it is probably inevitable that those with a particular furrow to plough will seize on the numerous gaps within police files, or apparent oversights within their investigation, to support their claims of a cover-up. One of the main arguments put forward in this regard relates to the missing physical evidence: the body itself, and the shoes found with it. Whilst failure to log the final resting place of the victim is troubling however, it is not obviously sinister. This item was in the hands of the forensic science laboratory, not the police, and is probably now buried in a pauper's grave (although enquiries at cemeteries in Stourbridge and the surrounding area have drawn a blank). But it is also hard to determine what would have been achieved by "losing" the body. There had been no match of the teeth but, if anything had subsequently come to light in this regard, the photographs would have sufficed for identification purposes. Most significantly, in the 1940s, there was a limit to what a dead body could tell you; the concept of DNA and matching bones to living relatives wasn't then even the stuff of science fiction. So, even if somebody did have an interest in protecting the murderer, the skeleton would not have been considered likely to yield many clues (and there was no indication at this stage that the case would become so enduring).

The claimed loss of the crepe-soled shoes was only brought to public attention by the reaction of the shoe repairer, Cogzell many years later, and whilst he was almost certainly shown a different pair, there is nothing necessarily disturbing behind this. The fact that he waited so long before coming forward probably prompted the police to believe that he was a time-waster. Where the remnants of clothing found in the tree are concerned, the likelihood is that they decomposed rather than were destroyed. The items found in a separate search of the wood (and identified as those discarded by the Smith family when camping in Nimmings Wood at the end of 1942) may provide a strong clue here: they are referenced in a memo written by Tommy Williams in October 1949, who wrote "I understand that with the passing of time this clothing has rotted and is not to be found anywhere at Stourbridge".

In terms of missing documentation, the arguments are, in some cases, different. A number of commentators have put forward the destruction of the coroner's report as "evidence" of a cover-up, but – however incomprehensible that it may seem now – this was merely observance of the retention policy of the time.[123] There are far more claims, though, arising from specific papers missing from files. One such is that not all the typed notes of Una Hainsworth's meeting with police made it into the official transcript. However, if this were a deliberate attempt to suppress information, then surely the handwritten notes would not have been

---

[123] John Lund, later commenting on the practice of destroying coroners' reports after 15 years, said that he personally found the policy astonishing.

Analysis

retained on file? Given the nature of police record keeping, too, could anyone orchestrating a cover-up be sure that nothing incriminating had got onto other files in error and would not later surface?

And what purpose would have been served by suppressing details of the search of the deposition site (except, perhaps, salvaging the dignity of the police who had supervised it so poorly)? Crucially, in terms of addressing cover-up allegations, it is hard to see who would have been protecting whom – and this is a view echoed by John Lund.[124] Author Andrew Sparke[125] has identified that, at the time that some of the early papers went missing (coinciding with police force reorganisation), a young clerk by the name of Stella Whitehouse was employed by the Worcestershire Records Office. She – under her married name of Rimington – would eventually rise to head up MI5. But Sparke himself acknowledges that only a dyed-in-the-wool conspiracy theorist would place any significance on this fact; and even if you do buy into the espionage theory, it defies belief that MI5 would have sanctioned placing the body of an agent inside a tree (and, if they had become aware of such an unauthorised act by one of their own, would surely have subsequently recovered it). If MI5 had approved the death of a spy, the only logical explanation would be that they were fearful of public opinion if they subjected a woman to such a fate. But if this were the case, surely a private execution and burial would have been the way to proceed.

If one discounts an MI5 angle, several other reasons could reasonably be put forward for a cover-up. It could be that the police knew the perpetrator to be dead but were suppressing details to protect innocent family members. Whilst this motive can't be completely discounted, it would seem to be unlikely. The number of potential suspects or witnesses suffering from mental health problems (interesting in view of "moon madness" being an initial line of enquiry) could also provide a reason for suppressing evidence. Tommy Williams in particular comes across as a humane individual who was very sympathetic to those afflicted, and this possibility cannot be completely dismissed. In light of press claims that

---

[124] As related by his son, UKTV broadcast, 2018.
[125] *Bella in the Wych Elm: In Search of a Wartime Mystery.*

Officialdom – The Forensics and Police Enquiries

the case had been solved, it could be argued that the police were satisfied that they knew the culprit but saw no benefit in sharing their conclusions if he no longer posed a risk to the public (for example, due to incarceration within a mental hospital). This would fit with Victor Crumpton (amongst others) being a suspect. In such circumstances – if the suspect were only identified as such late in the day – it might have been possible to keep key documents from appearing in official files.

Another intriguing possibility has been put forward fairly recently, on a website dedicated to the mystery. That is that somebody may have taken on the identity of the dead woman and paid the police to "lose" evidence so that their own identity should not be exposed. For the sake of completeness, its worthy of consideration – but not for long. In summary, if there has been an element of police cover-up, I would suggest that this would apply only to a wish to suppress a lack of consultation / cooperation between forces; to conceal the fact that the police may have been "duped"; or to protect somebody who was mentally ill. A corollary would be for reasons to protect somebody not involved in the killing itself but acting as an accessory after the event – something that will be explored in later chapters.

CHAPTER 11

The Travelling Community

At the outset, police identified the recent and regular – if unsanctioned – presence of Gipsies[126] / Travellers in the wood and, for very good reasons, concentrated much of their investigation in that area – certainly up until the appearance of the "Bella" messages.

A few words of clarification are needed here. At the time – as is still the case in parts of society today – many people were unaware of the real definition of "Gipsy", lumping in all Travellers with the Romany community. The "true" Romany Gipsies had a code of conduct and a traditional mode of dress, and it was in this context that Professor Webster and police sources probably drew the conclusion that "Bella's" clothing did not mark her out as a member of that population.[127] Belief that Gipsies may have had a central role in the case came from many sides, including – rather uncharitably – the Church. The local vicar indicated his belief that "gipsies" were involved whilst his warden, Mr A. H. Hodgetts, was adamant that "the Romanies, who have their own laws, [had] tried and condemned a gypsy woman". Like Hodgetts, proponents of the "true" Gipsy argument were quick to point out that the Romanies' code of conduct meant that they would deal with transgressions in their own way. This was true, but the ultimate sanction was usually expulsion from the community. There is no evidence to suggest that murder and subsequent placement of the body within a tree trunk was ever part of this code.

Many journalists of the time failed to draw any distinction between

---

[126] I have used this slightly more prevalent spelling throughout the book, purely to be consistent. I acknowledge that many feel that "Gypsy" is more correct, and have retained this where used by others in the context of direct quotations.

[127] A possible exception to this was the gold ring. Although not mentioned in this context by any contemporary commentator, this type of adornment was common in the Gipsy community but certainly not exclusively so.

The Travelling Community

Romanies and Travellers (who would also be most reluctant to involve the police in any domestic argument); and neither did the police themselves. At this time, too, the boundaries were starting to blur, with many traditional Romanies adopting a lifestyle that would not have been recognised or approved of by their forefathers. Interestingly, the only consistent use of the term "Traveller" is from within the group itself – Nalie Smith,[128] in particular, using the word within formal statements. In point of fact, a number of those mentioned in this narrative were descended from traditional Romany stock, although in many cases had married into Traveller families. Indeed, contemporary accounts do show signs of crossover, with some families adopting more settled lifestyles, whilst still fashioning and hawking clothes pegs, door-to-door. Many of the Travellers featured in this book had, indeed, had close family members marry into the "gorger"[129] community. As now, there was also a lot of suspicion attached to this sector of society, based partly on ignorance and mistrust. In this particular case, prejudices were later reinforced by the eccentric ramblings of Professor Margaret Murray. Those identified and interviewed by police in relation to the "Bella" missing person enquiries would mostly seem to have fallen into the general Traveller rather than traditional Gipsy category. By 2005 – the date of the police's Closure Report – the terminology used by police had at last changed, reflecting the more modern and informed usage.

A selective review of the police files might suggest that most of the travelling families to be found in the area at various times were seasonal workers involved predominantly in fruit and potato picking. Although there was, again, a lot of truth in this, a significant number were actually settled in informal camps for much of the year, sometimes being joined by members of their extended families; whilst others also had bases but would travel between work (often construction) contracts, staying on site for months or even years at a time.

---

[128] Part of the Smith family mentioned in Chapters 2 and 5.
[129] Non-Traveller.

Analysis

Evidence of occupation in and around Hagley Wood

There is some very contradictory "evidence" of just how many travelling families were camping in and around Hagley Wood before, during and just after the Second World War. Whilst some police interviewees suggested that camping in the area was well regulated, this was not the case. The statements of some farmers that only small and identified groups of Travellers were granted permission to camp is contradicted by the evidence of others. There may be numerous reasons for this, including irregular subletting by tenants. Some Travellers, too, were not particularly concerned with the niceties of obtaining permission and there may also have been an understandable reluctance on the part of landowners to confront any unauthorised occupiers – particularly adjacent to Hagley Wood Lane, which was very isolated. Some witnesses said that the Travellers never caused any trouble or unrest[130] – even though others spoke of vicious internecine fighting. Sifting through each of the witness reports, however, it would seem that Nimmings Field – the proximity of which made it most suitable for sorties into Hagley Wood – was not that regularly used by Travellers. Harry Willetts, however, had authorised members of the Smith family to camp there between December 1942 and January 1943; this was in response to a direct request from Felix Tate, who had moved them on from his land.

There was no restriction along Hagley Wood Lane itself, though, which provided plenty of opportunities for families to park their vehicles and take shelter in the wood. Many of the families that stayed along here did follow regular crop-picking (particularly pea and sugar beet) routines and would use the same stopping-off points at each of the various agricultural locations. Accordingly – and given the prevalent view that the perpetrator(s) may have known the location and properties of the deposition site – some Travellers would have had prior opportunities to become well acquainted with the adjoining Hagley Wood. Amongst these travelling families were undoubtedly a number of violent characters – some of whom had already killed. Surnames were widely

---

[130] Probably reflecting that whatever violence did occur did not spill over into the wider community.

used without entitlement, and common-law spouses often took the name of their partner, with some Travellers traditionally taking the surname of Smith, regardless of lineage. Further, identity documents were swapped around at will and often falsely claimed as lost, ostensibly to try and exploit food-rationing constraints. Such practices hampered attempts to trace individuals, both at the time and now (for research purposes). Of those families identified as worthy of interest at the time, each displayed some or even all of these tendencies, as discussed in the remainder of this chapter.

The Forrests

One of the major lines of early police enquiries was into the Forrest family and, as recorded within Chapter 2, they were able to cross-reference new witness reports to previous investigations. This was the family that had been moved on from Spout Farm, when neighbours had become concerned at the levels of violence being displayed by one of the men towards at least one of the female Travellers. Incidents reported had included a woman fleeing from her tent with blood spurting from a throat wound, and Felix Tate had spoken of witnessing a number of assaults involving (partial) manual strangulation. The police had been called at the time of the former, and had found evidence of strained and violent relations within the family. Ann Forrest's age was 36 years,[131] which was a good match in terms of Professor Webster's verdict on the murder victim.

Spout Farm was some 3 miles from Hagley Wood, but the reason for close police attention was Dorothy Lewis's later sighting of the Forrests' tent close to the wood. The timings are of great interest: although we don't have precise dates for each, the eviction from Spout Farm, the sighting of the tent near Hagley Wood and the investigation of screams emanating from the wood were all within July 1941. Mrs Lewis had said that the woman she had previously seen fleeing from her tent matched the description of the murdered woman. The fact that the witnessed

---

[131] Because of regular changing of identities, dates of birth must be treated with some caution. Ann Forrest's age has been taken from West Midlands food-rationing records.

Analysis

attacks involved wounds to / pressure being applied to the neck also suggests a possible fit. The police closed down this line of enquiry, however, because they had identified the domestic abuse victim as Mrs Ann Forrest, and found her to be alive. They had also found that Mrs Lewis was now not so sure about what she had previously claimed to have seen.

Taking this latter point first, there are a number of reasons why Mrs Lewis may have been reluctant to confirm her earlier story to police. It is one thing to tell a story to a friend in a pub and another to repeat it in a formal police interview. It is worth noting that she was sure in the first instance that the woman she had seen did correspond with the police description. Whilst others contradicted this, it may be that they were describing a different woman, who was nevertheless part of the same group. There may also be understandable reasons for a witness such as Mrs Lewis not wishing to fully cooperate with the police: she seems to have been linked to the wider travelling community herself, so may not have wanted to be seen as an informer. Allied to this, she may have been (naturally) reluctant to put herself in a position where she would be required to give court evidence against a violent man in a murder trial. Mrs Lewis's sighting of the Forrests' tent on the edge of Hagley Wood (opposite the Gipsy's Tent pub) is of potential importance.[132] We know from contemporary police reports that this was a very distinctive blue-and-green-striped square affair, quite different from those used by other Travellers. Although there were no other reports of this tent being pitched next to Hagley Wood, police did not explore this particular angle until some 18 months after the event, so not too much can be read into that. Accordingly, unless Mrs Lewis was telling a very large lie to impress her friend, this was potentially a good piece of circumstantial evidence.

---

[132] Also of note in relation to the Gipsy's Tent is that a relative of Jack Mossop's – a Nellie Law – was landlady here at the outbreak of the Second World War.

The Badger's Sett, 2019.

The police conclusion that they had successfully traced Ann Forrest is worthy of greater scrutiny. By the time that they caught up with her, she had separated from her husband (James). Interviewed twice by the police in April 1944, she agreed that she had been regularly subjected to violence. Yet she initially denied ever having stayed at Spout Farm, before admitting that this was, in fact, the case. More disturbingly, she claimed that her husband was dead, which was not the case, although Henry Forrest (James's brother) had died shortly before.

Tommy estimated the age of the woman that he had interviewed as being 42; this is older than her believed age, although within reasonable tolerance. She was far from the only member of the Forrest family to have misled the police, however. We have already seen that there was a tendency amongst travelling families to swap identities, but the Forrests did that on an industrial scale. In addition to the episode previously described (where James Forrest appears to have been masquerading as his own young relative), the family was later convicted for misuse of identity cards. Given this background, it is far from conclusive that the woman interviewed by police in April 1944 was actually Ann Forrest. Conversely, if it had been, there was no certainty that this was the same woman who had been regularly subjected to the regime of violence witnessed by others. It has to remain a possibility that the woman seen by Dorothy Lewis was murdered by James Forrest (or a relative) after the

Analysis

group had moved on from Spout Farm to Hagley Wood, and that the family conspired to conceal the truth.

It is also worth recording, in relation to the number of times that Manchester crops up in the narrative, that the Forrests were registered as living there in 1943.

Mary Wenman / Lee enquiries

In similar vein, the investigation into the apparent disappearance of Mary Wenman was closed down because an individual was traced. At an early stage, police looking into stories of a missing person from the wider Smith group, identified that Lennie – the wife of Danny Smith, and who had been hop picking the previous year – was no longer travelling with them. It transpired that she had died, and that a death certificate had been issued. But the background to this whole line of enquiry is fascinating, and further illustrates the difficulty that the police encountered in dealing with the travelling community. It also helps to demonstrate the complex inter-relationships existing within many of the families, and offers some additional pointers which may help in identifying the main protagonists.

To understand the dynamics at work here, it is necessary to go back to May 1896, when four "gipsies" (as described by the local press) named Joseph Loveridge, John Loveridge, Herbert Smith and William Smith[133] were tried for the murder of rag-and-bone man George Skerratt[134] ("also a gipsy"). The defendants were each listed as living on Hartlebury Common. Despite the evidence stacked against them, the charges were reduced to assault, and each received a sentence of just three months' hard labour. In June 1939, the Smith and Loveridge families were again in court, but not presenting such a united front. Two further Smith brothers – another William, 22, and 18-year-old Wisdom – were charged with the murder of John Loveridge, 43, who was probably the son of the John Loveridge who had appeared as a defendant in the earlier case. The brothers each gave their occupation as "labourer", whilst Loveridge was

---

[133] These were, indeed, two sets of brothers.
[134] Yet another surname that appears elsewhere. There is no obvious family link to the policeman of that name.

described in a press report as having been a "member of a gipsy encampment on Hartlebury Common". The same report went on to say that the victim "has been unofficial king of the [Gipsy] colony". Another press article labelled the Smiths as "two casual labourers from a gipsy encampment at Chadwick Bank, Hartlebury, employed on a local sewage contract", with their victim described as a firewood dealer.

A group, which included the three men, had been drinking heavily in the Angel public house at Stourport over a number of hours, when a dispute broke out over the ownership of a horse. Although the men left the Angel at 10 p.m., the dispute continued as they pushed their cycles back towards Hartlebury and, in the early hours of the following morning, a witness reported hearing "the most awful shouting and screaming, as though someone was receiving violent usage". Later that morning, Loveridge's body was found, on Hartlebury Common. Dramatically, the discovery was made by his brother, William, cycling to work across the common. The ubiquitous Professor James Webster, who would later examine and report on "Bella's" body, undertook the post-mortem, certifying that death was not due to natural causes.[135] By this time, the Smith brothers had been arrested and charged with murder.

Hartlebury Common, pictured in 2013.
(CC-BY-SA/2.0 - © Ian Capper - geograph.org.uk/p/5254031)

---

[135] The Deputy Coroner for mid-Worcestershire, however, expressed disappointment that Webster did not attend the inquest to give evidence.

Analysis

From the outset, Wisdom Smith was surly, displaying contempt for the whole legal process. He protested: "I did not have a fight with any one at all. I didn't know John Loveridge and had never seen him that I know of." It would emerge in court, however, that the Smiths and Loveridge were cousins, and that the two families had been in bitter conflict over a number of years. This enmity had, indeed, stemmed from a dispute over the ownership of a horse. In the event, and despite what many today would consider to be overwhelming evidence, neither William nor Wisdom Smith was convicted of murder. In October 1939, both were instead found guilty of the lesser charge of manslaughter. William received ten years' penal servitude, whilst his younger brother was given five years.

There is a lot to note of interest here, from both cases. Forty-three years after the earlier trial, the Loveridge Gipsy family was still living in the same place, confirming a level of permanence. The relationship between the Smiths and Loveridges (though greatly soured) also demonstrated the nature of some of the extended families to be found within the travelling community. The distrust and hatred of the police was well demonstrated by Wisdom Smith's replies to questioning, but the cases also reveal attitudes of police and judiciary towards the transient community. Arising from the 1896 trial, a sentence of three months' hard labour seems ludicrous, however it is viewed, for the death of a man following a beating. Even though William and Wisdom Smith received longer custodial sentences, at a time when the death penalty was in force for murder, their punishments also appear very lenient. Even at this time, there was a strong perception that the authorities much preferred to let these communities police themselves (if members of the public were not also involved); and that the killing of a Gipsy by one of their own was not afforded a high level of concern. It might be inferred, too, that Webster's non-attendance at the inquest reflected the same attitude. Further, tensions between the police and Travellers would undoubtedly have worsened had more severe punishments been handed down.

None of the above details, of course, appear on the Hagley Wood murder files. What is noteworthy, though, is that, when investigating the reported disappearance of Mary Wenman, the police (in the form of PC William Langley of Barnard's Green Police Station, Malvern Division) interviewed a list of Travellers which included those with names of Butler and Loveridge. Daniel Butler, of course, was identified as a member of one of the families who had camped in Nimmings Field. A close relative of his was Arkus Smith, who also commonly used the surname Butler, and Arkus was part of the wider family that included Wisdom Smith (both junior and senior). The Loveridges were also from the same clan that featured in the earlier court cases, alongside and against the Smiths – and the Hartlebury Common traveller site was visited by police as part of their "Bella" enquiries.

Although there is no clear evidence of a marriage tie between the Wenmans / Lees and the Smiths, they were well known to each other, and relationships were not often formally sealed in such communities. As with any extended family, relations were not always cordial, and some bitter disputes were recorded. Police efforts to trace Mary concentrated heavily on the Smiths and, as with their dealings with the Forrests, they encountered a lack of cooperation when dealing with them. They again found evidence of swapped identities and aliases being used, and there was heightened conflict arising from the fact that Mary's brother Caleb Wenman had served time for a serious assault on a police officer. Mary Wenman[136] was seemingly **not**, however, one of the party of Travellers that had camped in Nimmings Field in December 1942, after which rumours had circulated that one of their number had gone missing. It is no surprise, though, to learn that the facts have once more been confused.

When Bill Fletcher had first raised the possibility of Mary Wenman being missing, it was not at that time public knowledge that there was a body secreted in the tree. The discovery would not be made for more than another year. It is the case, however, that Ellen Drummond had expressed the clear view that, not only had a member of her community gone missing, but that it was a daughter of Charles Henry ("Charlie Boy") Lee. The police claimed that local enquiries were made and that they were unable to trace Mary Wenman. It was only after the discovery of the body and their review of outstanding cases that they now started

---

[136] To add to the scope for confusion, Edith Bull – common-law wife of Caleb Wenman – sometimes went by the name of Mary Lee. Born in 1898, she was probably too old to be considered as the murder victim.

searching for her in earnest. It is also probably safe to assume that rumours of a Traveller going missing would not have reached the gorger community until much after the event. This further suggests that some of the stories of missing females may have emanated from further back in time than the individuals would have been aware.

Indeed, although Fletcher's report (under the guise of an army colleague) of a missing woman dated from January 1942, it may be fairly assumed that the rumours would have taken time to reach him in his army barracks in Ilfracombe. Further confusion has arisen because of a police memo written by Tommy Williams on 5 October 1949, which stated:

> ... because this man [Fletcher] in 1943 wrote a letter to the police from Portsmouth using the name of a comrade ... to ask whether the skeleton had been identified and stating that he was interested in the whereabouts of a gypsy named Mary Lee.

Not only does Williams get the dates badly wrong, he confuses Plymouth with Portsmouth. But, more pertinently, there were clearly widespread rumours of a Traveller having gone missing well before the discovery of the body in Hagley Wood.

William (Bill) Fletcher's involvement

The number of times that Bill Fletcher's name features does make him deserving of special attention. Whilst police files do not specifically record any particular suspicions, Fletcher was interviewed several times in connection with a number of different aspects of the case. If he had no direct involvement in the murder, then he certainly had an unhealthy interest in it. Whilst Fletcher was not the only person to display such an obsession (Victor Crumpton, for example, was also fixated), he was the only one whose interest began *before* discovery of the body.

There are many reasons why Fletcher is worthy of greater scrutiny. Although details of his own antecedents are typically unclear, it does seem that, prior to settling in Halesowen, he was involved in fruit picking and vegetable harvesting as part of the travelling community. The Wenmans regularly stayed at the Jameses' farm at Illey, which was close to Halesowen. Fletcher was almost certainly the father of a child by Mary Wenman; he lived close to a number of the wall-message sites; knew many of the Smith family group;[137] and was a regular in the Lyttelton Arms pub – which (as with the Star) was a well-known haunt of Travellers. Like many of his extended family, he was suspicious of the police, which makes it surprising that he would try to get them to trace a missing "flame" in the first place. There were other organisations – such as the Birmingham Citizens' Society[138] – which would have been a more obvious choice. A possibility must be that Fletcher had heard, through the Traveller grapevine, that there had been a killing, and was concerned that Mary Wenman may have been the victim – precipitating a reluctant decision to involve the police.

In relation to the Nimmings Wood campsite incident, which arguably was behind the *Hull Daily Mail* article claiming that the case was close to being solved, Fletcher's actions also warrant attention. Although there is no specific mention within police reports that their circumstances were all checked out, there doesn't seem to be any real reason to suspect that any of the three women identified as camping in Nimmings Field "disappeared". Mrs Tate's recollection of a woman being missing is more likely to relate to a site further down in Hagley Wood Lane (as related by Harry Willetts). Nevertheless, Fletcher seems to have been very annoyed by the actions of his brother-in-law, Eddie Shearwood, in going to the police and reporting their conversation. Landlord George King told police:

> Two or three days after this conversation Bill Fletcher said [to me] "Sherwood [sic] must have told them. If you see DC Lee or Dancock tell them that Sherwood is one that exaggerates things and that there is probably nothing in the story."

It could be that Fletcher was concerned about being seen as a "grass" and upsetting the Smith family – whom we know to have contained some very volatile individuals. But it could, too, be seen as an admission of guilt, or evidence that Fletcher had something significant to hide. It is

---

[137] And may even have had a family connection.
[138] As was used by Mrs M. Lavin.

Analysis

also notable that Shearwood (his brother-in-law), had a similar fixation about the case. His involvement with the Nimmings Lane inquiry was troubling, although his contention that he had previously "forgotten" about the events he described can probably be attributed to his natural aversion to helping the police. His later claim to have found a shoe "whilst taken short" in the vicinity of the deposition scene must have been worthy of further consideration. Just why he should have been there in the first place raises numerous unanswered questions. And he, as Fletcher, was a regular drinker in the Star Hotel – from where many of the rumours about the case emanated.

The Bromyard camp

In the circumstances described in Chapter 9, the party that were camping in Bromyard in 1939 – which included branches of the Lee, Smith and Loveridge families – is deserving of close attention. In particular, the name of Bella Evans stands out.

As discussed, this name does not appear within police files and, indeed, has not featured in any accounts of the case until very recently, but has come to the fore as the result of new light shed on Traveller movements by Alex and Peter Merrill. Bella Evans' name, her age and the fact that she was part of the group which included Mary Wenman and Charlie Lee, all contribute towards a persuasive argument. Who, then, was Bella Evans? Once again, the informality of the travelling community and the commonality of the surname hamper investigation. There may well be a connection to the housemaid Sarah Evans, but they are shown as living at different sites within Bromyard. Bella is shown as residing on the same site as an Alfred Evans, two years her senior and also listed as a pedlar. With the caveats that are always necessary when trying to map such family trees, it would seem likely that the pair were brother and sister. The 1911 census shows children of these names living in Radnorshire (the Welsh county adjoining Herefordshire). If this is the right match, then Isabel Margaret Evans was born in the Kington District of Herefordshire to William Alfred Evans and Margaret (née Burton). Her birth was registered in the March quarter 1907. This might suggest that Isabel's birth was "out" by a year and, in the case of Alfred, the two sets of records also differ by a year. Amongst the travelling community, however, this would be far from unusual. There are also numerous newspaper reports suggesting that an Isabel(la) Evans was the victim of spousal beatings. Although the dates and circumstances of these incidents suggest that this was probably her grandmother (who shared the same name), this would indicate that domestic violence may have been a part of this family's norms.

Unfortunately – in terms of identifying a solution to the case – it is very unlikely that Bella Evans was our "Bella". Apart from the fact that the name used within the wall messages was almost certainly a red herring,[139] there is strong evidence that Bella Evans survived until 1987: a death certificate of that year shows a woman of that name dying in north Shropshire. This shows her date of birth as 1906, and other information also points to this being the same individual. It is, of course, possible that there was a swapping of identities, or even that the family deliberately bestowed her identity onto that of another family member to put police off the scent.

Evelyn Loveridge

A further alarming possibility, given some of the names already discussed, arose with the reported disappearance of Evelyn Loveridge in July 1941.[140] In the absence of any indication as to the results of this element of the police investigation, it may be tempting to speculate as to whether hers could have been the body in the tree. The name Loveridge is not that common; the date of her disappearance closely tied with Professor Webster's estimated time of death; and Evelyn was living just 8 miles from the deposition site. Not only that, but she is also linked by name to the Smith family (see earlier court case). Given that the Smiths and the Loveridges were known to be familiar with Hagley Wood due to having regularly camped on its edge, it might be surmised that her death could have resulted from the simmering feud between the families. This remained a possibility for quite a time during our research, although it

---

[139] See Chapter 12.
[140] See Appendix C.

transpired that gaps in official records were due to Evelyn and her husband's surname being wrongly transcribed as "Leveridge". It rather appears that Evelyn M. Brown had been born in 1910, and married Frederick Loveridge in 1937. By 1945, she seems to have been living back at Icknield Port Road and was still in the Birmingham area at the time of her death in 1998.

Dinah Curley (O'Grady) and the Lavins

Of all the names featured in police files, that of Dinah Curley has attracted amongst the least attention in any analysis of the case to date. This may be because the police were unable to verify her existence, and that their Closure Report appears to dismiss her as a viable line of enquiry. Yet they had pursued enquiries in this area from June 1943 and July 1944 and, whilst documentation of other areas of investigation is sparse, there are no less than 59 papers on file relating to Dinah Curley. She almost certainly did exist (although not necessarily under this name), and was part of a large travelling family.

The first issue to consider is why this name came to the fore in the first place. The list / partial list of missing persons as supplied by Birmingham City Police contains the names of 21 individuals or couples. Within this, there is nothing to make that of Dinah Curley stand out. She is one of 12 on this list with no known address and, amongst the others, there would appear to be persons of greater obvious interest. Certainly, Evelyn Loveridge and Mary Claypole would seem to have been better starting places, given the proximity of their addresses to Hagley Wood. The answer may be, of course, that all the names on this list (and others) were fully investigated by the police, but that the paucity of documentation makes the question rhetorical. The reason why so much attention was paid to Dinah Curley, however, almost certainly lies in the statement provided by Jack Lavin in July 1944 when he was finally tracked down by the police. This included the following: "I have never worked on the Birmingham–Worcester Road". This would be a most surprising part of any statement unless, of course, it was a response to a direct question. Accordingly, it may be fairly assumed that the police had reason to believe that Lavin – on the face of it the husband of the woman who had raised the missing person enquiry – **had** worked on the A456 road widening scheme.

In many ways, the Dinah Curley issue reflects the whole investigation in microcosm. There is uncertainty; dispute; a failure to properly document both events and police conclusions reached at the time; misuse of ID cards; withholding of information; and incorrect National Registration records. The original missing person enquiry was initiated by somebody claiming to be Mrs M. Lavin of 56 Stanley Street, Cheetham, Manchester. Police deduced that this was probably Mary Lavin, wife of John Edward Lavin, and asked their colleagues in Manchester to investigate. Enquiries initially found no formal record of anybody by the name of Lavin having lived at 56 Stanley Street, but a later police report identified that she had left there some two years previously.

The police did ascertain that this Mary Lavin had been friendly with a family called Lynch, who had lived at 32 Robert Street, nearby. The Lynches had moved to Haverfordwest in Pembrokeshire in May 1942, and the Welsh police were able to confirm that Mary had, for a time, stayed with them there. She had moved on again, however, and her forwarding address was in Ripon, Yorkshire. Police dispatched to this address found it to be a boarding house for working men. The landlady had no record or recollection of a Mary Lavin, but confirmed that John Edward Lavin had stayed there from 9 March 1943 for around six to eight weeks. Worcestershire Police now turned their attention to locating the man better known as Jack Lavin.

Jack Lavin was born in June 1916 in County Mayo, in a village that had also been his father's birthplace. At some point he and his father had travelled to England to find work, and both were registered as general labourers. Subsequently, Jack Lavin's movements would almost redefine the meaning of the word "peripatetic". Probably starting in London, the pair next moved to Bromley, Kent, where they are shown as residing on Registration Day.[141] They then switched to Gosport in Hampshire, after which Jack broke away from his father and moved to Morecambe, in (probably) December 1940. When he left Gosport, Jack claims to have

---

[141] September 29 1939.

taken his father's identity card in error. Ostensibly in pursuit of work each time, from Morecambe he moved to Cheadle Hulme, near Stockport (April 1941); Cannock (May 1941); Penkridge (Staffordshire);[142] Dumfries (April 1942); and then to Haverfordwest (September 1942). From here he moved on to the Ripon lodging house and subsequently lived in Northamptonshire, Crowborough (Sussex) and London SW3, where he was eventually detained by the Metropolitan Police and provided his statement. Despite his nomadic lifestyle, Jack Lavin had married in December 1941. His bride was Mary Dowling, presumably the individual who alerted the authorities to the apparent disappearance of Dinah Curley. The marriage took place in Stockport, where the couple would be registered as living – although there is no evidence of Jack ever working there. The likely reason for the couple choosing Stockport as a base is that there was a large contingent of Lavins living here; probably fellow immigrants from Ireland.

Intriguingly, Mrs M. Lavin's notification of Dinah Curley's disappearance was made in May 1941, seven months prior to Mary's marriage. At this time, Jack's partner would still formally have been Mary Dowling. Perusal of the local 1939 Register reveals a Mary Dowling residing at 36 Lawrence Street, Stockport, but with her surname crossed through and "Lavin" substituted. Other residents at this address were Edward Dowling, Jean O'Reilly, Michael O'Reilly and Bridget Murray. Whether Jack Lavin was also living here (between work contracts) as Dowling's common-law husband is unknown, but after their marriage the couple established a home almost next door, at 40 Lawrence Street. Rather belatedly, in September 1943, Stockport police tracked Mary Lavin to this address. Mary denied knowing anybody by the name of Dinah Curley, and flatly denied having made any missing person report. She advised that she had never lived in Manchester, nor had any relations there;[143] but it is of interest that the Lynch family had lived there, less than half a mile away from the address given by "Mrs M. Lavin" (and Stockport is itself pretty close to Manchester). Again, the

---

[142] Erroneously referred to as "Pinkerage" in police memos.
[143] Like her husband, she was of Irish descent, and most of her relatives still lived in Ireland. She did have a sister in Stockport, however and – quite possibly (judging by the 1939 Register entry) – a brother nearby.

lack of hard detail necessitates some reading between the lines, but it seems that Mary Dowling was probably related to the Lynch family. This would also explain why she and Jack moved to Haverfordwest when the Lynches went there. Although police had obtained a record of her staying at Worcester at one time (traced through her National Registration Identity Card number), she denied that she had ever been there. She confirmed that she had briefly lived at Haverfordwest, but said that this was the only time that she had accompanied her husband on any of the various contracts that he had worked on. DC Kelly, who had interviewed Mary Lavin, also reported that he had made enquiries at 12 Bird Hall Lane, Stockport, less than 2 miles from the Lavin family home. It is not explained how this connection was made, but it seems to have followed an interview with Mary Lavin's sister, Mrs Sorohan. The occupant here was recorded as being a Mrs Curley. She stated that she had lived there for many years, had no knowledge of a Dinah Curley, and was unaware of any missing relatives. This is odd, on many levels. The 1939 Register shows no mention of anybody by the name of Curley at this address, but lists a John Bernard Lavin and Mary Lavin as well as five others (including two by the name of Fletcher). John Bernard Lavin was still listed at this address right up until his death in 1956. Police attempts to trace Dinah Curley / O'Grady led nowhere. A search of historic records is hampered by the fact that, if part of the same extended family (which seems likely), she may have been born in Ireland. The most likely match that the authors can find is a Mrs Dinah O'Grady, born in 1914, and who was living in Chadderton – some 6 miles north of Manchester and just 12 miles from Stockport. If this was her, then she was not the murder victim, as she lived until 1974.

If it wasn't the wife of Jack Lavin who made the missing person report, it could conceivably have been the Mary Lavin at Bird Hill Lane but, in many ways, this isn't important. Similarly, the name ascribed to the reported missing person may not be too significant. As we have seen, many in the travelling community chose to use names to which they were not entitled; indeed, one police memo seems to name the alleged missing person as "Deria Curley Lavin".[144] Nevertheless, there was a clear

---

[144] This is handwritten by a member of the Metropolitan Police. Lacking detailed knowledge of the case, he may have made a transcription error.

Analysis

perception that an individual either related to or friendly with the Lavin family had gone missing, at a time when the police believed that Jack Lavin was working on the A456 road widening scheme. Opportunities to interview Lavin were missed. He had been pursued by Northamptonshire Police for non-payment of a fine, and they had been made fully aware of the Worcestershire force's interest. When arrested in Crowborough, East Sussex, for this offence, however, Lavin was released on settlement of the fine. It would not be until July 1944 that he would be formally interviewed in relation to the Hagley Wood case. At this time, he was living in London SW3, and the interview was conducted by a Metropolitan Police officer who – seemingly – had been provided with a list of question areas by Worcestershire Police. It is certainly disappointing that Worcestershire Police did not deem it appropriate to send one of their own officers (with a greater knowledge of the case) to interview Lavin. For, amongst the many interesting characters that appear in this saga, he appears to have been one of the most colourful – and with a number of questions to legitimately answer. By now identifying himself as an excavator driver and mechanic rather than general labourer, he had nonetheless managed to leave several jobs without providing any forwarding details. He had been prosecuted by the Ministry of Labour and National Service at least once for absenteeism; and, additionally, both reported the loss of an ID (National Registration) card and been found using a card that was not his (notwithstanding that he put forward a case that this was in error). As well as being pursued by police for non-payment of a fine, he had further been charged with housebreaking by the Northamptonshire force.

When Lavin denied that he had worked on the A456 road widening scheme, this was probably in the reasonable belief that the Metropolitan Police would not pursue the issue. Even if he was telling the truth, he undoubtedly had some knowledge of the area. In addition to having been registered at Cannock, which is just to the north of Birmingham, in May 1941, he had told a former landlady at Dumfries that he had links to the English Midlands. There was also probably more to his wife than first meets the eye. Lavin could account for his movements for much of the rest of the time, but not for the spring / summer of 1941 – the most likely time of the murder according to James Webster. At the time of the

The Travelling Community

air raid following which Dinah Curley's disappearance was reported (May 1941), Lavin acknowledged that he was employed by Sunleys of Northampton,[145] yet the police did not appear to bother to follow up with the company to identify on which site he was then engaged. Jack Lavin would also claim that there was another family of the same name in the Reddish[146] area of Stockport, and this in itself seems quite suspicious. The police were unable to find any evidence of this other family (although they may not have looked too hard), and National Registration records did not suggest that it existed.

It is puzzling why the police Closure Report concluded (many years later) that the motive behind this missing person report was financial gain. It is difficult to see how an insurance claim could have been made for an individual if she didn't really exist. The police were obviously convinced at the outset that Lavin had worked on the A456 scheme which would, at the very least, have given him the opportunity to have become acquainted with Hagley Wood. They also had reason to believe that Mary Lavin had been in Worcestershire, and what reason would she have had to lie about this? It is possible of course, given Jack's record for petty theft, that there were other misdemeanours that he was trying to distance himself from, although he would have been aware that the police would not have made such strenuous attempts to trace him for a minor matter. Police enquiries in this area seemed to end very soon after the "Bella" messages had surfaced and diverted resources. In the same way that, 34 years later, the Yorkshire Ripper inquiry was so badly derailed by a message posted by a sick hoaxer, could the outbreak of graffiti some four months before Lavin was apprehended have distracted attention from one of the case's most promising leads? Something else which is of worthy of mention (for reasons discussed earlier) is that two individuals in this episode had the name of Fletcher. One of these was listed as a potato picker, and married into a Lavin family at around this time (the union being recorded in Yorkshire). Some members of the Lavin clan were also identified as seasonal fruit pickers, although the paucity of available information precludes establishing a link to Bill

---

[145] A plant hire firm involved with numerous national contracts.
[146] Erroneously recorded at "Redditch" in some police documents.

Fletcher. Another discrepancy within the police's Closure Report was the statement that they had not interviewed Mary Lavin. This was not the case: although it was local (Manchester) officers involved, she had been questioned. The significance of the Lavins within this saga remains a real puzzle.

Kenneth Patten

Kenneth Patten is only in the frame as a potential suspect because of Vivienne Coss's statement, but deserves closer consideration. The obvious conclusion is that Coss was an attention seeker, but not all the facts support this. Coss herself advises that the alleged events occurred only six months prior to discovery of the body in the tree. Whilst it might be argued that she could have merely got her timings wrong, she had consciously noted at the time of the discovery that the events she had witnessed took place only a few months previously. Within her statement, she does not come across as deluded, but her story is implausible in parts, and some of what she related had been in the local press.

Although arguably not strictly a Traveller, Kenneth Patten's nomadic lifestyle hampers attempts to identify his movements around this time. He seems to have lived much of his early life in Nottingham, but can also be traced to Gloucestershire and the North East, in addition to Manchester. This much can be confirmed by his numerous court appearances and prison sentences – mostly resulting from petty theft. In court, Patten would claim in mitigation that he suffered from asthma and bouts of anxiety caused by an incident when serving in the RAF; and that it was for this reason that he struggled to hold down a regular job, forcing him to turn to crime. He died in 2002, in Surrey.

What may be pertinent is that, in December 1942, Patten was bound over for two years for stealing a coat belonging to the Hon. Audrey Lyttelton, daughter of Lord Cobham, from the Hagley estate. This would coincide with the time of the incident which Vivienne Coss related (where the police were allegedly searching for Patten). If her version is correct, then it is difficult to see why Patten – a persistent petty criminal – would have been so worried by the police looking for him in relation to car tyre offences (as he had claimed) or the theft of the coat. It may be that he was concerned that some more significant misdemeanour had come to light. Judging by his criminal record, he could have stolen more expensive items (he would later receive convictions for jewel theft) from the Hall, which had not then been identified or reported as missing. But, if he had been involved in some way with the Hagley Wood murder (even after the event), it would have given him powerful reason to be more fearful of the police. Even if there had been no news of the discovery of the body at this stage, he would still have been understandably jumpy.

If, for the time being, we rule out the apparently incompatible timings, there is some detail in Coss's statement that is worthy of further examination. There is no doubt that Coss and Patten did know each other, and she disclosed some further information that was not in the public domain. This included that Patten had a relationship with a girl by the name of Sheila – something which Patten himself confirmed during his police interview at HMP Wandsworth. Even though police records suggest that he was only in the Hagley area for about three weeks, Patten had lived with her for much (if not all) that time. Coss knew little about Sheila – apart from the fact that she was working as a Land Army girl, and had previously lived in Manchester. Police had managed to confirm that she had a friend, Peggy Bottomley, who had visited the couple at Hagley, and it was at Bottomley's house in Chorlton-cum-Hardy, Manchester, where Patten was subsequently arrested for the coat theft.

Patten himself (during his interview at Wandsworth prison) added more detail, saying that, after leaving Cheltenham in August 1942, he had been hitch-hiking around the country, arriving in Stourbridge in October the same year. Here he had met up with Sheila, who (in her Land Army capacity) was living in a cottage near the main Hagley Hall gates. Yet, even though Patten had lived with Sheila, he claimed to be unable to recall her surname. At the point of his arrest, it was only a number of days – certainly no more than six weeks – since he had left Hagley, and he was now in Manchester, apparently living with Sheila's close friend. Even given Patten's dissolute lifestyle, it seems unlikely that he would have been genuinely unable to recall Sheila's full name.[147]

---

[147] And surely, Peggy Bottomley could have supplied it, too.

Analysis

The entrance to Hagley Hall (2018), just a few hundred yards from the Lyttelton Arms.

It was PC Pound's assertion that he had seen the woman in Manchester which seemingly ruled out the police considering this "Sheila" to be a possible victim. Yet this is strange. If Patten had left Sheila to live with her friend, would the three of them really end up sharing a house? It would again seem unlikely. A more alarming scenario is that Patten had murdered Sheila – possibly to pursue an affair with Bottomley, who could also have either been involved – or been an accessory.[148] If this were the case, Patten (and possibly Bottomley, too) would surely have been keen to keep her full name from the police. There is, however, a much more logical explanation. Patten had a sister named Sheila May Patten, and it would seem likely that it was she who was living in Hagley Hall – with Patten (who had no permanent home) staying there when he could. If this were the case, it is easy to see why Coss would have jumped to the wrong conclusion. It would also explain why Patten "couldn't remember" her surname: he was a thief who may well have stolen other things from Hagley Hall; if it had become known that his sister had brought him into the house, that would have reflected very badly on her. It would also be far more plausible that Patten was having an affair with his sister's best friend rather than being part of a ménage à trois.[149]

---

[148] And that the "Sheila" seen by PC Pound was a different person.
[149] Regardless of other issues, the body in the tree could not have been that of Sheila May Patten. She married a man named Frederick Comins in Nottingham in 1947, and lived until 2009.

The Travelling Community

The strange events described by Coss have her driving Patten to Hagley Wood at night and lending him her dog. One interpretation of this could be that his purpose was to properly dispose of a body that had already been hidden there – or was checking that a disposal site had not been disturbed. If so, he would have undoubtedly been nervous, and the presence of a dog (Patten being a dog lover) would perhaps have helped to calm his nerves. Could this be a realistic possibility? Alternatively, having a dog with him might present a credible reason for being in the wood (even if it might be for reasons of poaching). Patten's arrangement with Sheila seemed to give him wide access to the Hagley estate and at least some of its buildings and, through his friendship with Vivienne Coss, he also seems to have established a position of trust within the dairy firm run by Mr T. F. Parsons.[150] These contacts and accessibility may have afforded him the opportunity of hiding a body before some more suitable and long-term resting place could be found. The dairy, for example, may have given him the chance to have stored the body in a freezer; whilst this might be expected to slow the decomposing process, it could be that rapid thawing could later have accelerated it. Alternatively, the body could have been stored in a warmer place which aided the decomposition process and persuaded Patten that he must find an alternative site. Such factors could have distorted Webster's assumptions on timings. Had the body been in a state of decomposition when placed in the tree, this would also better explain how some of the bones became detached and ended up outside it. Patten's access to a van could, again, have aided him in this regard.

Excepting that she may have been a fantasist, one questions what Coss would have gained by deliberately lying in her interview. She was in the company of her husband, as well as the detective inspector leading the investigation. Assuming that there are no missing papers on this line of enquiry, the police actions are disappointing in the extreme. They should not have read much into Patten's insistence that he hardly knew the area, because he was a regular offender who must have known full well how to

---

[150] It is intriguing that one of the 14 men visiting the Birmingham fruit market at the time that the first wall messages appeared was a Mr Parsons of Selly Oak (see Appendix H). Selly Oak is not far distant from Hagley, but it is not known if there was a connection.

Analysis

work the system. He flitted from place to place and may well (like many Travellers) have had prior knowledge of Hagley Wood and the opportunities it afforded to secrete a body within, even before 1942. More significantly, there is no indication that Mr T. F. Parsons, the dairy owner, was contacted as a witness. Had Patten really turned up at his house at 10.30 p.m. to ask him to return Vivienne Coss's dog, he would surely have been able to recall such a bizarre event. And, had he confirmed this, Patten would have had some serious explaining to do.

As a corollary, could Kenneth Patten, with his nomadic lifestyle, have befriended the same Travellers who were camping in Nimmings Field? Certainly, he was in the area at around the same time, and it is conceivable that he could have helped to move a body from one location to another. Patten was one of many in this saga who seems to have pulled the wool over the eyes of the authorities. A final point in relation to him is that, despite his frequent flitting from place to place, his sister did seem to have a more settled lifestyle, and Patten would spend time living with her, particularly in Manchester. Her address in Manchester[151] was only 7 miles from that of Jack Lavin, and less than 4 miles from where the Lynch family had lived.

---

[151] Wood Road, Whalley Range, Chorlton-cum-Hardy.

CHAPTER 12

Provenance of the Wall Messages

Responsible for capturing the imagination of the public, the wall messages certainly took investigations in a new direction. But how much relevance should be afforded them? There have been many theories put forward as to whether they provided any real pointers to the killer, or the background of the victim. In some quarters, they reinforced views that the victim could have been a prostitute – "Hagley Bella" and "Hagley Wood Lubella" perhaps being nicknames attributed by clients that signified a girl's "patch".

Arising leads

If the messages were genuine, the most straightforward (but not necessarily the most likely) interpretation is that somebody knew the identity of the victim but did not want to contact the police directly. There are many – particularly those who live on the wrong side of the law – whose personal code prevents them from speaking to the police but, nevertheless, are not prepared to condone murder. A police memo from April 1944 claims that the "Burgess List"[152] at Old Hill was checked and that "[all] female and male persons whose Christian or surnames contain either the names Bella, Luebeller, Christabella or other similar" were investigated, but that nothing significant was gleaned. It is not identified whether this search was subsequently extended to other parts of the West Midlands. It is strange, though, that the police took this action after seemingly determining that there was no substance in the "Lubella" / "Luebeller" references. The subsequent messages had to

---

[152] Strictly speaking, this was the burgess roll. Electoral registers included all people who could vote in parliamentary elections, whilst burgess rolls additionally listed those who could only vote in county borough elections.

either be copycat graffiti or, if not, referred to a diminutive form of Lubella, and to subsequently pursue missing or potentially missing persons who answered to any form of "Bella" is contrary to their earlier conclusions. It is possible that the police were by this time responding to public agitation, with the name "Bella" having permeated the public consciousness. Regardless, from this point onwards, the focus was on anyone known as Bella who had not been seen since early 1941. This exercise could not, of course, have included all members of the travelling community.

Whilst the forensic science laboratory staff were of the view that the initial messages – those at Old Hill and the Birmingham fruit market – were probably written by the same hand, care must be taken with such assumptions. Handwriting analysis was a science very much in its infancy at this time; the laboratory was less than categoric in their assurances; and handwriting experts to whom copies of the writing have been shown (in relation to this account) are less than unanimous in their opinions. Of the four direct leads that resulted from the wall messages (missing women by the name of Bella), only one of the names would seem to have been that of a prostitute. Of the other three, two (Bella Beech and Bella Tonks) were relatively easily traced. The police also initially believed that they had tracked the other – Bella Luer. They later acknowledged, however, that the person of this name that they had located was probably not the one they were looking for. Nevertheless, the evidence for hers being the body in the tree is very weak, being based only on her forename and the fact that she had moved from London to the Midlands. It might, even more tenuously, be argued that her employment record may have led to her sacking and a need to earn money through prostitution. Whilst this could explain her presence in Hagley Wood, and hers is the name that might be best be corrupted to Luebella, it is a very long shot.

Bella Lawley

That left just Bella Lawley, a known prostitute, and for a long time she seemed to offer a very promising lead. Although she was ultimately traced and eliminated from enquiries, her circumstances justify closer scrutiny. Amy Isabel Shemwell had been born in Cannock on 6 January

Provenance of the Wall Messages

1906, to parents Richard and Clara (née Davies). When she was five years old, her family was resident at High Mount Street, Hednesford, Staffordshire. In June 1927, at the age of 21, she married Frank W. Lawley. It would seem that this was yet another "shotgun" marriage within this story, as a girl named June Millicent was born in Cannock in the September quarter 1927, to a woman with the surname of Lawley. June, unfortunately, died in 1934, the same year that the birth of another girl – Beryl A. K. Lawley – was recorded (in the March quarter) at Birmingham. During this first marriage, it seems that the woman was known as Isabella Lawley, a name which appears on some official documents.

It appears that Isabella's marriage to Frank Lawley was not a success, however, as in 1935 she is shown as living at 34 Trafalgar Road in Mosely, with a family named Evans. Police records show that her landlady was a Mrs James – although the latter is not recorded as residing there. There was a hotel in the same road where a James family was shown, and the likely inference is that this was an area with cheap commercial lodgings and bedsits, with the Jameses probably owning a number of these establishments. Also of interest within electoral records of this time is that a George Brittain – married to Norah Elizabeth (née Allard) – is shown nearby (at 37 Trafalgar Road). Much later, Isabella would marry George Brittain. This was after the death of their respective spouses but, in reality, they were in a relationship a long time prior to that. The 1939 Register lists Isabel at 235 Edward Road, Birmingham – a row of bedsits, not far from Moseley. Her occupation is shown as "retired housekeeper", probably reflecting the custom of the time that women gave up their employment on marriage. George Brittain is shown at the same address, and it seems clear that they were living as a couple (on the original Register document, Isabel's surname is initially shown as Brittain; this entry has, however, been crossed through and "Lawley" is substituted in the manuscript).[153] It would seem that Frank and Isabel Lawley had probably separated soon after the death of their first child and the birth of their second – not a unique scenario in this saga. Another of the "unknowns" is who was caring for her daughter, Beryl, in

---

[153] It was only when Frank Lawley died in 1947, that the way was open for the pair to marry. The marriage did not take place, however, until 1950.

Analysis

these early years: she is not listed as living with Isabel in 1939, and neither was she officially with Isabel's parents. She survived childhood, however, and lived into adulthood.

Another point of note within the electoral records of 1935 is that a family by the name of Kendrick is shown as living in Trafalgar Road (at No. 49). It may be questionable how well Isabel was acquainted with the Kendricks generally, but police files show that this name was one of a number of aliases that she used. For at this time, Isabel was clearly leading a chaotic and disordered life – and may even have been living part-time with one of the Kendricks. There were three families with the name Kendrick living in the Moseley area, very close to the Payne family.[154] A further – and more intriguing – possibility is that Isabel took this name from the father and son in Moseley who also ran a tea shop at Hagley Causeway (as discussed below).

Separated from her first husband and with no obvious form of income, it was clearly difficult for Isabel to survive. It was in these circumstances that she seems to have turned to prostitution. Details of this part of her life are, of course, sketchy, but it was a fellow prostitute who came forward to report her absence in the wake of the wall messages. The police clearly believed that this was a worthwhile lead, and devoted a significant level of resources to finding her. Their investigation tracked her down (via her former Trafalgar Road landlady) to her parents at 93 Gorsemoor Road, Heath Hayes, near Cannock. They confirmed that Isabel Lawley was still alive – and had, presumably, made a decision to renounce prostitution, disappearing from the scene. It may well have been that the gossips of Hasbury – less informed than the police – interpreted this disappearance as confirmation that hers was the body found within the tree.

If Bella Lawley had been working the local area, she would have been known to numerous residents of Hasbury. One of these, living behind the Rose & Crown, had the surname James, and another that of Allsop. In a case that never fails to highlight intrigue and possible coincidences, a trade directory of 1932 shows a family named Allso [*sic*] residing at 34 Trafalgar Road (i.e. just three years before Bella Lawley is first shown

---

[154] One of whom (Fred) was among the group of youths that discovered the body in the tree.

there). If one assumes that this is a misprint, it would provide further evidence of a link between the James and Allsop families, and to the Hasbury addresses featured in the wall messages. However, further research shows that Allso is a family name, albeit very unusual.[155] It is just possible that this was a branch of the Allsop family who, for whatever reason, had decided to drop the last letter of their name. Of far more significance, though, may be that when attempts were being made to trace her, one of her former landladies was found to be a Mrs James; could this be another link between Bella and the occupants of houses behind the Rose & Crown?

In summary, then, Bella Lawley ticked a lot of boxes. Christened Amy Isabel, Isabel and Isabella were her names of choice, which clearly lent itself to the diminution "Bella". Next, the prostitute who reported her disappearance worked the Hagley Road. It is not unreasonable to assume that they would have worked adjacent patches, and thus the term "Hagley Wood Bella" may well have been applied to her. The fact that Bella at one time used the surname (Kendrick) of the proprietors of a tea shop in Hagley Causeway is also very intriguing. A tea shop would be a good base for a working girl at the time, particularly in cold weather, and it may be that the father or son would have been able to ferry her to and from her Moseley home (close to where other Kendricks also lived). Lawley does not seem to have shared the generic profile of prostitutes of the day, and operating out of a tea shop would have marked her out as a cut above the rest; this could account for the line "Hagley Wood (Lu)Bella was no pross". A further reason that could have linked her in the minds of the public was that Bella Lawley would have been 34 or 35 years of age at the time that Professor Webster estimated that the victim died – fitting very much with his estimate of the victim's age. The wider significance of all this is that, although hers could not have been the body in the tree, Bella Lawley's sudden absence could have led people to draw that conclusion – and arguably provide the rationale behind some of the wall messages.

---

[155] At the time of writing, there would appear to be only 17 families with this name in the UK, the majority living in the Midlands.

Analysis

More likely origins

It is not unprecedented for murders to spawn anonymous messages, either in the form of graffiti or – more often – letters. Reasons may include to deliberately waste police time (possibly due to a grievance); to settle old scores (through implicating an adversary); mental instability; the need to feel important; and to attract publicity. In the unusual event of these messages being written by the killer, the motive is often to goad the police. In some cases, such messages may originate from journalists, who wish to stoke publicity and keep the case alive. In this case, for reasons that will be explored subsequently, this seems a quite believable scenario.

The first ones that came to attention were in the fruit market in Birmingham, and were probably courtesy of a hoaxer or journalist (or somebody linked to a journalist) – copying the messages in Old Hill that had not so far been openly discovered. These messages all referenced "Luebella" or "Luebeller" – and nothing has come to light to strongly suggest that there was anything significant in this choice of name. Any link to witchcraft is obscure and would mean buying into the absurd theories of Margaret Murray. But all this is almost certainly over-analysing the situation. Although the self-proclaimed psychic Zita Boyden had little else to offer of practical use in any review of the case, she did make an interesting point in relation to the possible origin of the name "Bella". She suggested a link to the song "Bella Bambina". Whilst many people associate this song with Matt Monro, it was written in 1939, and recorded by Gracie Fields in the early 1940s. Popular with servicemen, the literal translation is "beautiful girl". In view of the number of soldiers in the area at the time, this could be considered pertinent in relation to the wall messages. The likelihood, though, is that the name was probably chosen because it was exotic and memorable – in the way that, for example, "Who put Mary in Tree" would not have been. Most of the subsequent daubings were probably of the copycat variety, and, had they been by the same hand, why would the name be spelt in different ways – "Luebeller", for example, being significantly different from "Luebella"?

In some ways, the graffiti at Heath Town was of particular interest: it

Provenance of the Wall Messages

is more of an "outlier", with no obvious link to Hagley (either geographically or via direct transport). Heath Town is now a fairly anonymous settlement outside Wolverhampton, but at the time it was home to the Mander factory. Mander's was a huge operation, based on an 18-acre site which had been purchased from the Government Disposal Board between the wars.[156] It had started off producing paint and then, following a merger, became one of the largest manufacturers of printing ink in Europe.

This particular daubing was reported by the Mander's employee, Stanley Ray, and it must have been a possibility that whoever wrote the message(s) here was an employee who commuted to work. Although Heath Town once had its own station, the line had been closed in 1910, however, the Mander factory was nearer to Wolverhampton Station. It was only a four-minute walk from the station to the factory site and, for those alighting on the northern platform, the route would have taken them through Sun Passage / Sun Street railway arches. Anybody from the Hasbury / Halesowen area who worked at Mander's should have been of interest to the police, but there is no evidence that this was a line of enquiry that was pursued. Stanley Ray was probably exaggerating when he described himself as a chemist (the likelihood being that he was rather involved in the paint- or ink-production process), and would have been aged around 22 at the time of the murder. Whilst not in any way suggesting a personal involvement, he lived at Selly Oak. This is 7 miles from Halesowen and 5 miles from Birmingham. Whilst none of the 14 market traders who had visited the Birmingham fruit market site of the first messages and were investigated by police had any obvious links to Heath Town, two did live at Selly Oak.

Hagley Road references

The most insightful set of daubings, however, would seem to be those pointing to addresses within Hagley Road (as previously discussed in relation to Bella Lawley). The police interviewing of Hagley Road property occupants within the parameters identified is certainly

---

[156] It had been a wartime munitions factory, producing phosphorous poison gas during the First World War.

Analysis

thought-provoking. Their records suggest a very tight-knit community, with some branches of the same family living cheek by jowl, and occupants included four families who had each been living there for over 30 years. The four families who could claim this longevity were the Willetts (father and son), the Allsops, the Basterfields, and the Moores. Research does not identify anything interesting about the Moore family in relation to the Bella case, but the others all warrant further scrutiny. It may be recalled that a Basterfield – Harry – would come forward some 30 years later to claim that he was part of a Home Guard unit regularly patrolling Hagley Wood during the war.

There is nothing obvious about Samuel Allsop senior's background and history to link him to murder (he appears to have been in no trouble with the police and to have lived a settled existence) although, of course, history is littered with killers who have lived a double life. But it is strange that he should fail to disclose that his only son, Samuel Charles Geoffrey Allsop, also lived here when on leave from the RAF. Could Allsop senior have deliberately hidden the existence of his only son because he feared that he was in trouble? The younger Allsop was another who warranted greater scrutiny by the police. Born in 1921, he would have been around 20 at the time of the murder – and his background makes troubling reading. He had been born in the family house, as had his sister. His sister, however, had tragically died at just 18 months, and this understandably cast a long shadow across the family. Samuel attended schools in the area and, after leaving in 1935, had a succession of low-grade jobs with local employers before being called up into the RAF in 1940 as a leading aircraftman. At this point he was aged $18\frac{1}{2}$, but his short RAF career was marred by regular bouts of sickness, which were mainly diagnosed as "stomach trouble" (and probably stress-related). He was known to be courting Hasbury girl Mavis Jones, but his parents strongly disapproved of the relationship. They believed that the couple had separated, but it seems that Samuel continued to see Mavis without their knowledge. From a family torn apart by grief, the young man was prone to anxiety, and his parents had rejected his choice of partner. Could this background have led to a situation where some catalyst – for example, being taunted by a prostitute if he failed to "perform" – had pushed him over the edge? Or could he even have murdered Mavis

Provenance of the Wall Messages

Jones? If the graffiti writer really was trying to identify someone at this specific address, then he is the likely – and most realistic – candidate. An alternative scenario is that the author of the messages was trying to settle a score with the Allsop family, possible in revenge for their treatment of Mavis Jones. It does again appear that this aspect of the police investigation was less than satisfactory. However, one of the questions that they should have asked can now be answered: Samuel Allsop junior didn't murder Mavis Jones. For, in 1945, he married a Lilian M. Jones, and it would seem that this was the young lady in question.

Another deception perpetrated by Samuel Allsop senior was in telling the police that he had lived at the Hagley Road address since 1888. This is not borne out by the relevant census data. Yet there was still more which would (or at least should) have interested the police, which he didn't disclose. The 1891 census records showed both Samuel and Isabella Allsop at the family home at 56 Prospect Hill, Redditch. At this time, Isabella Allsop was 18 years old, and listed as a needlecase maker. In 1894, Isabella had married Arthur Sealey, and is shown as still living at Prospect Hill, Redditch – (but a few doors away at No. 38) in the 1901 census. But – and it's a big "but" – Isabella was also being shown as single and living at 404 Hagley Road within the same census! So, Samuel had a sister who sometimes also went by the name of Bella, but of whom the police were not aware.[157] Something else of which the police did not become cognisant was that the Bella James identified as occasionally living at this address was (in all probability) a relative of Samuel's brother-in-law.[158] It could, alternatively, even be that Bella James and Bella Sealey were the same person, but that records had become confused.

If the police were negligent in not following up these Allsop family leads, they were even more so in their enquiries in relation to the Willetts. The fact that the Willetts had the timber concession in Hagley Wood – and thus both unfettered access to the wood and legitimate reason to be in it at all times of the day – would appear to be highly significant in relation to the rumours circulating at this time. Not only that, but Nimmings Field

---

[157] At around 70 years old at the time of the discovery of the body in the tree, this could not have been hers.

[158] And quite possibly related to his close neighbours.

Analysis

– quite central to the Traveller rumours – was tenanted by Harry (Charles) Willetts. It has not been possible to find a direct link between Ernest / Walter and Harry Willetts, but there is some circumstantial evidence to suggest that they may have been distant relatives.[159] It is easy to see how, in these circumstances, the messages could have been written by somebody who had picked up on the rumours and these links, and felt that the Willetts family may at least have helped to hide and / or move the body. In this case, too (as probably at the fruit market) the name of "Lubella" would have been taken from the earlier messages and not necessarily indicate any knowledge of the victim. If the one reference to a specific number in Hagley Road (404) was not erroneous, then it might indicate a belief that Samuel Allsop senior had helped the family who had been such close neighbours for over 40 years.

Although accepting that police practices have changed over time, it does seem disturbing that Tommy Williams seemed to interview the Willetts as the family friends that they were, rather than more formally as potential witnesses or suspects. Walter Willetts' view that the victim was not a local woman could be construed as a useful piece of local knowledge, but could equally be interpreted as an attempt to mislead (if Willetts himself had an involvement or was covering for somebody). Willetts certainly appears to have had some strong views on the case. In defence of Williams, though, if he had by this time identified the message writer (which would not be totally inconsistent with other events) he may have felt justified in not pursuing this angle.

There must also be a slim possibility that some of the Hasbury graffiti references may have been to Harry Truman, who at one time lodged with his mother at 324 Hagley Road. Whilst Truman can probably be dismissed as a candidate for the murder, his possible involvement was clearly being discussed within the Rose & Crown, as evidenced by police interviews with Edward Hall. The fact that Truman also had a house close to the site of other graffiti at Upper Dean Street, and was known to mistreat women, would also have provided ammunition to those locals who wished to point the finger at him. It is further germane to record that, in the words of DC Lee: "it would appear that Truman had an

---

[159] Family trees dating back to the 1840s do not identify a close familial relationship, but places of birth and apparent links to the travelling community suggest a likely connection.

intimate knowledge of Hagley Wood and the surrounding countryside". It is just possible that somebody was trying to "frame" him, or even that Truman (who seemed to share some of the less pleasant character traits of Jack Mossop) had taken another lover and then killed her to prevent his wife finding out. But most certainly, the timings rule out his former mistress as being the victim.

Suspects / candidates for authorship

There are a number of individuals whose names feature within the police files and elsewhere who were considered as possible suspects in terms of having written at least some of the messages. In terms of candidacy, some are much more plausible than others.

Victor Crumpton

It was his letter of 23 November 1953 to Sidney Inight, following another article about the case within the *Wolverhampton Express & Star*, that seemingly resulted in Victor Crumpton first coming to full police attention. His written references to the "chalkings" in Old Hill are of great interest. Old Hill, with which Crumpton was so familiar, is some 2 miles north of Halesowen – which was then much smaller than it is now. But it was here (in all likelihood) that the first "Bella" message appeared in 1943. Crumpton's extensive knowledge of some of the graffiti messages was, he implied, gleaned from PC Horrobin. Just why a police officer would confide so deeply in a member of the public – particularly one perceived to be unbalanced – is open to question, but it seems that a number of officers were on first name terms with Crumpton, treating him as a harmless and friendly eccentric. It could just be, however, that Crumpton's assertion about PC Horrobin's apprehension of the graffiti author put some wheels in motion. Although from a distance this might seem unlikely, the lack of coordination between forces may have meant that such an incident – if it had taken place – had not been relayed by the Staffordshire force (Old Hill station) to the Worcestershire CID at the time. Whatever Tommy Williams may have felt about Crumpton's state of mind, he would have been duty-bound to follow up this lead with Horrobin, and within just five days, Williams had advised at least one

Analysis

newspaper that the graffiti evidence had been dismissed "as the work of a crank". It is difficult to put an alternative spin on this: Williams presumably felt that the culprit had been identified and that, in his opinion, there was no further mileage in pursuing this angle. This is disappointing in a number of respects. The fact that there is nothing directly relating to this within the police files could, arguably, point to deliberate suppression of the facts (to protect a guilty party). More likely is that Williams – who had been involved in the case from the start – felt that it was unnecessary to record this development or, more probably, that it would be embarrassing for the police to document such a glaring failing in communication protocols. It is frustrating that we accordingly don't know whether his conclusions were verified by others, or whether they applied only to those daubings at Birmingham and Old Hill (specifically referred to within the *Birmingham Daily Gazette* article). Secondly, it would be very useful to know whether Victor Crumpton – almost certainly residing in Old Hill at the time – had been the scribe, and that his tale was, in part, autobiographical. Crumpton claims that the culprit lived at Halesowen and worked at Netherton Ironworks (and there is no indication that he himself ever worked in that industry).

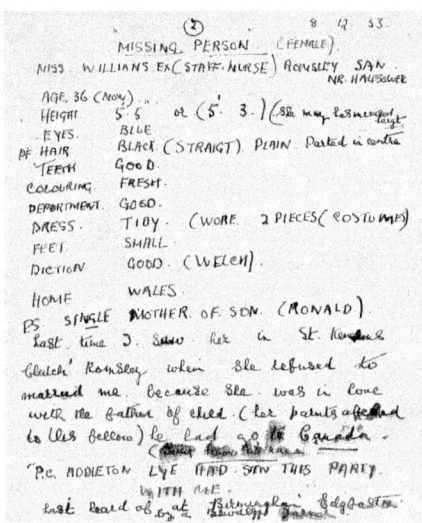 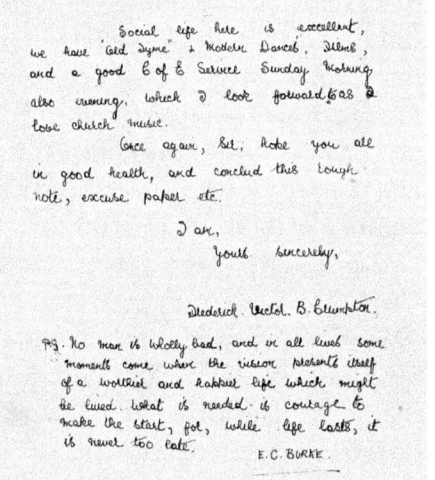

Samples of Victor Crumpton's handwriting, which did seem to deteriorate in quality when he was under stress. (West Mercia Police)

Provenance of the Wall Messages

In his letters to Williams, some ten years after the event, Crumpton sometimes prints his words – and some of the characters do arguably display similarities with those on the wall chalkings. But this is far removed from being conclusive.

Horace Henry Edmonds

Another issue of possible relevance is that the individual named in police reports only as H. Edmonds, who called in to the fruit market area of Birmingham when the "Bella" messages appeared there, also lived at Old Hill. Research identifies him to be Horace Henry Edmonds, born in 1898, and he is obviously of interest to anyone studying the case. Unfortunately, there is little within police files which relates to him. One item which does exist is a manuscript note by Tommy Williams which states "Telephoned DC Venables Old Hill who knew Edmonds and was quite satisfied that he knows nothing of this matter". When interviewed again subsequently, Edmonds stated that he had not seen the (fruit market) message until someone drew his attention to it. This is another of the many examples within the inquiry of a witness or potential suspect being on friendly terms with a police officer. There is no suggestion of anything untoward here, but the possibility again exists that judgement may have been impaired.

If the strange account of the apprehension of the graffiti author outlined by Victor Crumpton was true, then it could even be that it was Edmonds who was accosted by PC Horrobin.[160]

John H. Jones

Another avenue relating to the wall daubings – and which seems to have been more thoroughly followed up – was the behaviour of John H. Jones, the young man who had visited the *Birmingham Daily Gazette* offices to view their files on the Hagley Wood murder. The police not only successfully traced him, but satisfied themselves that he was a harmless "misfit" rather than a person of genuine interest. From their notes, this would seem to be a logical conclusion. Certainly, both Tommy Williams

---

[160] Crumpton lived at Harcourt Road, whilst Edmonds lived in Halesowen Road. Halesowen Road is a long thoroughfare, but at one point is only a few yards from Harcourt Road.

Analysis

and Dr Harrison of the forensic science laboratory were convinced that Jones's handwriting (and ability to spell) did not match that of the message writer.

Bill Fletcher

Bill Fletcher's name appears so many times in this analysis, and he was interviewed on several occasions by the police. Although not obviously suspected by the police of writing the messages, he must be considered a candidate. To recap, once he discovered that Mary Lee was safe (and not having access to all the facts), he could have realised that the rumours were true, but related to another Traveller. In such a scenario, whilst not wanting to be seen to help the police directly, he may have been looking to offer a few pointers via messages left in prominent places.

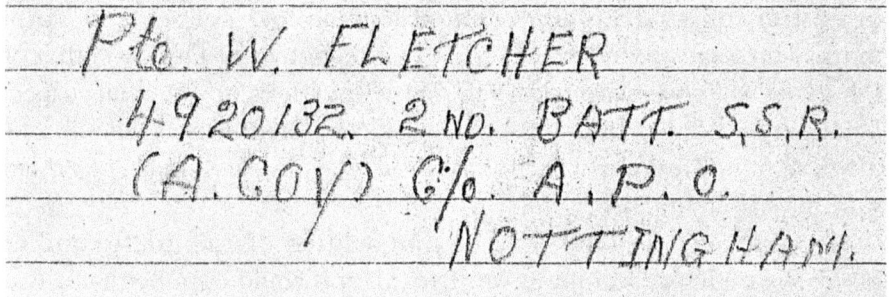

Fletcher's capital letters (specifically the letters "H" and "T"; top) arguably show similarities with those in some of the wall messages (below). (All images courtesy West Mercia Police)

In this regard, it is useful that there is a copy of what purports to be his handwriting on file. This is from the letter that he wrote to the police seeking help in tracing Mary Wenman (Lee). The letter in question is well written and in an apparently educated hand, which (as explored within Chapter 10) is a little surprising in the context of the travelling community. This is not being elitist or intended as a slur; many of the Travellers in this saga were illiterate, and in the habit of signing documents with a mark (cross). Whilst it might be tempting to speculate that the letter may have been written by another, it does appear to be very similar in style to that which he initially claimed was written by his army colleague, Haywood. Given this deception, it is hardly likely that he could have asked the same person to have written both letters on his behalf.[161]

The Palmer family

Further names worthy of consideration are those of Jack and Charles Palmer – respectively landlords of the George Inn at Halesowen and the Hill Tavern at Clent. Jack was, of course, additionally involved with the removal of a dead horse from the area, in strange circumstances. Another Palmer was a timber merchant with business on the edge of Hagley Wood, and one of the "Bella" messages (of that genre which implicated the residents of Hagley Road) was on his timber yard boundary wall. In the context of the wall messages and the pointing of fingers; that the pubs involved were hotbeds of rumour about the case; that there was an employment link to Eddie Shearwood (brother-in-law of Bill Fletcher); and that the timber business would almost certainly have brought family members and employees into contact – possibly conflict – with the Willetts family, may all be of significance.

In summary, though – and despite the high profile that these messages achieved – it doesn't seem that there can be any great value attached to the wall messages in terms of identifying the victim or killer(s). There may be more significance in terms of perceptions, but there appears to be no real reason to question Tommy Williams' 1953 assertion that "the claims within the wall messages are false".

---

[161] If a third party had been involved at this stage, it would seem likely that Fletcher may have turned again to his army chaplain, A. G. Harper. Whilst his (Harper's) own letter is on file, it is typewritten, so offers few clues in terms of handwriting.

CHAPTER 13

Una Hainsworth's Story

That spying lies at the root of this case has become so much a part of the folklore surrounding it that its origins have been overlooked. Although rumours of spies having been in the area had long been rife, the reason that most people have now heard of the case is down to the testimony of Una Hainsworth. As we have come to expect with this case, however, nothing is straightforward. Both Una Hainsworth and her first husband, Jack Mossop, were highly complex characters, and it is necessary to examine their backgrounds and relationship to obtain a better understanding of events and motives; also, to set in context subsequent events. Included in any analysis must be Una's second husband, Alfred. For a time, he was lodging with the couple and was almost certainly conducting an affair with Una whilst Jack was still living in the marital home. This would undoubtedly have affected the family dynamic, and probably Jack's mental health – as would circumstances surrounding the Mossops' children.

Mossop family backgrounds

Jack and Una Mossop

The relevant part of Jack Mossop's family tree starts with George Crump marrying Mary Ann Stanford in 1879.[162] Together, the couple ran the Boycott Arms near Claverley, and, between 1880 and 1891, had six children. The last of these was Charlotte ("Lollo") – who would grow into something of a local beauty. When she caught the eye of Edward

---

[162] There are discrepancies within local records regarding Mary Ann's date of birth and marriage. It seems from this distance that she lied about her date of birth to avoid the requirement to obtain her parents' permission to marry; and subsequently claimed to have married two years later to hide this deception. It also appears that she may sometimes have gone by the name of Smith.

Una Hainsworth's Story

Percy Mossop, her parents were appalled. One of 13 children (not all of whom survived to adulthood), Percy Mossop was widely described as "a bit of a character", which is rather a polite way of portraying an out-of-control youth. He was part of a gang whose antics earned them the nickname "the Seven Sods", and most people gave him a very wide berth. Against her parents' wishes, the couple went on to wed and, for a time, Lollo became estranged from her parents. Briefly, though, it seemed that marriage might have tamed Percy, who threw himself into the family steeplejack business, and Charlotte bore him two children: Jack, born in August 1912, and – a year later – Louis.

It was not long, unfortunately, before Percy reverted to his old ways, and the Crump family struggled to suppress their renewed contempt for him. Then, tragedy struck: at the height of the Spanish flu epidemic in 1918, Charlotte contracted the virus and died. The Crumps felt that Percy Mossop could not be trusted to bring up his two sons and, accordingly, made alternative arrangements for the boys' care. Six-year-old Jack went to live with his aunt (Charlotte's sister), Mary Ann, who was now settled at Coseley under her married name of Jenkins – and who was also in the licensed trade. Louis was entrusted to the care of another of Charlotte's sisters, Eliza (who was by now married to Sidney Maiden).

The Boycott Arms, close to Claverley (which forms part of its postal address) was once run by Jack Mossop's grandparents. It is an impressive inn which still operates today.

Analysis

Overlooking beautiful Shropshire countryside, in an extension to Claverley churchyard, are the graves of members of the Crump family. That on the right of the right-hand picture is the resting place of George and Mary Ann Crump, whilst next to it is that of their daughter Charlotte and her son Jack Mossop (Charlotte's grave is engraved with her nickname of "Lollo").

Louis is recorded as saying that he had "little time" for his father. It seems pretty clear that Percy had little interest in his sons, either. Soon after his wife's death, he took up with another woman, Violet Catherine Vant. Despite her bearing him another five children, Mossop refused to marry Violet, telling her rather callously that there would "never be a second Mrs Mossop". He would die at the age of 54, in Birmingham. Louis features little in the story hereafter, but at various times in his life was both a road-haulage contractor and, perhaps inevitably, given his family connections, a licensee.[163] He lived to the age of 82.

The two boys indisputably had had an unfortunate start to life, losing their mother and then – as they may well have seen things – being rejected by their father. Understandably, Jack now formed a very close bond with his aunt, but his behaviour was somewhat wayward – and he developed an early taste for alcohol. Whilst still a teenager, probably the last thing that he needed was to meet Una Abel. Yet, only a month after turning 20, he had married Una, who herself was just 18. It is very

---

[163] Running the Ivy House Inn at Coseley – a pub whose previous managers had included his maternal grandmother.

doubtful that the couple married for love: their son, Julian, had been born a month earlier.

By contrast, little has been recorded of the early days of Una Ella Abel. Born to parents Frederick Rowlinson Abel and Rhoda Gertrude (née Smith), she appears to have had two older sisters: Annette Rosannah Thirza and Eugenia Stella. The family lived at Wombourne, near Wolverhampton, where other close relatives were also based. It is worth noting that Mary Ann Jenkins (Crump) had connections to Wombourne – and was also landlady of the Waggon & Horses pub there when Julian Mossop was born.[164] It may be that it was this connection that resulted in Jack and Una meeting in the first instance.

Extract from Una's birth certificate. The spelling "Wombourn", without an "e", was in use until the late 1940s. (Crown copyright)

Una and Jack's marriage was also rocky from the outset, and it certainly didn't provide a good environment in which to bring up a child. Although Una claimed in her police statement that Julian was living with the couple, she was a compulsive liar. Jack Mossop's former workmate Bill Wilson said, "They [Jack and Una] did not hit it off too well. I never saw the boy of the marriage. As far as I know he never lived with them.[165] Lived with the grandmother, I thought it was the sister."[166]

Details of Jack Mossop's early employment are sketchy. In 1934 (at the

---

[164] Further keeping things in the family, Eliza Maiden would also spend a time managing the Waggon & Horses.

[165] Julian did seem to have lived with Una and Jack early on, because the whole family was registered at the Waggon & Horses at one time. Wilson's comment confirms that this was only a short-lived arrangement, and it appears that Mary Ann Crump once more took on a fostering role for a young Mossop.

[166] This comment further demonstrates the complicated nature of the family dynamic: Mary Ann was Julian's great aunt.

Analysis

age of 22), he was registered as a dairyman, [167] resident at Bridge House, Wombourne – the cottage assigned to the Waggon & Horses inn. We know this because records identify that he was declared bankrupt at the time[168] – perhaps explaining why he felt unable to look after his son; although his own dysfunctional childhood may well have been a larger factor.

Massey Ferguson, Banner Lane, Coventry. This was the former Standard Aero Works' Banner Lane Factory, where Jack Mossop once worked, pictured in 2005. Built in 1939, it has since been demolished. (CC-BY-SA/2.0 - © David Stowell - geograph.org.uk/p/47171)

By 1936, Jack was employed in Leamington and working for Lockheed, an automotive parts manufacturer which, soon after, diversified by moving into the aircraft parts industry. According to Una, in 1937 he joined the Airwork Service Training (AST) Corps,[169] which trained reserve pilots in the RAF, as a pilot officer. This meant a posting to Hamble near Southampton, but it was to be only a brief stint.[170] Just

---

[167] Una Hainsworth would claim that he was a trainee surveyor whilst living at Wombourne – possibly another illustration of the need to treat her statements with caution.

[168] Entry in *The Edinburgh Gazette*, 09/11/1934.

[169] There is no record of an organisation named as such, and it must be assumed that, whatever he joined, it was a forerunner of the RAF's Air Training Corps (ATC) – which was not founded until 1941.

[170] An alternative version of events has it that it was 1934 when Mossop joined the AST.

Una Hainsworth's Story

why he left the AST could offer an important insight into the case, but that in turn depends on the credibility of Jack's own account. For he would later tell the story that he had been invalided out of the RAF after suffering head injuries (jokingly claiming that he had crashed his plane too often). Whatever the truth surrounding his discharge, the following year Jack returned to the Midlands. By 1938, he was working for Armstrong Siddeley[171] as a fitter. The following year, he was employed by the Standard Aero Works,[172] which was also in Coventry. It is most likely that it was whilst he was working either at Armstrong Siddeley or Standard Aero that Jack and Una moved into their first marital home: 39 Barrow Road, Kenilworth. They would spend the bulk of the rest of their married life at this address, and Jack would bring many of his workplace and pub friends back to the house. It was here in 1940 that, allegedly, Una was introduced to the mysterious van Ralt – the Dutchman with the Rover car.

Money was far from being the only source of friction within the Mossop marriage. Jack was undoubtedly gregarious, and rarely gave his wife any notice of the many guests that he would bring back to the house. Reflecting his own interests, most of these were mechanics or car enthusiasts. Probably of much greater significance, though, in addition to his liking for copious amounts of alcohol, was Jack's philandering. He fancied himself as something of a ladies' man and it is said that he also acquired and took to wearing an RAF officer's uniform to which he was not entitled. The reality, however, is probably that he just continued to wear his old AST clothes. Leaving Una's relationship with Alfred Hainsworth aside for a minute, in her interviews with police she claimed that her finding of other women's clothes in the marital home was the reason for her leaving him in December 1941. Her assertion that the marriage had been in a bad way for a significant time before the pair eventually separated was reinforced by colleagues and friends of Jack's, when subsequently interviewed by police.

Jack did not divulge to his wife from where his additional money came,

---

[171] The engineering group which produced aircraft engines as well as luxury vehicles.
[172] Firstly, as a fitter at No. 1 Factory; then (from November 1940) transferring to No. 2 Factory, Banner Lane, where he worked in the assembly shop.

although we only have Una's word that it existed. She claimed that it might be from spying, but – if there was, indeed, some extra income – there are other more likely sources. There is a possibility that his father may have left him some in his will[173] (and Bill Wilson suggested that he wouldn't even have told his wife of a windfall, let alone shared it with her). A more likely source is suggested by the rumours that Jack may have been an active black marketeer (or "spiv") during the war. He fitted that particular profile, being good-looking, popular with the ladies and a flashy dresser. Moreover, he had access to a car[174] and, presumably, petrol coupons. Another school of thought was that he may have had a role as a pimp – but this is highly speculative. Because whatever extra money was coming in never made it as far as the family budget (or because Jack spent too much of his income on alcohol and socialising), Una was forced to take in lodgers – mainly from Jack's workplace – to make ends meet. These included Bill Wilson and, later, Alfred ("Jack") Hainsworth.

Jack Mossop's lifestyle and obsession with cars resulted in him appearing before the courts a number of times. On one occasion, in April 1940, he was fined 10 shillings for each of four motoring offences, including driving without a licence. This prompted the court clerk to comment that he "did almost everything wrong that he could". Although never prosecuted for any major misdemeanour, there were plenty who believed that Jack was active in petty crime. Not that Una herself was a paragon of virtue, either: over her life she ran up a series of debts which she resisted settling, and she was not averse to the occasional "midnight flit" to avoid facing her creditors. Whilst there may be a degree of mitigation if she was being deprived of household income, her actions caused considerable ill-will in the community and police files record that "Una Hainsworth is well known [to us]".

Julian Mossop
Julian Mossop shouldn't really have much of a role to play in this story, but was – bizarrely – for years categorised as a suspect in police files, despite being just 11 years old when the victim was discovered in Hagley

---

[173] Percy Mossop's estate was valued at £425 in 1936, equivalent to £20k in 2020.
[174] This was in addition to the unreliable Rover car.

Wood. It seems barely possible that the police may have believed that he was present at the time the crime was committed; could have helped to dispose of the body; or else had some knowledge of the crime gleaned from his father. But, for whatever reason, police continued to monitor his movements and whereabouts until he emigrated at the age of 21. There is a lot that is of interest about Julian on police files, but none that has any obvious value in relation to the murder. He had numerous run-ins with law, was convicted of theft, and acquired a significant criminal record before sailing to a new life in the United States. Whilst it would be wrong to visit the sins of the son on the parents, it does add to the picture of a family not well disposed to observing the niceties of the law, nor particularly moral. He died in 1998, and was buried on New York's Hart Island.

Jill Kyra Mossop

Within her police statement, Una Hainsworth unequivocally states that Julian was the only child of her marriage to Jack. There appeared no reason to contradict this, and she made no mention of a girl – Jill Kyra Mossop – who was born on 19 November 1941. Birth certificate detail leaves little doubt that the girl's mother was the same Una Mossop who, at the time, was still married to Jack. Interestingly, the child's birth was not registered until 2 January 1942 – over six weeks later. The documentation points to the registration having been undertaken by Jack Mossop (identified as the father), who was by now living apart from his wife. This in itself raises some questions, not least because the law required registration within six weeks, so Jack was presumably liable to a fine for non-compliance.

Another point of note is that the birth was registered as having taken place at 124 Warwick Road, Kenilworth. This was not a hospital but a private house and whilst it was not unusual for births to take place at home, this was not an address at which either of the Mossops were ever formally recorded as living.

Analysis

Columns:-	1	2	3	4	5
No.	When and where born	Name, if any	Sex	Name and surname of father	Name, surname and maiden surname of mother
52	nineteenth november 1941 124 Warwick Road Kenilworth M.D.	Jill Kyra	Girl	Jack Mossop	Una Ella Mossop formerly Abel

Birth certificate of Jill Kyra Mossop. (Crown copyright)

Barrow Road, where the Mossops were previously dwelling (and where Una would claim in her statement that she stayed up until December 1941) does connect to Warwick Road, but the only readily accessible record[175] shows just an Arthur and Alice Douch residing there in 1939. Given that Arthur is shown in these records as an aircraft engineer, and that much of the surrounding housing was occupied by the staff from the nearby aeronautical works, it is reasonable to assume that Una may have been temporarily lodging with another workmate of Jack's.

At first sight, Jill Mossop now disappears from official view, never to be heard of again. But a search of recorded deaths under the name of Hainsworth is more productive. This reveals a certificate recording the death of a Jill Hainsworth on 7 January 1942, although her middle name is shown as Myra rather than Kyra – requiring some explanation. The name Myra was in much more common usage at the time (later falling out of popularity with the conviction of Myra Hindley for the Saddleworth Moors murders); the writing on the original birth certificate is not clear, and it is easy to see how such confusion could arise. Given that there is no record of the birth of a Jill Hainsworth at the appropriate time, and that the death occurred at Nuthurst, Shrewley (where Una and Alfred were known to be later living), there can be little doubt that this

---

[175] The 1939 Register.

Una Hainsworth's Story

was the same girl. An inquest was held two days later, and the death was notified by Alfred Hainsworth on 12 January – five days after the event, but only ten days after Jack Mossop had registered her birth. It might be seen as surprising that Alfred didn't notice that her middle name had been wrongly entered on the death certificate; grief, though, could have been a mitigating factor.

Within her statement, Una advises that she left Jack in December 1941 (possibly on the 13th of the month), which is fully consistent with the above events. She states that she was "forced" into this action and that "we" then lived at Henley-in-Arden. As Julian was in all probability still living with his great aunt at this time, it can only be assumed that her use of the word "we" signifies that she was now openly living with Alfred Hainsworth (and this would explain why Jill Mossop's name changes). The timings are highly significant: three and a half weeks after giving birth, Una leaves her husband and moves in with her lover. A further three and a half weeks later, the child is dead. It is interesting that Bill Wilson says within his statement that Una only moved in with Hainsworth after her husband had died; this strongly suggests that Una's extra-marital affair with Hainsworth did not become common knowledge for some time.

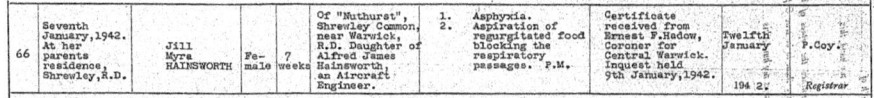

Extract of Jill's death certificate. (Crown copyright)

Alfred Hainsworth

Born in Coventry in May 1917, Alfred Hainsworth had spent time in the RAF before (uncannily reflecting Jack Mossop's short stint in the services) being discharged after just four months. In September 1940, he joined Standard at Banner Lane. It was here that he met and worked alongside Mossop, and the two men soon formed a close bond. Their shared interest in fast cars was undoubtedly a factor in this and, before long, Hainsworth was invited to lodge with the Mossops at Barrow Road. A further address is recorded for him in Kenilworth, before the move to Nuthurst House at Shrewley.[176] It was to here that Una moved after

---

[176] Very close to Henley-in-Arden.

Analysis

leaving Jack, and the couple married in September 1943, at Meriden. At this point, Una was once more heavily pregnant.

Alfred Hainsworth remained in the same post with Standard until 1944, when he transferred to their Aircraft Production Division, Ansty Aero. He left there in 1945, starting both a pig-farming business at Shrewley Common and a florist's at Warwick. By this time, Una had given birth to two further children: sons born in December 1943 and January 1945. Later, Alfred would land a job that he really would have coveted, working in the motor trade for Cyril Kieft[177] Racing of Wolverhampton in a role which sometimes entailed him driving to and working in France. In 1951, the couple returned to Kenilworth.[178] By now, there had been another addition to the family: a daughter, born in November 1946. There had sadly been a second infant mortality, too, with a further daughter dying in March 1949, only a few days after her birth. In August 1953, the family moved to Four Acres, Long Acre, Claverley. Soon after, in November 1956, a final child was born to Una, who was by now 43 years of age. This was another girl.

History does not tell us a lot about Alfred Hainsworth, but he appears to have been a better choice of husband than Jack Mossop. He was prepared to take his stepson, Julian, under his wing and, at various times, employed him in both of his known businesses. There is nothing to suggest that Hainsworth's business ventures were a great success, but his own father seemed to have been a much more astute businessman. By far from the only person in this saga to be involved in the pub trade, for 32 years he had been the tenant licensee of the Brickmakers Arms at Berkswell (Balsall Heath). When he died in 1956, some six years after retiring, he left an estate in excess of £4,500 (equivalent to around £410k at 2020 prices).[179]

---

[177] This was his place of employment as advised by Una Hainsworth in her police statement of December 1953. She wrongly stated this as being "Cecil" Kieft within her police statement.

[178] It seems that the address for at least part of this time was 71 Randall Road, Kenilworth.

[179] There are numerous different indices that can be used to calculate the changing value of money. Throughout this narrative, income values have been used (rather than, for example, the real price of purchasing power index).

Una Hainsworth's Story

The Brickmakers Arms, (a former farmhouse) at Balsall Heath, pictured in 2018. (CC-BY-SA/2.0 - © Richard Law - geograph.org.uk/p/5718837)

It would appear that the Hainsworths later made an unsuccessful attempt at starting a new life in Canada. At some point, Alfred travelled to North America and, on 1 February 1957, Una and their four surviving children joined him. They left from Liverpool, and their home address was given as Mill Cottage, Lane End, Mathon.[180] Just over four months later, however, the whole family returned, travelling back from Montreal to arrive at Plymouth on 9 June. This could arguably have been an extended holiday, but the fact that their return address was given as the Swan Hotel, Stratford-upon-Avon, suggests that they had not planned to come back. In either case, it would seem likely that the trip would have been financed by a legacy from the estate of Alfred Hainsworth senior.[181]

All that can be gleaned of Alfred Hainsworth over and above this level of detail is a civil action that he took against a Cardiff firm, in 1948,[182]

---

[180] This is a small village in Herefordshire, near Great Malvern, Worcestershire.
[181] Although he left all his estate to his widow, Nellie, it would not have been unusual for her to have passed some of this on.
[182] This appeared within articles published in the *Western Mail* and the *South Wales News*, February 1948.

Analysis

which showed him to be working as a "fruiterer". This is far too late to be considered as relevant in terms of the writing of the "Bella" wall messages, but does beg the question of how he became involved in that particular business.

Lucy Stephens

Lucy Stephens was the young Welsh woman who – according to Una Hainsworth's version of events – disappeared from Brick Bridge Cottage with her husband's money. It is doubtful that she was a relative, although this could have been so. If it was the case that Una was trying to plant the seed that Lucy Stephens (by virtue of being known to Jack Mossop and then disappearing) was the murder victim, this can be dismissed for the reason that she is recorded as living until 1994.

"Confession" and death of Jack Mossop

When Una made her statement to police at the end of 1953, she maintained that it was in March or April 1941[183] that Jack Mossop had returned home in the early hours, and confessed that he and "van Ralt" had stuffed the body of "the Dutch piece" into the hollow trunk of a tree. After leaving him in December of the same year, Una claimed to have seen Jack only three more times before he was admitted to the county mental hospital. These contacts were apparently arranged so that Una could retrieve furniture and other possessions. She implied that Jack had been prevaricating, claiming that he "thought [he] was losing his mind as [he] kept seeing the woman in the tree and she was leering [at him]. He held his head in his hands and said: 'it is getting on my nerves, I am going crazy'."

Even if the story told by Una properly reflects what Jack told her, it does not necessarily accurately portray events. If Jack Mossop was a murderer, then he may have massaged key details to present himself in a better light. In view of what Una said and the subsequent events, his mental state was key,[184] although the detail contained within his death

---

[183] In some accounts, wrongly stated as April 1942.
[184] At this stage it is not helpful to discuss whether or not Mossop could have been involved in a spy ring; this is considered in more detail within Chapter 14.

certificate[185] could be used to argue several different scenarios. Chronic nephritis is symptomatic of severe kidney disease, and this and myocardial degeneration (a disease affecting the heart muscle) suggest that Jack was in an exceptionally poor state of general health for a 29-year-old. Both conditions could be seen to be the result of excessive drinking. Cerebral softening – also shown on the death certificate – covers a multitude of sins, but these include traumatic brain injury, and it would be appropriate to consider Jack's claim to have received head injuries whilst in the AST in this context. For somebody in such a poor state of health, his personal life collapsing around him and alcohol his only refuge, perhaps nothing further was required to drive him over the edge.

When interviewed by police, Bill Wilson – one of Mossop's closest friends – expressed astonishment that he could have taken part in a murder, believing that, whatever his faults, he was not capable of such violence,[186] or even assisting an offender in such circumstances. Against this, psychiatrists will argue that coercion, stress or panic – particularly if mixed with alcohol – can make people behave in the most unexpected ways; and it is quite possible that remorse and regret at being involved in the death of another could cause a mental collapse. Wilson would also go on to say that Mary Ann Jenkins (Crump) had asked him what was worrying her nephew / adopted son; Wilson had replied that it was probably marital problems, but advised that "she did not seem satisfied [with that]". There is, however, another possible explanation for Mossop's breakdown, which has not previously been put forward. If Professor Webster's timings were correct, around 11 months passed between the murder and Mossop's admission to Stafford mental hospital, and some might argue that this is an unusually long time if the events were directly linked. There was, however, only five months between Jill Kyra Mossop's death and Jack's incarceration. Could this have been the real catalyst? Whilst the natural assumption is that Jack would have been aware that Jill was not his daughter, if this were not the case, then a number of interesting scenarios present themselves. It could have been,

---

[185] See Chapter 6.
[186] Wilson stated that Mossop "couldn't hurt anyone".

for example, that he believed that the new arrival would bring him and Una back together. Like his own father, Jack had been a poor parent, judging from the fact that he was unwilling / unable to look after his first born (Julian), and perhaps saw this as a last chance to sort out his life. The death of his only daughter, or the discovery that he was not her father may have been sufficient to have caused an emotional meltdown. If this were the case, the additional revelation that his wife would shortly leave him for good may have precipitated a fresh surge of binge drinking that tipped him over the edge.

The austere St George's asylum that was home to Jack Mossop in his last days, pictured post-closure. (Both photos copyright Glen Hayes)

Credibility of Una Hainsworth's allegations

The fact that Jack Mossop was now dead meant that it was – and remains – very difficult to verify a lot of the details of the story imparted by Una Hainsworth. What we do know for certain is that Mossop had a huge drink problem. Bill Wilson would later tell police: "He was having trouble with his wife and he used to drink a considerable amount. A very heavy drinker … I did not realise how heavy until after he had gone and people told me."

The most important part of Una's story hinges on what happened in the car when the protagonists allegedly left the Lyttelton Arms. Newspaper reporting of Una's statement suggests that the occupants of the car must have doubled back on themselves. One interpretation could be that the girl was killed after they had passed Hagley Wood, but the articles do not convey that. Further, turning right off the Bromsgrove

Una Hainsworth's Story

Road into Hagley Wood Lane would also represent an unnecessary and pointless detour. It is further confusing that the police drew a tentative conclusion (which is repeated within the Closure Report) that it would be unlikely that Mossop would have driven to Hagley Wood to deposit the body, as it was not on the way back from the Lyttelton Arms pub to his home at Kenilworth. This is a very strange deduction: if "Bella" was already dead, it would be illogical to drive around with a body in the car looking for a suitable burial spot on the way home. Mossop was well acquainted with the local area and would have known that Hagley Wood, just a short distance from the pub, would present a number of possibilities. And, far from representing a major detour, this was on a practicable route home. Whilst it is natural to read into this that either Jack Mossop or Una was telling an unlikely tale, it does not appear that these details were supplied by Una, and the inference is that the press may have wrongly interpreted the information that they had.

So, why should we not take what Una told Wilfred Byford-Jones and the police at face value? A better question would be: *where should we start?* From the outset, it must be stated that Una Hainsworth is far from being a credible witness. Apart from her cavalier attitude to debt, she had come to the attention of the police for other petty misdemeanours. Her statements contain numerous inconsistencies, some of which – for example, her assertion that her son (Julian) was always living with her – were probably designed only to present herself in a more favourable light. It does seem highly significant, though, that she deliberately withheld from the police the existence and death of her daughter, Jill. With Jack Mossop's state of mind being so important to the investigation, she suppressed a piece of information that could have provided a satisfactory and logical alternative explanation for events.

Without insight into her background and duplicities, Una's story is, at first sight, persuasive. There is, however, very little that can be confirmed to independent sources, and it is necessary to consider her possible motivation. She did not come forward until 1953, some nine years after the discovery of the body, and aspects of her story are difficult to take at face value. That she was unaware of the murder at the time is hardest to accept, particularly as missing person reports indicate that the news had reached as far as India. The wording of her statement rather smacks of somebody protesting too much. It could also reflect somebody having been coached in what to say. So, what was Una's real reason for going to the press at this time? There was a reward on offer of £100, which equates to around £2,000 at 2020 prices, although there is no record of money having changed hands. Of course, even if Una wasn't acting in the public interest, it doesn't mean that elements of the tale were all untrue, or that Mossop was not implicated in murder. It is even conceivable that Mossop had divulged details of a murder that he had carried out and that Una had invented van Ralt as a means of trying to lessen her former husband's culpability. On the other hand, if Una was still bitter over the way their married life had worked out – or even felt that Jack was in any way responsible for the death of her daughter – she would surely not have thought twice about maligning his memory. Either way, the fact that Jack was dead by this time meant that an explosive story could be told without anybody being able to contradict it. As previously discussed, the police hardly pulled out all the stops in their efforts to trace van Ralt, although it may be that, even at this early stage, some officers were unconvinced by Una Hainsworth.

It is interesting that members of the extended Mossop family believe that their ancestor was a murderer. Judith O'Donovan is one such, saying (without qualification) that Mossop was often at the local pub,[187] drinking with a Dutchman called van Ralt; and that he later confessed his crimes to his grandmother [*sic*], asking her for money to facilitate an escape. It is reasonable to assume that, if Mossop was confiding in Una, then he would also tell his aunt, to whom he was very close. It is difficult, however, to know just how much reliance can be placed on information that has been passed down through generations of a family; history is written by survivors, and it is quite likely that it was Una Hainsworth who planted the seed within the Mossop family that their forebear was a killer. Indeed, Judith O'Donovan's statement, rather than validating the existence of van Ralt, strongly suggests this.

---

[187] This is most likely to be the Boycott Arms, with which Mossop's family had a connection. It could, however, have been the Plough, the Crown, the Woodman or the Kings Arms – or a combination of these.

Una Hainsworth's Story

There has been speculation over why Una Hainsworth used "Anna" as a pseudonym. There may be many reasons behind this, but nothing concrete that would offer any obvious insight. One of the wall messages (that at Mucklow Hill) did refer to "Ana" rather than "Bella" or "Lubella", but this was not widely viewed as being by the original writer(s). A conspiracy theorist might read anything into the choice of name, but it may just have been selected completely at random.

There are also some further unexplained notes within two police documents, which both appear to be linked to the first *Anna of Claverley* letter. The first of these handwritten papers – to continue a long-running theme – contains the names of two pubs. One is the Labour in Vain: although there were a number of pubs with this name at the time in question, it is most likely to be that at Yarnfield, just to the north of Stafford. The name "Mrs Johnson" is shown alongside,[188] and the likely interpretation is that the police had tentatively deduced that the landlady, a woman by the name of Annie Johnson, should be included on their shortlist of possible authors (prior to Una Hainsworth identifying herself). The notes also recorded that Annie Johnson had relations at the Crown at Iverley, near Stourbridge, and only some 5 miles from Hagley.

The annotation within the second police note is potentially more interesting. There is nothing contextual, just a list of names and partial addresses. The first name is illegible, but underneath are the words "1936 Royal Hospital Ear & Throat Dept"; then "Brick Bridge Inn Claverley"; followed by: "Dr Lee Dutch Army Hospital New — [illegible]"; "Lt Col Wilfred Byford-Jones Lower Hall Beckbury"; and "Lou Daughter of Mervyn Mander". There is also a telephone number (Ryton 21), and Directory records show this to have been that of Wilfred Byford-Jones.[189]

---

[188] The only other time this name appears in this narrative is in relation to Wilfred Byford-Jones. Johnson was the maiden name of his second wife, so this could just relate to his mother-in-law – but it's another very long shot.

[189] Ryton-on-Dunsmore (near Kenilworth) being the local exchange.

Analysis

The Labour in Vain, Yarnfield, left, 2014 (CC-BY-SA/2.0 - © J. Thomas - geograph.org.uk/p/6173375); and The Crown, Iverley (2011, (CC-BY-SA/2.0 - © Chris Whippet - geograph.org.uk/p/2289348)

If these references are, indeed, in direct response to the first *Anna of Claverley* letter, then they are interesting on a number of levels. Given the contents of the letter, it is understandable that the police would have sought to confirm Wilfred Byford-Jones's details (as the journalist who wrote the article that sparked it), and also that they would have identified an appropriate contact at the Dutch Army Hospital. The mention of the Royal Hospital is puzzling, but the other two names are intriguing. As we have seen, the Brick Bridge (Waggon & Horses) is at Wombourne, not Claverley, and had strong links to the Mossop / Hainsworth families. Had the police already included Una Hainsworth's name amongst their list of "suspects" at this stage? The name Mander has already been mentioned, as it was near the Mander factory that the outlier "Bella" graffiti was found. The Mander family was particularly influential (Mervyn's father being the local MP), but it becomes clear from scrutinising newspaper reports at the time that Mervyn Mander also had a link to the small village of Claverley.[190]

Where the elusive Dutchman is concerned, Una certainly hedges her bets. She claims to have met him only the twice and, in saying that his name was "something like" van Ralt[191] she leaves herself plenty of room

---

[190] In 1935, the engagement of Mervyn Mander to the German Elizabeth Mettlich was announced. The newspapers reported that the couple had met in Claverley.

[191] In addition to "van Raalte", some sources present the name as "van Raalt". It cannot be assumed that the police spelt the name the same way as Una Hainsworth did, and their later summary report favoured the use of "van Ralt".

for manoeuvre. She would certainly have been aware that there was a large Dutch community in the Midlands at the time,[192] and that Dutch spies were believed to have been fairly active in the country. There was a lot of distrust arising from ignorance (with many, during the war, assuming from their names that they were German) in parts of the community, so adding a Dutch connection to the story would have been very logical.

The closest we have to confirmation that van Ralt may have existed was a police memo referencing a telephone conversation between DS Murray of the Coventry force and WPC Florence Hill. Murray had spoken to the manager of the Coventry Hippodrome – a Mr Newsam – and mentioned the name "van Ralt" to him. Newsam advised: "although it [the name] rang a bell, [I] was unable to think anything about it". This is far from conclusive, and "van" is a common part of many Dutch names. But, for a theatre manager, the name probably should have rung bells, as there was a blind pianist and organist of the time by the name of Stanley van Raalte. In addition to having been engaged to play the summer season at Butlin's Skegness Holiday Camp in 1937 and featuring on BBC Radio in both 1939 and 1941, he had also appeared in theatre at nearby Daventry.[193] If Newsam had heard this in a show-business context, it is quite possible that it was a name that Una Hainsworth had picked up through the same sources – given her connections. Alternatively, she may just have chosen the name from a brand of silk stockings that was then very popular.

---

[192] Wolverhampton was a centre for Dutch immigrants, whilst the HQ of the Dutch army based in the UK was at Wrottesley Park (in nearby Perton), where there was also a hospital staffed by Dutch nurses.

[193] There are records of a travelling entertainer by the name of Sydney van Raalte, too, at a similar time; although the likelihood is that this was the same individual.

Analysis

The Coventry Hippodrome, on the corner of Hales Street, opened its doors in 1937, becoming the Coventry Theatre in 1955 and the Apollo in 1981, before closing in 1985. It then suffered the ignominy of becoming a bingo hall until it was finally pulled down. Shown are Hales Street, in 1981, left (CC-BY-SA/2.0 - © FCG - geograph.org.uk/p/3907829); and Coventry Theatre demolition in 2002 (CC-BY-SA/2.0 - © E. Gammie - geograph.org.uk/p/1139017)

Una admits that she had no evidence that van Ralt was a spy, and that her suspicions were based on Jack's financial circumstances, which seemed to improve whenever van Ralt was in town (and we know that there may have been other reasons behind this). Also highly important in the context of Una Hainsworth's story is her claim that: "Van Ralt was in the back [of the car] and then she [the unidentified spy] fell over towards my husband". Although Una heavily implies that this was due to intoxication, it has been interpreted by some as indicating that the female spy had been given a lethal injection. They point to this as supporting the spy ring theory, as agents did have access to chemicals that could have been used for such a purpose. Yet, as we have seen, the absence of part of the hyoid bone would now point to strangulation being a more likely cause of death of the tree victim. Unless the spy was so drunk that she was unable to resist, it is likely that an attempt at strangulation would have at least induced a struggle; in a full or partially full car, the driver would surely have been aware of such an action taking place. This is a long way removed from the victim being seated upright one minute and then slumping over the next.

Van Ralt is the key character in Una's tale, but the police failed to identify anybody by that or a similar name who was in the area at that time. The one person they did trace with any connection to the area was a young teacher who had once visited the Malvern Hills for a holiday.

Una Hainsworth's Story

This was tenuous to say the least, although one does wonder just how hard the police pursued this particular angle. There was certainly a family of van Raaltes at Market Harborough, just 40 miles from Kenilworth. One of these would have been of an age that would be typical of a sex killer, although there was nothing to connect him to the crime. Perusing other contemporary records, there was a further (possibly related) van Raalte family in another north Staffordshire village (Hanley). It does not appear that the police were ever aware of the existence of either family.

Perhaps most significant was that none of Jack's workmates could place the name, or anyone fitting the description of van Ralt. If he did exist, then this is highly surprising. Bill Wilson – who from police transcripts and actions comes across as one of the few credible witnesses in the whole case – indicated that he and Mossop were part of a clique of car enthusiasts, which also included Vic Draco (who, in common with Jack Mossop, had a number of driving convictions) and Ted Peck "who knew most people who were circulating in the district". Given that car ownership was still quite a rarity, Mossop's weakness for drink and socialising, and the closeness of the local community, such acquaintances would surely have been aware if he had been spending time with a mysterious foreigner with a Rover car (quite a luxury at the time) – regardless of whether he was a spy. Rovers were a particular interest of both Mossop and Wilson and, indeed, they had joint ownership of such a vehicle, although this was a very run-down model which hardly (if ever) ran. Further, are we to believe that two or three men (including one who was able to drive) were so inebriated that they each believed that forcing a drunk woman into a very narrow tree trunk was an appropriate way of getting her to sober up as Una had said? This aspect alone defies rational analysis. Lastly, is it really likely that anybody would have actively recruited Jack Mossop as a spy? Whilst there are examples of Second World War spy rings displaying an alarming lack of competence, it really is stretching credibility to suggest that Mossop could have been earmarked for such a role. An habitual drunkard, and as such not the sort of individual who could be trusted to keep a secret or capable of maintaining a deception, he would have made an exceptionally poor choice of contact for an agent. If Jack Mossop was a killer, then his

Analysis

lifestyle suggests that a far more likely victim would have been a woman picked up in a bar, quite possibly a prostitute.

There are two further intriguing areas of Una's statement and believed testimony: an address within Coventry, and the potential involvement of an ice-skating showbiz act – and there was a likely link between the two. A lot has been made of a show-business connection, but much of it is based on Una's mention of the performer Frack. This led to the Coventry Police undertaking some detailed investigation of acts appearing at Coventry Hippodrome. The connection here was the boarding house at 9 Grosvenor Road. This was just a mile from Coventry Hippodrome, and well used by acts appearing there, as well as local workers (in the words of Bill Wilson: "everyone was a lodger at Grosvenor Road"). Una was probably familiar with the set-up, having, by her own admission, spent time there and mixed with show-business people. It was there, too, that the Mossops may have met the Swiss performer "Hansruedi" (Hans Rudolf) Mauch, one half of the act going by the name of Frick and Frack. For many at the time, their only pre-war contact with foreigners would have been through local theatres, so this would build on subconscious xenophobic prejudice. It would have been quite easy for Una Hainsworth to throw in a name like this to exploit such bigotry and add credibility to her story.

A show-business act, undertaking regular travel around the country, would certainly have provided spying opportunities, but there is no evidence of Frick and Frack being in any way implicated, and there is nothing to suggest that they were ever on police or MI5 "radar". Neither was there anything in the background of the two men to suggest that they should have been of particular interest to the authorities. The pair were performing in Coventry up until 1938, but did not appear there again until post-war. Shipping manifests show them both leaving Southampton for New York (aboard the SS *Normandie*) in November 1938.[194] A flight record completed by Werner Groebli (Frick) has him flying back from the US to Europe (Paris) in April 1946, and shows him as having been on tour in the US for the

---

[194] The manager of the Coventry theatre told DS Murray that there were no ice shows anywhere in the country during the war, due to the difficulty of obtaining stages.

full intervening period.[195] To scrape the bottom of this particular barrel still further, there is one ice performer of the time whose name might be contracted to Bella. This is one Maria Belita Jepson-Turner (born 25 October 1923), who was known professionally as Belita the Ice Maiden – and had both performed at Coventry and subsequently appeared in at least one film with the duo.[196] She, however, lived until 2005.

Compatibility with other events

To further test the plausibility of the spying story recounted by Una Hainsworth, it is worthwhile considering its elements against the few known facts. Firstly is the timing of the events she describes. Una claims that it was April 1941 when her husband came home in a state of great agitation, confessing to his part in a murder. In other circumstances, it might be questionable whether her recall could be that accurate after 12 years, but the fact that she was pregnant at the time would certainly be a reference point. It also fits in with the parameters for the victim's death (April–October 1941) as advanced by the pathologist. It is not fully consistent with the victim apparently wearing summer clothing, and nor does it fit with the screams heard within Hagley Wood and investigated by the police, in July 1941. Neither factor, however, can be used to rule out her version of events.

One arguably unrelated action may also be worthy of note here: in February 1942, Jack Mossop had reported his car as missing. The "Bella" files do not provide any details of this, and the only reference is within Bill Wilson's statement. From this, it is clear that the police must have asked Wilson about the car, and that Wilson was totally oblivious to the fact that it was reported stolen – despite his joint ownership – some 11 years earlier. There is nothing in either Una Hainsworth's typed or written statement to suggest that she introduced

---

[195] This does not necessarily preclude Groebli from any involvement in the crime, as he could have been trying to create an alibi for himself – however unlikely this may have been. No such details can be traced for Mauch however. It also does not accord with a newspaper report of Frick and Frack appearing at Coventry Hippodrome in 1945.
[196] *Lady Let's Dance.*

Analysis

the matter, so the obvious inference is that it came from other police files. Wilson's reaction on being told this suggests a number of possible scenarios, including that:

- there had been a misunderstanding
- Mossop was trying to perpetrate an insurance fraud
- Mossop may have had another ulterior motive.

We know that, at this time, Mossop's mental health was beginning to crumble, for whatever reason. Amongst more likely explanations, it could be that he had in fact committed the murder, or at least been involved in it. In his agitated state he may have been convinced that the body would soon be discovered and that his car had been seen in Hagley Wood Lane, so was trying to create a false alibi by reporting his car as stolen. Not thinking rationally, he wouldn't necessarily have realised that the evidence would show different timings. But Mossop's lifestyle was so dissolute by this stage that it is just possible that he had simply forgotten where he had left his car. He was also known to have owed money to a relative (a butcher) however, and the car being taken as surety is a much more probable scenario.

CHAPTER 14

Other Spy Ring Theories

As identified within Chapter 7, part of the reason that Una Hainsworth's outlandish claims have attracted such prominence is that – whether by design or accident – she provided others with the opportunity to develop their own beliefs about spy rings that may have operated in the area; and that these included the journalists Ladislas Farago and Donald McCormick.

Ladislas Farago

The argument put forward by Farago seems believable at first sight, but soon unravels. The "master spy", Karl Dickenhoff, is revealed by Farago to be, in real life, Hans Caesar, and described by him as an "amnesia-stricken inmate of an asylum". But Hans Caesar was actually a successful Midlands jeweller, who was not only alive, but still working in the West Midlands. And, rather than having undertaken any incisive journalistic research, Farago had just reproduced parts of an ill-informed story that had first appeared in a trade magazine.

The reality was that Hans Paul Caesar, a German-born businessman, had followed in the footsteps of his uncle to become established in the Birmingham jewellery business between 1934 and 1939. The Birmingham Jewellery Quarter suffered some fairly intense bombing during the subsequent hostilities, and, even only a few weeks after the war had ended, there were fears that the market would become swamped with cheap imports from Germany. In a bid to counter this, *The British Jeweller* published an article on what it described as "the German Menace". Its author, W. Stewart-Turner, posed the question: "Are we going to buy from Germany?" and then criticised those who would take the attitude that, if they didn't, others would. His article further went on to state that: "It should be remembered that the German stone dealer, Hans Caesar, who resided in Birmingham for seven or eight years, was a

Nazi agent, and used his knowledge of the district to lead a bombing attack on Birmingham in which the jewellery district was badly damaged."

This article was full of similarly outrageous slurs, but reflected attitudes of the time: distrust of the Germans was prevalent, and destroying the reputation of the only German national that many of these traders would have encountered as part of a marketing strategy would have seemed legitimate to some. But, whilst *The British Jeweller* had only a limited circulation, these utterings were given a much wider audience when picked up by the *Evening Despatch*. On 13 June 1945, this newspaper ran the headline: "BLITZ ON BIRMINGHAM – You can blame Hans for this". This, and a follow-up article the next day, told how Caesar had "pinpointed raids on Midland's *Hatton Garden*". Further claims were made, including that a girl in the jewellery trade had picked up a German broadcast at 7.30 one morning and heard the announcer boasting about the bombing of Birmingham, "and the work of their good friend Caesar".

Whilst a degree of nationalism was understandable, to suggest that Caesar had orchestrated the bombing of the Birmingham Jewellery Quarter was ridiculous. Caesar was a Nazi sympathiser, but there was no basis for such an allegation. The further claim that a girl in the trade had picked up a German broadcast and heard an announcement about Caesar, was also demonstrably false. Whilst propaganda announcements (including those, famously, by "Lord Haw-Haw") were a feature of the Second World War, individual names would never be mentioned in circumstances where the agent was embedded and might have family in the area. The fact that the newspaper acknowledged that only one person claimed to have heard the broadcast must also be significant (as it would be just about impossible to disprove). One of the *Despatch's* articles additionally carried a picture of Caesar holidaying at his mother's "luxurious house" in Idar-Oberstein (within the German jewellery district), which had no purpose other than to stir emotions – and ride the anti-German sentiments of the time.

It is true that Caesar had travelled back to Germany at the start of hostilities, where he had enrolled in the German infantry. Rather than directing bombing operations on Birmingham, however, he had been sent to the Russian Front. Surrendering in 1941, he would remain in captivity until repatriated in 1949 – at which point he returned to resume his former career in the Midlands. His reintegration into English society would have been difficult in any event, but was made even more so by these claims made against him. Whilst he must have heard the rumours, though, he seems at that time to have been unaware of their origin. This would all change when Farago published his *War of Wits*, in which he conflated *The British Jeweller's* erroneous tale and that of Una Hainsworth.[197] Now, the flawed arguments achieved both greater prominence and more credibility. This is partly because Farago was a prolific writer who had achieved some acclaim, although his work still probably wouldn't have registered much in the West Midlands had it not been for the *Birmingham Post* precis of his "findings", under the headline: "The Spy Caesar of Edgbaston". Whereas Caesar had been in no position to challenge the similar accusations previously made against him (being held within a POW camp), he now read them at first hand. Outraged, he took immediate action to successfully sue both the newspaper and Farago's publisher (Hutchinson & Co.). Presumably, neither party was keen to identify the real source of their story for fear of exposing their own poor practices. It is quite remarkable – though not much out of keeping with this whole saga – that a piece of propaganda nonsense that had first appeared within a low-circulation trade magazine should now achieve international attention. Indeed, just how such an article could do the rounds and then be presented as irrefutable fact 11 years later says a lot about journalism of the time. It is also noteworthy how Farago – some of whose work was critically acclaimed[198] – was also panned by some critics, one of whom would say that he "was the most successful disinformer or dupe".[199] But he is far from being the only journalist within the saga to whom this criticism could be applied.

---

[197] It is also of interest that Farago introduces a known agent – Jan Willem Ter Braak – into his narrative, and suggests that he was a spymaster who could provide the key. In Britain for five months, Ter Braak is generally believed to have been the German agent at large for the longest time.
[198] In particular, his biography of George Patton.
[199] Stephen Dorril, within *MI6: Inside the Covert World of Her Majesty's Secret Intelligence Service*.

Analysis

Donald McCormick

When Donald McCormick picked up the cudgels, he fell into a number of the same traps as Farago. As previously discussed, his book *Murder by Witchcraft*[200] is full of ambiguities. At times, he suggests that the underlying reason for the murder of "Bella" lies with the occult, or at least attributes it to the practice of astrology. Whilst it is documented that many senior members of the Nazi Party placed a lot of store in astrology, it defies reasonable belief (as McCormick implies) that they would track a woman halfway across Europe to murder her simply because her predictions had angered authority. *Murder by Witchcraft* is a strange, rambling account which mixes spying with witchcraft although, to be fair, whilst his pronouncements in relation to witchcraft cross the boundary of rationality, some of his theories in relation to spying are quite well argued, and accord with what was known at the time. Whether McCormick was the first to "see" the Abwehr papers is open to question and, given his track record, it is more likely that he had spoken to somebody else who had claimed to have viewed them. It is also arguable that McCormick did speak with Franz Rathgeb and Frau Cremer, although this does not mean, of course, that Rathgeb and Cremer didn't have their own agenda; nor does it mean that their version of events was correct. It is plausible that there was an agent (whether going by the name of Clara or any other) who was earmarked to be parachuted into the Midlands, but far less likely that the plan was executed. It is also credible that the agent may have previously worked in the area and acquired a local accent. As with many of the theories put forward, however, there is a huge leap of faith between a spy going missing / being unaccounted for and a connection to the body within Hagley Wood. Speaking later, McCormick did acknowledge that there was no proof that this woman (Clara) was ever parachuted into the country, and also that there was no suggestion that she would have been dropped anywhere near to Hagley Wood. The Verbindungsstab / Abwehr records allegedly reveal that she failed to make contact with her handlers, and was presumed missing. But the alarm bells really start to ring at the point

---

[200] Confusingly, McCormick also wrote under the name of Richard Deacon and one edition of this book bears that name.

that McCormick identifies the agent previously embedded within the Midlands and who was coordinating events as Karl Dickenhoff. For this is the same "spy" – with the alternative name of Hans Caesar – identified by Ladislas Farago.

As with Farago, some of Donald McCormick's early work was well received, but his reputation has not stood the test of time. His output was also prolific, but his journalism has been exposed by numerous commentators. One of these, Paul Newman, has spoken witheringly of McCormick's "fraudulent career",[201] and points to him fabricating documents which he claimed related to the Jack the Ripper case. McCormick's theories concerning Frau Dronkers were picked up and developed by other commentators to suggest that "Bella" could in reality have been Marie, the wife of Johannes Marinus Dronkers. This, though, serves more to illustrate just how the internet allows wild rumour to become established. For, although Dronkers was married, this was to Elise Antoinette Eleanora Seignette (born in Den Helder [Holland] in 1893). This would have made her close to 50 at the likely time of "Bella's" demise (as opposed to the 35–40 upper age range of the victim attributed by Professor Webster). There is also evidence to suggest that she was still in the Netherlands in 1942, and that she probably died there two years later.

Clara Bauerle

McCormick did not identify Clara Bauerle as the possible victim but, as others before him, he planted seeds that subsequent writers would nurture. Most prominently, it was the journalist Allison Vale who took things forward when the MI5 files were disclosed under time-limitation protocols. At face value, the argument that she put forward was very persuasive and, at the time, was viewed by many as conclusive. It unravels, though, in the face of the diligent research undertaken by Josef Jakobs' granddaughter, Giselle (Gigi) Jakobs. This proves that Bauerle's

---

[201] In February 2009, Under the Shadow of Meon Hill, by Paul Newman, revisiting both the "Bella" and Charles Walton murders. In defence of McCormick, some key source documentation that Newman refers to was not available to him when he undertook his research.

cannot have been the body in the tree, not least because she died in Berlin on 16 December 1942[202]. Vale is a far more credible journalist than many who appear in this saga, but she made some basic mistakes. Firstly, by incorrectly linking Clara Bauerle to a piece of graffiti that allegedly read "Who Put Clarabella in the Wych Elm?"[203] Secondly, Bauerle was between 5' 10" and 6' tall, obviously at odds not only with Professor Webster's estimate of Bella being under 5' in height, but also later suggestions that she may have been up to 5' 8". Thirdly, there is no evidence that Clara Bauerle ever visited the UK, and it seems that Vale mixed up characteristics of Bauerle and her compatriot Karla Sofie Bauerle who, being born in 1906, was a year younger. Karla Sofie Bauerle had visited these shores in the 1930s, although Vale's contention that the victim spoke English with a Brummie accent acquired through working in the music halls of the West Midlands seems to have come straight from the pages of *Murder by Witchcraft*. Within that, McCormick had in fact been referencing Lehrer's alleged mistress and, whilst stating that Clara had acquired a local accent, had not linked this to her working in show business. To her credit, Allison Vale has subsequently acknowledged the work undertaken by Gigi Jakobs and, in correspondence, agreed that this rules out Bauerle being "Bella".

The reality

Despite each of the spying theories having a core of believability, there is nothing that points to this as providing the key to solving the mystery. Yes, the West Midlands were most certainly of interest to the Nazis, but, whilst early on the police may have been hamstrung by a lack of access to intelligence records (due to disclosure rules), MI5 have repeatedly since claimed that they are confident that there were no spies operating in the

---

[202] Her death certificate records the causes as pneumonia and veronal poisoning. This has been widely interpreted as being an accidental overdose. Veronal is a barbiturate which was then widely used to treat mental illness, but often used as a sleeping pill; unfortunately, individuals soon develop a tolerance, leading to the intake of progressively larger doses to achieve the same effect – which is sometimes fatal.

[203] Further, one would question whether an agent would be allocated a codename that so closely resembled her real name.

Other Spy Ring Theories

Midlands of which they were unaware – let alone one that was murdered. Nor has anything come to light from files later released under Freedom of Information legislation to contradict this. The respected Nigel Jones[204] and others have consistently stated that all spies were quickly rounded up; and strangers seeking information would have been easy to spot and apprehend. What the work of Farago and McCormick rather suggests is that it is very easy to take a few facts and embellish them to suit any favoured argument, particularly when the public has already bought in to the wider concept.

Both within the Bella narrative and more widely, the calibre of spies operating in the UK throughout the Second World War has been greatly exaggerated. This applies to some of those featured in this account, who have been wrongly portrayed as experts in their field. Josef Jakobs, for example, was typical: as the last person to have been executed in the Tower of London, he has been depicted by some as being one of the greatest threats to national security. But his was a sad story, and he seemed to have been more of a danger to himself than to others. He was largely a victim of the incompetence of the Nazi regime, which sent poorly prepared agents on missions that had virtually no chance of success. In similar vein, the agent Jan Willem Ter Braak[205] was no mastermind. Farago inserts him into his own analysis in a bid to demonstrate that he had identified a major spy ring, but he was just a convenient figure on which to hang a conspiracy theory. Indeed, others have since tried to link Ter Braak to the Bella case. McCormick claims that Caesar was an associate of Ter Braak, and further links him to Clara, the spy that he alleges may have been parachuted from a plane between Birmingham and Kidderminster. Ter Braak was in all probability only a very minor player, and was found dead in a deserted public Cambridge air-raid shelter, with a bullet in his head and an Abwehr-issued pistol by his side. Despite the inevitable multitude of conspiracy theories, it seems that he had just run out of money and committed suicide in a fit of depression, rather than taking his own life to protect Nazi secrets. There is absolutely no evidence that he even knew

---

[204] Within the UKTV documentary.
[205] Also known as Engelburtes Fukken.

Analysis

of the existence of Hans Caesar, and there would appear to have been few opportunities for the two to have met.

Looked at as a whole, the spy ring theories soon unravel. Most have a journalistic fiction at their heart and, where this is not demonstrably the case, the claims defy logic. Such an example is the account of Squadron Leader William Douglas-Osborn's chance encounter with Canadian soldiers. In fairness, Douglas-Osborn is not here to amplify this view, or to explain his son's claim that his preparedness to talk about what he had witnessed changed over time. Peter Douglas-Osborn is now very much identified as an expert on the case, and he has spoken widely to the media about his father's recollections. Nevertheless, not too much should be read into his father's alleged change of stance. Whilst Douglas-Osborn senior subsequently clamming up about the incident is presented as corroborating evidence, in reality, the war affected those involved in many different ways – and there may be numerous reasons why an individual may choose to block out incidents (if, indeed, this was the case). It also flies in the face of William telling his son in detail about the later incident. This is a very difficult tale to buy into, because of the coincidences involved in William firstly encountering and befriending the very Canadian personnel responsible for cataloguing the Abwehr records; the description of "Bella" striking such a chord with them; and them being so open with such still-confidential information. An alternative explanation is that, in the post-war euphoria of the time, the Canadian soldiers told Douglas-Osborn something that they thought he would want to hear.

CHAPTER 15

The Occult And Related Angles

Although there is very little of relevance that can be read into the various theories and suggestions put forward by psychics and students of black magic, they must – for the sake of completeness – be considered.

The Hand of Glory

As identified within Chapter 4, all that even tenuously connected the murder of Charles Walton and the body in the tree in Hagley Wood was geographical proximity, and it was only the intervention of Professor Margaret Murray that gave the theory any hint of authenticity. Her linking of the two cases was quite outrageous, although dismissing the notion that witchcraft was behind the murder doesn't necessarily preclude the possibility that some may have believed this to be the case. For those so minded (and probably addicted to conspiracy theories), there is a link between the Hand of Glory and the name Bella, although mostly for those who hail from the North East. For it was in Yorkshire and County Durham – even as late at the 18th century – that witches did a good trade in selling these gruesome "trophies" from hanged felons, robbers and thieves, for up to an incredible £50 a time. One of these artefacts was allegedly used in an infamous attempted robbery of an inn on the Brough–Bowes Road on a wild October night in 1797. According to the well-told tale, disaster was avoided only by the actions of a faithful servant girl – who went by the name of Bella. But for this to be the reason for that name appearing on walls in the West Midlands must be the most remote of possibilities.

Murray's Hand of Glory argument cannot, anyway, be sensibly put forward in this case. As previously discussed, there is nothing in official sources to suggest that either hand was found separated from the rest of the body. This argument anyway still overlooks the simple fact that, even if the perpetrator of the crime believed in this nonsense, the Hand of Glory would only be of use if in their possession. There is no precedence in witchcraft for severing the hand and then burying it. And, whilst there were some bones missing from the hand once the skeleton had been reassembled, both Professor Webster and the police were convinced that any missing bones had become separated from the body through the action of animals. Some sources have suggested that no bird or animal would be capable of accessing the bole of the tree from the top, and then emerging with a part of the body, but this is disingenuous. Other bones were also found outside the tree, and from this it is clear that there were holes within the trunk through which ground-based creatures could enter and exit. The hand could even have protruded when the body was left in the tree (and the limited light in the wood may have prevented the killer[s] from noticing this). Alternatively, if wounds had been inflicted by knife, there may have been some defensive injuries inflicted on the wrist and hands, facilitating subsequent removal of hand bones by animals. Similarly, if the body was in a state of decomposition when hidden, parts could have become more easily detached, but there is no real reason that either hand had been deliberately detached. In short, we can speculate as to how the hand and other bones may have become separated from the body, but after 18 months or more there could be a number of possibilities – and none supports the Hand of Glory speculation.

Other witchcraft connections

Murray also claimed that Bella, Isobella and Luebella are "all to be found in lists of witches' names". There is no great body of knowledge to indicate that the names quoted by Murray are any more associated with witchcraft than others; nor that entombing a body within a tree is a hallmark of witchcraft. Further, her attachment of significance to the "Bella" messages being written predominantly in Halesowen ("a Midland town that has in the past produced some occult phenomena") is typical of her approach. Many claims have been made that certain parts of the country are occult "hot spots", and Halesowen seems to be no "busier" than anywhere else. Yet Murray seems to ignore the obvious: that Halesowen just happens to be rather close to the murder scene.

Professor Murray was undoubtedly a clever and remarkable woman and, in her middle years, was widely respected as an Egyptologist. The newspapers loved her because she was unconventional and outspoken, and was good for sales. The reality was that, in old age, Murray became even more eccentric and publicity-seeking,[206] and, after her death, she was widely discredited. Although a pioneering archaeologist and anthropologist, one commentator wrote that she had "a tendency to see witches everywhere". Despite ongoing beliefs in some quarters that witchcraft was prevalent, when *The Independent* newspaper[207] ran a story in 1991, no local person questioned could identify any current occult activity within Hagley Wood. More pertinently, although some outsiders would claim that Hagley Wood had been a hotbed of such activity, nobody – including local historians and a journalist involved in breaking the story at the time – could find any credible evidence to support such claims having foundation back in the 1940s. It is the case that old letters found in the archives of the *Black Country Bugle* suggested that sabbaths were once regularly held in Hagley Wood, while the pub opposite – the Gipsy's Tent – was associated with hauntings and other occult goings on, but this was years before the Second World War. Geoff Pardoe, the Hagley representative of the Worcestershire Local History Forum, is on record as saying "if it [the death of 'Bella'] was witchcraft, it's the only incident of its kind that I've heard of round here. I've never come across any of it."

As with Murray's account, the parts of McCormick's *Murder by Witchcraft* that relate to the occult are characteristically full of contradictions. The rather confused and confusing narrative starts with a heavy implication that the murder of "Bella" and that of Charles Walton some four years later were connected; although McCormick does later admit:

---

[206] At this time she was in her 80s.
[207] *The Independent* newspaper is the one national newspaper to have given regular prominence to the case in recent years.

Analysis

To avoid any possible confusion one point should be made … there is no link whatsoever, not even a remote one, between the Hagley Wood and the Lower Quinton crimes.

And, whilst McCormick himself acknowledged that some of his theories lacked firm evidence, he still tries to lay the murder of "Bella" at the door of the occult, or at least attribute it to the practice of astrology.

The *Cone of Power* argument is also almost too ridiculous to consider. The only reason for including it in relation to the "Bella" inquiry is that some adherents of this particular brand of fantasy have suggested that the body in the tree may have been connected to a Midland enactment of *Operation Cone of Power* – with the ante being raised through the offering of a human sacrifice. Researcher Philip Heselton has suggested that similar rituals were carried out by covens around the country, and that some of the older members of these covens willingly gave up their lives so that the ritual would have greater chance of success. This has fuelled speculation, in some very select quarters, that "Bella" was a willing victim, but it probably goes without saying that there is no evidence whatsoever to support either this or the absurd notion that any human sacrifices were made in support of the war effort.

Psychic leads

The likes of "psychics" George Elwell and Zita Boyden should never really have been given the oxygen of publicity, and the grief caused to the Bradley family illustrates just why that is the case. Yet there are, nevertheless, some interesting elements to be found within Zita Boyden's letters. One is her suggestion concerning the possible origin of the name Bella within the wall messages, as considered within Chapter 12. The various references to Holland and Canada, a services uniform and mental instability can all be linked to claims made by others, but one name put forward by her is arguably of particular note. This is Louis Mellor. Boyden, in one letter, comes up with his surname and then, in another, the first name. There was a Louis Mellor who, in 1930 (when 22 years of age), was charged with murdering his landlady with a hatchet at Stoke-on-Trent. He was, however, found guilty but insane and detained

The Occult and Related Angles

at His Majesty's pleasure. Records from then go cold, but it is just about possible to argue that he could have been released and was free to commit murder in Hagley Wood some 11 years later. More logically, though, Zita Boyden probably read about this incident, either at the time or subsequently.

CHAPTER 16

The Deceptions of Wilfred Byford-Jones

The lack of any hard evidence to support the more outlandish theories around this case begs the question of how so many wild ideas managed to become planted in the public consciousness. Any high-profile and unsolved murder will undoubtedly give rise to conspiracy theories, but they are usually much better argued and more valid than those surrounding this case. Even where the less sensational claims are involved, those who came forward with information still only did so many years later – often after renewed media attention – and with proponents usually demonstrating that they had their own axes to grind.

Any objective analysis identifies that, after the initial police investigation was scaled down, it was only media coverage that kept the case properly alive. This is not unusual in unsolved murder cases, even as far back as the late 19th century, the media drove a lot of what happened in the investigation of the Jack the Ripper murders. In this case, a number of unscrupulous commentators – journalists and authors – worked hard to feed the public appetite, and were happy to use gullible, confused or credulous "witnesses" for their own purposes. Along the way, some disturbed members of the public were drawn into the picture through media appeals, and their involvement moved attention away from the journalists themselves. We have already seen how Ladislas Farago and Donald McCormick managed to bend the truth for their own purposes, but there is one individual whose actions fuelled most of what is now in the public consciousness and who, when interest in the case began to wane, reignited the fire. That man was even (allegedly) asked to assist the police in their investigations. By now, his identity should be clear. But just who was *Quaestor*, and what motivated him?

Wilfred ("Bill") Byford-Jones

Byford-Jones was seemingly born in Dudley in 1905, although, typically for a man so practiced in deception, for much of his life he claimed to be at least two years younger.[208] Entering journalism at the age of 18, by 1929 he had attained the role of *Wolverhampton Express & Star* Foreign Correspondent. The following year he married 22-year-old Winifred Louise Dawson, and their only son was born in September 1931. It appears that they probably also had two daughters. Certainly, there were girls born in March 1934 and September 1942 under the name of Jones, with the mother's maiden name recorded as Dawson; the ubiquity of the surname, however, makes confirmation difficult.

By 1950, Byford-Jones was a highly respected pillar of the community: a war veteran who had risen to the rank of Lieutenant Colonel; aide of Field Marshal Montgomery; distinguished journalist; expert on the Middle East; and author of several acclaimed books. Yet all was not as it would seem – or at least as Byford-Jones himself would like people to have seen it. The image that he portrayed of himself (with a Latin pen name to boot) was rather grandiose, but somewhat disingenuous. For, although there was nothing fraudulent about his use of the title Lieutenant Colonel, this had been bestowed as an honorary rank (major being the highest "working" level that he achieved during the war). And, whatever he had made of his life, his beginnings were modest. Far from being the aristocrat that he made out, he was the son of a humble fruiterer – Ehud Jones – and his wife, Mary Elizabeth (née Byford). Whilst there are plenty of examples within this account of working-class children being given their mother's maiden name as a middle name, this was not the case for Wilfred. Nor was it the norm at this time to transform a maiden name into a double-barrelled surname on marriage. [209] And if further evidence was required that his was not an

---

[208] On a shipping register of 1960, his date of birth has been entered as 27/07/1908.
[209] He seems to have adopted this affectation during the war years. Any investigation of the precise role of Byford-Jones in this story is partly hampered by inconsistent use of his double-barrelled surname. On some documents – including his second marriage certificate – he is named only as Wilfred Jones, and within others his name is not always hyphenated. In 1963, he did formally change the name to Byford-Jones on his wedding certificate.

Analysis

upper-class or privileged family, then this is provided by a newspaper article of 28 June 1902, just three years before the birth of Wilfred, and relating to his father. The *Alcester Chronicle* reported:

> On Sunday morning PC Pheysey found a man wandering about a field at Barnt Green. He took him to Bromsgrove Police Station, where he gave the name Ehud Jones of Blackheath. As he was suffering from the effects of drink he was taken to the workhouse and placed in [the] custody of two men. In the evening he borrowed a knife on the pretext of desiring to cut some tobacco, and having diverted the men's attention by asking them to look through a window he cut his throat. The master and doctor were summoned and although it was a severe wound in the throat it was stitched up.

Few pictures of Wilfred Byford-Jones are known to exist. This is taken from one of his books,
Oil on Troubled Waters.

Alongside his duties on the *Wolverhampton Express & Star*, Byford-Jones researched and wrote extensively, having several successful books published before the outbreak of the Second World War. Some of these were largely compilations of articles that he had written for the newspaper, and most drew on his life in and love for the villages and places of Staffordshire, Shropshire, Warwickshire and Worcestershire. The earliest was *Both Sides of the Severn* (1932), and this was quickly followed by *Midland Leaves* (1934) and *Vagabonding Through the Midlands*

(1935) – describing a canal boat trip that he undertook with his family. *Midland Murders, Hauntings and Odd Characters* (1936), demonstrated his interest in matters of local crime and sensationalism, whilst a later biography of the polymath Francis Brett Young also drew on his liking for and knowledge of the area in which he himself grew up.[210] A further book – *I Met Them in the Midlands* (1937) – comprised sketches of 50 Staffordshire and Shropshire men and women from all walks of life. This was another compilation of interviews initially conducted for the *Express & Star*, for which Byford-Jones had travelled the length and breadth of the two counties, searching out likely people to interview.[211] It further demonstrated that he had a knack for getting people to tell their life stories; and an *Illustrated London News* review of a later publication commented that Byford-Jones had "a remarkable capacity for establishing sympathetic contacts with people".[212] A number of his books featured the villages of Claverley and Wombourne, as well as the parish of Rowley Regis. Throughout, Byford-Jones speaks widely of his love for frequenting village pubs.

According to Byford-Jones's own memoirs and subsequent media interviews, he spent most of the war in Egypt and Cyprus, serving in the Intelligence Corps, and also working as Chief Liaison Officer for Field Marshal Montgomery's staff. In 1944, following the withdrawal of Germany from Greece, he was part of the small British contingent sent by Churchill to accompany and support the returning Greek government.[213] During this episode, he claims to have intervened to save the life of Georgios Grivas (the leader of the Greek-Cypriot nationalist guerrilla organisation), who had been captured by communists. At the end of the war he travelled to Hitler's bunker, reporting that he

---

[210] Brett Young had been born in Halesowen, and had a career mapped out in medicine. On suffering injury in the First World War, he had to reconsider his career, and concentrated on writing both novels and songs. He is best known for his series of *Mercian* novels, set in the Midlands and Welsh Borders. Young wrote a foreword for Byford-Jones's *Both Sides of the Severn*.

[211] One of the interviewees was Sir Geoffrey Le Mesurier Mander, radical MP, industrialist and chairman of Mander Brothers Ltd (and with, as we have seen, connections to Claverley).

[212] *Illustrated London News* book review, 24/10/1959.

[213] Force 140.

Analysis

interviewed many "witnesses" who were adamant that Hitler had escaped (with a stand-in taking his place); then claimed to have worked as a member of the British legal team at the Nuremberg Trials. In later years, he would relate that he had served in the regular army for 20 years.

Any independent review of Byford-Jones's life and times identifies him to have been a very complicated and conflicted individual. Whilst some of his wartime claims can be verified, the details of many cannot. Byford-Jones *did* apply to join the Intelligence Corps, but was rejected. Although a subsequent application was successful, this was post-war, and within the Army Reserves. Back in April 1940, he was instead appointed as an army press officer in Kenya, although before he could take up this post, orders changed, and he was sent to take up a similar role in Alexandria, Egypt. Press and liaison work would seem to have comprised the bulk of his war service, and the only accessible references to him having served Montgomery are within his own writings and the interviews that he himself gave subsequently. Similarly, whilst Byford-Jones clearly did serve in Greece and subsequently received the Greek Medal of Military Merit, it would seem this was fairly routinely awarded to all who were there; again, the only mentions of Byford-Jones's involvement with Grivas seem to be from within his own writing. Further, although it seems that Byford-Jones was at the Nuremburg Trials, evidence understandably points to this being as a reporter – certainly not as a member of any legal team (for which role he would have been singularly unqualified). Finally, having been in the Territorials at the time of his call up and then serving as reservist until being obliged to retire on reaching the age of 50 (in 1955), it is just possible that he clocked up 20 years' military service – but he most certainly couldn't legitimately claim to have served in the regular army for that length of time.

Something else worthy of mention is a letter that Byford-Jones wrote to the Ministry of Supply in October 1951.[214] In this, he claimed that he could prove that the astonishingly successful Spitfire Fund – "the whip-round that won the war" – was his idea. He wrote:

---

[214] The Ministry of Supply had absorbed the Ministry of Aircraft Production in 1946.

The Deceptions of Wilfred Byford-Jones

Early in the war before I was sent to Africa I conceived the idea of towns, federations and firms raising money to provide their own Spitfire. I made a speech about it under the chairmanship of Sir Robert Bird, Bart, ex. Conservative M.P. for Wolverhampton. I wrote an article about it and got the blessing for the idea from Lord Beaverbrook by telephone. I raised the money for the first Spitfire in the British Isles and four months later explained my idea to scores of people by pamphlet and word of mouth. The result was that the idea caught on and when I was sent abroad to join Lord Wafell's staff similar funds were being raised all over the country.

But the Ministry of Supply rejected Byford-Jones's assertions. The reason for this was explained in a letter from the minister himself, the Rt. Hon. G. R. Strauss, to Captain J. Baird, MP for Wolverhampton North-East (who had taken up Byford-Jones's case). He wrote:

I am afraid that I still cannot accept his [Byford-Jones's] claim. I readily accept his claim to be the inaugurator of the Wolverhampton Spitfire Fund, but the fact is that a fortnight before he suggested in the Wolverhampton Express & Star that that a fund should be raised to buy Spitfires, we received £10,000 from Jamaica to buy a Spitfire.

It seems that there may well have been more to this, and Byford-Jones even escalated the matter to Prime Minister Winston Churchill. But, where Byford-Jones is concerned, it is often very difficult to work out just where the truth begins and ends. What it does confirm is that he was a proud man, who would name-drop at the slightest opportunity. It additionally demonstrates that he had most definitely not severed his links with the *Wolverhampton Express & Star* during the war years.

Throughout his career, Byford-Jones seems to have taken incidents which had an essence of truth and embellished both them and his own involvement or importance to quite an alarming extent. An official of the Foreign & Commonwealth Office intriguingly described him within a briefing note as having a "lively intelligence with a small *i*". Although this statement might be open to interpretation, it would suggest that he was describing somebody with an enquiring mind, but who was not as clever

Analysis

as he would like others to believe. This is certainly the impression that one gets from studying Byford-Jones's career, and his attention to detail – essential if you are to maintain a deception for any length of time – was poor. Returning to full-time journalism – and the *Express & Star* – in 1945, Byford-Jones seems to have been popular with some of his colleagues, one of whom described him as "a very cheeky character, full of wit and charm". It was reported that, when he and his young bride turned up at the paper's Queen Street office, his contemporaries would greet them with the cry: "*Quaestor* Mighty!"[215] He now also drew on his war experiences to write extensively on the Middle East (and, particularly, on oil production). One of his books on the oil crisis – *Adventures with Two Passports* – was particularly well received, and included material he had gathered from interviews that he had conducted (or claimed to have conducted!) with Colonel Nasser and King Hussein of Jordan. Another,[216] however, earned the comment: "the work is uninformed" from a reviewer.

It would seem that the separation resulting from the war years took a toll on Byford-Jones's marriage. It is one area of his life that he doesn't appear to have written about, but the fact that his wife subsequently re-married confirms divorce, rather than widowhood. Soon after the war, he met and then later (in 1947) married his second wife, Cynthia Johnson – 17 years his junior. By now, Byford-Jones was something of a large fish in a small provincial journalistic pond, and was highly prized by the *Express & Star* management in terms of maintaining circulation figures. He clearly cared deeply for the community that his newspaper served, too, and was responsible for establishing a Poor Children and Widows' Christmas Fund. His popularity and loyalty to the newspaper was rewarded with a series of promotions, which saw him achieve the post of Assistant Editor in 1952.

---

[215] It should not be assumed, however, that he was popular with all his fellow journalists. There were some who were jealous of his popularity and others who felt / realised that he took short cuts in his work.
[216] *Quest in the Holy Land*.

The Deceptions of Wilfred Byford-Jones

The entrance to the imposing Beckbury Hall, pictured in 2018. Although Wilfred Byford-Jones was fond of giving this as his address, he actually lived in the Lower Hall – a small, timber-framed 16th / 17th-century building within the grounds.

After their marriage, he and Cynthia set up home in the small Shropshire village of Beckbury. Beckbury is only some 7 miles from Claverley, where – at various times – Jack Mossop, his aunt, his son and the Hainsworths all lived; and which featured quite heavily in many of Byford-Jones's books. The couple were still there in 1953, when the first *Anna of Claverley* letter surfaced. Even now, this area is very sparsely populated; immediately post-war, these villages were more like hamlets with even lower levels of habitation. In the late 1950s, Byford-Jones left the Midlands and moved to Machynlleth, in Powys (west Wales).[217] In 1960, however, he set sail to South Africa, possibly with a view to staying there, where his son was living (and where other members of the family would also settle). But, from this time, his movements are again somewhat unclear. At some time unknown, he returned to Wales. He continued to write prolifically, and his books were regularly reviewed in the *Western Mail*. Whilst his output was undoubtedly impressive, he made the extraordinary claim within an interview for that newspaper that a new book would be his 113th. This was made in 1959, however, by that

---

[217] It is assumed that this is where his family roots lay. One of the last references the authors can find to him living in Beckbury are within an article describing his son's wedding in March 1957.

time, the authors have been able to find evidence of only 12[218] having been published.[219] He would go on to write at least a further seven books.

The lovely Shropshire village of Beckbury, once home to Wilfred Byford-Jones.

There is so much within the above to suggest that Byford-Jones, for all his charisma and popularity, was a fantasist, and embroiderer of the truth. It would be natural to assume that his interest in this unsolved murder developed following his return to the Midlands after the war had ended, in 1945. This may not, however, be the case. We don't have any independent verification of his movements during wartime, and the likelihood that his wife gave birth to a daughter in 1942 also suggests that he was not exclusively out of the country. He did seem to have spent time in North Africa in 1944 and claimed to have been in Germany when Hitler took his own life, but there is no reason why he could not have come back to the UK in between.[220] Indeed, in one of his own articles, he writes of "flying out from London" at the time of Hitler's death (April 1945). More certainly, at this stage of the war, there would have been less restriction on communications, and he would have been able to keep in

---

[218] Including two published under his pen name *Quaestor*, by the *Express & Star*.
[219] It is, of course, possible that the newspaper erroneously printed 113th as opposed to 13th, but with Byford-Jones it is difficult to take anything for granted.
[220] Byford-Jones's movements from mid-1944 to early 1945 are particularly unclear.

regular touch with those back home. Accordingly, there is every likelihood that he was not only aware of the developments in the "Bella" case but was, towards the end of the war, contemplating a full-time return to civvy street and his old journalistic duties.

Back in his old job, and probably as a result of the police stance that involvement of the media could be crucial in helping to solve the Hagley Wood murder, Byford-Jones seemed at times to be very well-informed of their enquiries. It may well be that he himself engineered this cooperation, and he would claim that no lesser person than the Chief Constable formally assigned him with responsibility for ascertaining the true identity of the allegedly anonymous letter from the member of the public (Una Hainsworth). He further alleged a personal friendship with Inight; if true, this could have developed over the course of the inquiry although, equally, may have pre-dated this time. There are also occasions where Tommy Williams (or Sidney Inight) [221] may have selectively informed parts of the media.

Byford-Jones and Una Hainsworth

Major events in the whole Bella case – and arguably also in the newspaper career of Byford-Jones – were the *Anna of Claverley* letters. Una Hainsworth's story is so contrived that a member of the public[222] who wrote to the police on the case in 1968 described it as "a cock and bull story ... full of holes and piffle" and questioned why the police had even looked into it. This individual also described "Anna" as "a liar an imposter and a romancer". This was so obviously the case that it is surprising that such conclusions had not been reached many years earlier – if, indeed, they hadn't. Probably the only bit of her ridiculous story that is true is the sad fact that her first husband died a broken man in a mental institution. Whilst Una may have thought that she was doing no harm to a dead man, her story blackened his memory, and no doubt caused further anguish to his family. But what prompted Hainsworth to come forward in this way? One doesn't have to look too far for the answer.

---

[221] Sidney Inight, as with Tommy Williams, would appear to have been promoted during the course of these events, being later identified within newspaper reports as Assistant Chief Constable.

[222] This was J. G. Bowers.

Analysis

For, rather than these two worlds colliding only because Byford-Jones's articles pricked Una Hainsworth's conscience, it is clear that the two were well acquainted long before that; and the many inconsistencies within Una's letters and stories scream "fake" at every turn. The fact that Una Hainsworth lived a colourful, eventful life does not, of course, in itself make her party to a criminal deception. In the event, though, it seems that Byford-Jones chose Una to "break" a story for the reason that her husband had died in mysterious circumstances, and thus could not refute their outlandish claims. But she was a most unsuitable ally in so many ways. Her attention to detail was also very poor and, within her first "anonymous" letter to *Quaestor*, there are numerous errors and betrayals. So much so, it is surprising that Byford-Jones didn't get her to rewrite it. But, by then, he had become complacent. At a time when journalism was more respected than now, and anything in print was more-or-less accepted as gospel, he probably felt that nobody would see fit to question his version of the truth.

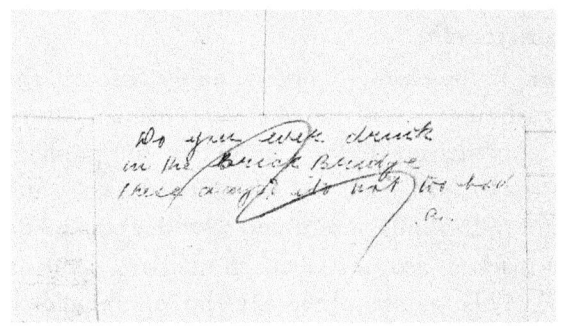

Deep within the police files is this additional clue to Anna of Claverley's identity.
(West Mercia Police)

Leaving aside the issue of whether Una was the type of person to act in the public interest, the most obvious observation to make is that an anonymous letter should not identify the sender. Yet, in a final paragraph (which has been crossed out), Una enquires about a mutual friend. Byford-Jones did acknowledge that he was responsible for striking out these additional words – allegedly for editorial reasons prior to publication. But of even greater significance is another brief paragraph written by her and which has also been crossed through. The photocopy of this is buried within a police file, but it would appear that the original was written on the back of one of the other sheets (Una tended to write on just one side of each piece of paper, so this could have been overlooked by others). This read: "Do you ever drink in the Brick Bridge these days? It's not too bad." This suppressed reference adds to the large body of evidence that Una Hainsworth and Wilfred Byford-Jones were known to each other. On the face of it, Byford-Jones and Una Hainsworth moved in very different circles and would have had very little in common. Nevertheless, Byford-Jones was a gregarious individual, and his fondness for village pubs has already been established. The Brick Bridge was, of course, the local name for the Waggon & Horses at Wombourne, the pub where not only was Byford-Jones known to drink, but where Jack and Una Mossop had once lived (when Jack's aunt was landlady there). Byford-Jones was also very familiar with Claverley (particularly through his connections with the Mander family), where Una Hainsworth was then living.[223] Furthermore, it is highly likely that Byford-Jones, with both his knowledge of the local villages and his journalistic contacts would have been well aware of the real circumstances surrounding the tragic death of Jack Mossop – and alert as to how they might be used.

There is something further which may have led to Una Hainsworth and Byford-Jones becoming re-acquainted. We have seen that Una had lost two children, in 1942 and 1949. Byford-Jones and his young wife were desperate to have a family, but lost the only two children they had – one at four months of age, and one at 18 months. These tragic events happened in 1948 and 1951 and provide another plausible link. It is surely quite possible that Byford-Jones and Una may have met up again at local hospitals, or even in some form of early counselling group. But it is more likely that they had never lost contact, and that these ordeals brought them closer together.

---

[223] It is worth noting, too, that in the street where Byford-Jones grew up, there were several residents who were related to the Crumps (Jack Mossop's extended family).

Analysis

The Waggon & Horses, Wombourne, as it is today. The Wom Brook runs alongside, and it is easy to see why the pub was once more commonly known as the Brick Bridge.

In her first letter, Una explains why she is writing under a "nom de plume", a term more widely used in the 1950s than is the case today (where "alias" or "pseudonym" are more usual), but one which still wasn't in everyday usage. It was, however, a phrase much favoured by *Quaestor* himself. Una's summation: "the one person who could give the answer is now beyond the jurisdiction of the earthly courts" is a surprisingly dramatic piece of prose to be used by a 1950s housewife, and has the ring of a journalist about it.[224] And Byford-Jones's second article[225] included his opinion: "I think that the murderers – one man could hardly carry out the operation – were local men or were acting under local guidance." Nobody had hitherto suggested that the 12-year-old murder was a joint enterprise, yet, the following day, the newspaper office allegedly received Una Hainsworth's initial letter putting forward this very scenario. Although letter writing was afforded a much higher priority then (in the absence of suitable alternatives) than

---

[224] Further circumstantial evidence lies in the fact that the content of Hainsworth's two letters seem quite different in style – suggesting different authorship.
[225] On 20 November 1953.

now, this was a very quick turnaround if "Anna's" response hadn't already been drafted. But Anna's letter is actually dated 18 November – i.e. before the newspaper article to which she purports to be responding!

Crucially, within her formal police interview, Una refers to having put "sufficient clues in [my] letter which should have helped to have identified me". This strongly suggests that the police challenged her about her past association with Byford-Jones, and that she was now trying to cover herself. Byford-Jones, of course, did not feel so inhibited, still claiming some four years later that he had used his great powers of deduction to identify "Anna" when he saw her "for the first time" in the Whittington Inn.

Byford-Jones and the wall messages

Whilst Victor Crumpton and others may well have had some questions to answer in relation to the wall messages, it is no doubt that they were journalistic gold, and it is interesting to speculate whether and how Byford-Jones may have been involved. Regardless of his whereabouts at the time, Byford-Jones had strong family connections to Halesowen, near to where the early messages appeared, and also to Wolverhampton, where another was later found. The latter was the one close to the Mander Brothers' factory, and he had become acquainted with the Mander family through his journalistic work. Not only that, but the site was close to the *Express & Star* offices – and also on the route between there and Byford-Jones's home in Beckbury.

It was the graffiti in Upper Dean Street that was the first to shoot to prominence and this, it will be recalled, was in the fruit market area. Intriguingly, two of the 14 men identified by the police as having visited the Birmingham fruit market immediately before the messages appeared there, had the surname Jones.[226] Once again, the ubiquity of this name precludes establishing whether either was related to *Quaestor*, although it is worth reiterating that his father, Ehud Jones, was recorded as being a retired fruiterer within official records. Before dismissing this notion as yet more speculation, it may also be pertinent to record that Byford-Jones

---

[226] The same list contains the names Edmonds, Taylor and Parsons which also appear elsewhere within investigations; although, similarly, the commonality of these names hampers research.

Analysis

had a nephew by the name of Douglas Wood, and obituaries of Cynthia Gregory (Byford-Jones's second wife) suggest that the two men had been very close throughout their lives. Could one of his family have been the mysterious "Mr Wood" who had written to the police claiming to be the author of at least one of the Birmingham messages? Whilst it is tempting to attribute this letter to a crank, it could be that one of the Woods[227] had been involved – writing some of the messages or priming another family member or contact to act – but, having seen how the situation had escalated out of control, then decided to put the matter straight and write to the police, before losing his nerve. Even if Byford-Jones had been on war service at the time, this would not exclude a contact such as Wood having written the messages. Of course, it could have been another journalist who sowed the seed for *Quaestor* to water on his return from the war. Whatever the reality, it would certainly not have been the first time that a journalist may have planted "evidence".

Even if he wasn't behind them, *Quaestor* must have been delighted at how the wall messages were received (and reported by others, as well as himself). It should also be borne in mind that the residents of the houses behind the Hasbury Rose & Crown (implicated within some of the messages) included a number of members of the Willetts family, and that there were links between a branch of this family and the Joneses. It is not, unfortunately, possible to find a close family tie, but Ehud's aunt married a Willetts and, when the family was living in Halesowen, electoral records show numerous Joneses and Willetts living alongside each other. Implicating Walter Willetts – who owned the timber yard behind the pub, had some firm views about the case and was also friendly with Tommy Williams – might also be seen as a good journalistic tactic, particularly if the journalist already had a working relationship with Williams. Developing this concept further, could it be that PC Horrobin had been made aware that the graffiti artist apprehended by him had links to *Quaestor* and was persuaded to keep quiet? In such a scenario, when Crumpton "spilled the beans", PC Horrobin would have had no

---

[227] Harry Wood, was Wilfred's brother-in-law, married to Wilfred's sister. It would appear that Douglas was Harry's son (so, technically, Cynthia's nephew). The ages would suggest that he would have been too young to have been involved in the wall messages, although his father wouldn't. The family lived in Long Lane, Hagley.

option but to come clean. This would provide a logical explanation of why Williams so suddenly stopped confiding in Byford-Jones and then let a rival newspaper break the news that the wall messages were a red herring.

Byford-Jones and Warwick Plant

Warwick Plant is yet another of the enigmas that characterise this case. On the surface, Plant – a trainee accountant – was from the same sort of well-to-do family that Byford-Jones liked to pretend that he himself was, and would seem to have no reason to fabricate a story. That Plant did come forward to the press at some subsequent point was established very much later in the piece (in the new millennium), when author Joyce Coley made contact with a local newspaper and was put in touch with a journalist who confirmed that his newspaper had previously interviewed him. This, of course, is far from confirming that his sister contacted the police immediately after he returned home on leave from the RAF in 1944, and she allegedly showed him the *Daily Sketch* newspaper article. There is no mention whatsoever within surviving police files of the Plant family and, further, the author has been unable to trace any contemporaneous newspaper article which reflects an interview with him or his sister. If Plant was telling the truth, it seems unaccountable that a local newspaper wanted nothing to do with the story: because of the furore stirred up by the "Bella" messages, anything that was remotely relevant was gobbled up by the press.

Warwick's description made this Bella a very good "fit". She was described as being short of stature, which was a good start in terms of Webster's conclusions. She allegedly had uneven teeth and, similarly, the fact that she was a foreigner is promising in terms of explaining there being no flurry of reports of her disappearance. Far more compelling, however, is the matter of the footwear: the conclusions that the victim's shoes were probably too large for her frame and that their quality was inconsistent with the rest of her clothing very much fits in with the circumstances of her acquiring the shoes, as described by Plant. The coroner had also ventured that the victim of the unsolved murder was "obviously not in the 'higher flight'" but "nor [was] she a ragamuffin … she is, moreover, a type of person who may have been rather neglectful

Analysis

as to her appearance and habits". This would again very much fit with Plant's "candidate". If his testimony is to believed, then Bella's drunk and abusive landlord would be a prime candidate for being the murderer. If this were the case, the likelihood is that he would have killed her first and then taken the body to the wood by car, increasing the chances of discovery; it is unlikely that he would have been able to lure his victim to the wood on any spurious basis. Once again, this is a line of enquiry not followed by the police for the reason that Plant's evidence does not feature in their files. Plant claimed to have seen the landlord following the disappearance of Bella on two separate occasions, but that he was too scared to confront him. This could be the case, although it must be pointed out that he was in his twenties at the time and not the young boy implied by numerous sources.

Being charitable, it is possible that the siblings' concerns were reported to the police, and there are a number of reasons why a visit by Plant or his sister may not have been recorded by them. We know that there are gaps in police records, and we certainly don't know who was on duty at the time of their alleged visit. In wartime, there was a shortage of uniformed staff, and civilians were often used to man the front desk. There is no guarantee that there would have been a police officer to speak to, or that any message left would have been passed on. It may even have been the case that there was a spate of missing person reports in the wake of the newspaper articles and that, as a result, the police were wary of accepting just another unsupported claim. Perhaps, too, (assuming that Plant's sister approached the police on her own) social attitudes of the time would have played down the significance of a report from a young woman. The overwhelming likelihood, however, is that neither Plant nor his sister went anywhere near either a police station or a newspaper office in 1944. This is one of many examples of claims being made after the event, with very little to back them up. So, why would Plant lie about contacting the police, be reluctant to visit them, or invent a story which would cast them in a poor light? The answer might well lie within a previous incident involving the two parties, which had led to a lot of bad feeling.

Back in July 1938, a jewel robbery had taken place at a house in Hagley. Some £2,300-worth of goods were taken, but what would make this a notable and high-profile case was the fact that the victim was C. F. Walters, the England and Worcestershire cricketer. Six arrests were swiftly made and the names of the accused featured prominently in local and national newspapers, up until their court appearance in November the same year. One of the men arrested was Warwick Aston Plant.[228] His offence was to have been found in possession of a travel clock from the burglary, and he was charged with receiving stolen goods. Plant claimed that he was unaware of the fact that the clock was stolen, and it seems that he may well have been telling the truth: he maintained that he had been given the item by a friend after his wristwatch had broken. The judge clearly believed him, and Plant was duly discharged. It would seem, though, that this incident resulted in a major loss of goodwill between Plant and the police – who believed him to be guilty.

It is (just) possible that Plant's mistrust of the police stemming from this incident meant that he didn't come forward as he had claimed – but later realised that he should have done so. The most compelling argument against Plant's story, however, is that nobody else reported the woman's absence at the time. By his own account, this Bella was an accomplished singer who was popular at both the Three Crowns and the Mitre. The two establishments were well frequented; surely her sudden disappearance would have been noticed by others and, once the "Bella" messages had started to appear, someone else would have notified the police (even assuming that she didn't use a different name when performing)? And Plant claimed that his mother had a close, personal connection to Bella, so why didn't she go to the police herself? There may be a number of reasons that could be put forward to explain a reluctance on her part, including concern that she might be contravening licensing laws by allowing an "alien" to work in her pub and thus feared losing her licence; that she believed her children had already made a report; or that she feared reprisals (Plant stated that Bella's landlord was reputed to be a very violent man). But the police had never identified Mrs Plant as the purchaser of a pair of the distinctive crepe-soled shoes, and a much more believable reason is that this Bella was a figment of Warwick Plant's imagination – with the name selected to fit with that appearing in the wall messages.

---

[228] Warwick Aston Plant is another whose middle name reflected his mother's maiden name.

Analysis

If so, what would have prompted Plant to make such claims so long after the event? Once again, the most obvious answer would be Wilfred Byford-Jones. Whilst Byford-Jones was dead by the time that Joyce Coley interviewed Warwick Plant, it would seem likely that when Plant did first come forward (but not in 1944), it would have been to speak to him.[229] Despite their tenure at the upmarket Three Crowns Hotel in Brierly Hill, there had been a long history of pub management in the Plant family, particularly on Warwick's mother's side. A common belief is that, rather than the Three Crowns in Brierly Hill High Street, Plant's parents ran the Gipsy's Tent opposite Hagley Wood – but this is not the case.[230] More to the point, however, the Aston family (on his mother's side) had a strong connection to Wombourne, which included the running of the Waggon & Horses / Brick Bridge pub at the turn of the 20th century – the very same pub that Charlotte Mossop (née Crump) would later take on, in the village where Una Abel was born and her family had roots. It was also a pub with which we know (thanks to Una's carelessness within her letters) Byford-Jones to have been acquainted. It is certainly easy to see how a journalist with links to the area could have used Plant for his own purposes. The "evidence" that Plant provides is so good that, indeed, it appears too good to be true, particularly the shoes being a poor fit. By his sighting of her in a field next to Hagley Wood, Plant lends credibility to the possibility that she had been forced into working as a part-time prostitute – which would account for her familiarity with the area, and explain why she might take a client there. But such a sighting – from a bus that just happened to be passing – must be regarded statistically as highly improbable. And some of the detail that Plant provides is wrong. He states, for example, that the distinctive crepe-soled shoes were cream and tan in colour. Yes, there was a discrepancy in the official reporting of

---

[229] The fact that there is no evidence of an arising article could be down to the fact that, by this time, more editorial control was being exerted over Byford-Jones (see below).

[230] This confusion may in part have resulted from the interviewing of the Gipsy's Tent landlord, Harry Chambers, by the *Birmingham Daily Gazette* back in April 1943 (soon after the body was discovered). He advised that "so many strangers call here that it is impossible to remember them", and it seems that this statement has been erroneously linked by some to Plant's tale. In 1939, electoral records show the Gipsy's Tent being managed by the Law family.

the shoe colour; but the reports stated that they were either black or blue. Confusion between these two colours is understandable given the time that the shoes had been exposed to the elements; there is less likelihood, however, that they could have been confused with a cream and tan pair. Nevertheless, Plant's story would be fully consistent with Byford-Jones – whose failure to pay attention to detail is regularly exposed – having "fed" the information to him. Alternatively, it may just be that so much time had elapsed that Plant had forgotten exactly what Byford-Jones had previously told him.

Byford-Jones and Zita Boyden
Byford-Jones's journalistic contacts stretched far and wide. Chapter 8 has alluded to the fact that some of Zita Boyden's strange "insights" reflected the theories of others which were not in the public domain at the time. Some detail that she provided was consistent with what Una Hainsworth would subsequently come out with (for example a Dutch connection) and, following the publication of receipt of the first *Anna of Claverley* letter, Boyden even speculated upon the physical appearance of "Anna". But one doesn't have to look too far for an explanation: in a letter to the police dated 26 November 1953 (i.e. less than a week after the *Anna of Claverley* letter), Boyden acknowledges that she had already spoken with (and visited) "the journalist Wilfred Byford-Jones".

Byford-Jones and Victor Crumpton
Byford-Jones would almost certainly have been acquainted with the family of Victor Crumpton, too. The Albrighton Hunt used to meet regularly at St Kenelm's Hall at the time that the Crumpton family lived there. This would have entailed regular liaison between the two parties, and Wilfred Byford-Jones was a supporter of the Albrighton Hunt – if not one of its members – who also reported on it. Further, his writings frequently referenced the parish of Rowley Regis, and Crumpton's service as a councillor there provided another point of likely contact.

Byford-Jones and others
Even where Byford-Jones was not directly involved, he created grounds for speculation by others. The danger within this is that even reputable

Analysis

journalists can become sucked in, as we have already seen. But there may even have been connections between him and a number of the other discredited authors who feature in this narrative. Whilst, for example, there is no firm evidence to link him and the Hungarian Ladislas Farago, such a connection cannot be discounted. The two were of the same age, and had a keen interest (and wrote about) both espionage and events in North Africa in the Second World War. It is possible that they could have met post-war, and that it was through Byford-Jones that Farago learned of the existence of the obscure Edgbaston jeweller, Hans Caesar. It may also be relevant that *War of Wits* was published at around the same time that ITV broadcast the programme claiming that the "Bella" case had been solved. Not that it would have mattered much had the two not been acquainted: Farago was an unprincipled journalist quite happy to accept what had been printed in a trade journal if it would help sell copy.

Nor has it been possible to find any definitive link between Donald McCormick and Byford-Jones. But the former does seem to have based a sizeable amount of his writing on the *Anna of Claverley* correspondence, and related newspaper articles. Whilst this is hardly conclusive, McCormick has been widely pilloried for his rejection of anything approaching the truth – which makes he and Byford-Jones natural allies. It could also be that Byford-Jones and the Home Guard volunteer Harry Basterfield were known to each other. The Basterfield and Jones families were both prominent in Halesowen, living in close proximity, and Byford-Jones was a vocal advocate of the Home Guard organisation. Then there is the evidence of John Swindon, who reported seeing a soldier entering the wood with a girl. Although not coming forward until seven years after the event, he claimed to be able to precisely date the episode. The fact that this was the first day of the fishing season does add some credibility to his claim, but it is puzzling that he could be so sure of the year – and, indeed, in his initial police statement he gave it as a year later. The fact that he came forward in response to a newspaper appeal does not necessarily link him to Byford-Jones but, once again, the possibility has to be considered.

The Deceptions of Wilfred Byford-Jones

Byford-Jones and TV claims that the case had been solved

At no point did Byford-Jones lose interest in developments, and he was highly aware that returning to the "Bella" mystery always paid dividends in terms of newspaper sales. Between 1949 and 1952, though, he was strangely quiet. This was probably due to the fact that his bosses were now exerting an appropriate level of management control over him. It was presumably his promotion to the post of the newspaper's Deputy Editor in 1952 which gave him a new lease of life. He still bided his time before – in November 1953 – writing his pivotal article on the case. Within just ten days of publication, Una Hainsworth had come forward with her fantastical tale; Victor Crumpton had told Tommy Williams about his alleged encounter with PC Horrobin; and Williams himself had told the press unequivocally that the "clue to Bella was false". The results of this brought home the ongoing power of the press, but Byford-Jones was still not satisfied. However, due to the hornets' nest that had been stirred up, and the attention that was probably now being focused on his own role, he had to be careful. Things accordingly again subsided, until 1956, in which year the TV programme in which it was claimed that the case had been solved (as related within Chapter 9) was transmitted.

Could Byford-Jones's influence really have extended this far, though? Whilst he had a role with the BBC by this time,[231] the programme was made by rival company ITV. To fully explore this issue, it's necessary to look through the police files, which contain part of a puzzling draft (and unissued) police statement purporting to announce that the case had been solved. This is undated, but was prepared just after the Whittington Inn meeting. It reads:

> Owing to the hunch of a regular army reserve officer, who hides behind the nom de plume "Quaestor", I was given a vital clue on the Wych Elm case which has enabled the 11-year-old mystery to be cleared up at this late date.
>
> This is very satisfactory since we have, in the course of investigating this, one of the most baffling mysteries of modern times, travelled many

---

[231] He had taken on this additional post at roughly the same time he became Deputy Editor of the *Express & Star*, in 1952.

Analysis

hundreds of miles, interviewed and read 1 [*sic*] letters of thousands of people and followed up many clues.

"Quaestor" was fascinated by one aspect of [the] case – the aspect cannot be divulged since 1 solution of the crime opens up a wider and more important investigation and He collected on many facts as possible [*sic*], had long interviews with 1 assistant chief constable, and later met me on two occasions. I also showed him the clues. He obviously was anxious to help me

After visiting Hagley Wood and writing out his deductions "Quaestor" was able to hand to me a[n] anonymous letter from a person who claimed to know who committed the crime: and later he was present when I actually met the person + obtained certain facts.

I carefully listened to 1 story and later made investigations and I can now say that the following represents the explanation of the remains found in the wych elm tree in April 1942.[232]

[then follows 4 horizontal lines]

Further inquiries being made into another aspect of the matter. It's not possible to give names and addresses [*sic*]

As well as being sympathetic to, and complimentary of, *Quaestor*, this draft looks as if it may be in his own distinctive hand! It is surprising why, within this, the date of discovery of the body has been changed from 1943 to 1942. Both Byford-Jones and all the senior police officers were fully aware of the timings, and it may be yet another example of the journalist failing to pay attention to detail. The strong likelihood is that this draft would have been prepared soon after the December 1953 meeting between Una Hainsworth, the police and Byford-Jones. The statement that 11 years had elapsed should not be taken too literally, as the author may have assumed that the letter would not be issued until the following calendar year.

---

[232] This date was originally written as April 1943, but subsequently changed.

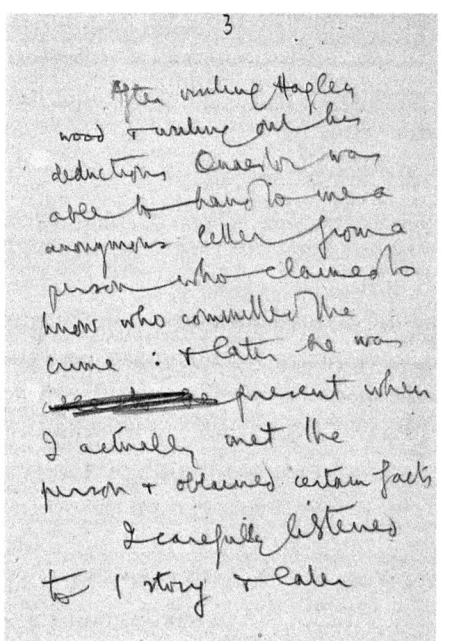 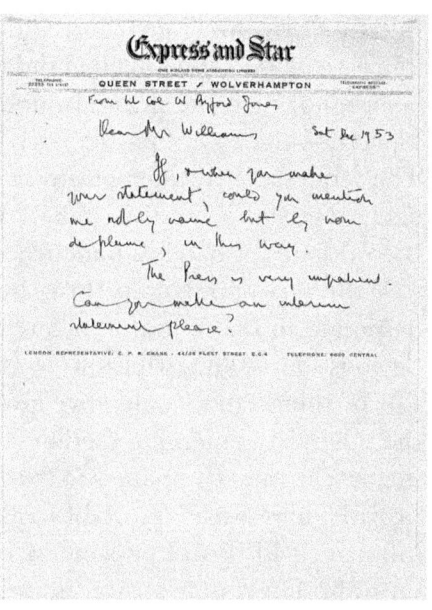

The distinctive writing and word linkage within the undated police document claiming that the murder had been solved (contained within police files; left). The document on the right is a letter from Byford-Jones to Williams and includes the term "nom de plume". (West Mercia Police)

The obvious inference is that Byford-Jones was trying to build on his earlier deceptions by taking credit for solving this historic and sensational crime. If further proof were needed, the next document on the police file is from him, and dated 19 December 1953. Addressed to "Mr Williams", it states:

> If, and when, you make your statement, could you mention me not by name but by non de plume, in this way. The press is very impatient. Can you make an interim statement please?

This is quite revealing. It demonstrates just how desperate that Byford-Jones was to publish his scoop, and it also confirms his fondness for the phrase "nom de plume". But of even greater interest is his keenness for his real name not to be used – something also evident within the draft press statement. This may be for journalistic reasons, but could also be attributed to him not wishing all readers to know his identity. At this time, bylines were very widely used, and the public were often unaware of the individual behind them; if Byford-Jones's own name had been used, then the general public may well have linked him to other aspects of the case – particularly his association with Una Hainsworth. The request for a statement to be issued clearly fell on deaf ears, most likely because, by this time, Williams had either seen through Byford-Jones or had lost patience with him.

With this opportunity lost, by 1956, Byford-Jones was becoming desperate to find ways of taking his story forward. Television was the obvious source and, whilst his work with the BBC was more on the radio side of things, this would have given him an insight into the workings of the other and emerging medium. If he could persuade one of the two major television companies to take an interest in the case, then this would provide him with a suitable vehicle. But how could he have both influenced ITV and persuaded James Webster to perpetuate such an untruth? The simple answer is: probably without too much difficulty. TV investigative journalism was in its infancy at this time and it would be misleading to say that today's exacting standards of editorial control did not apply; rather, there was almost no control over the programme-makers whatsoever, and no independent checking of facts. Another newspaper journalist – Michael Green – writes in a volume of his autobiography[233] of his move from print to television journalism at this very time (1956). Despite having absolutely no experience of the medium, Green managed to secure numerous commissions, sometimes of whole series when he had written only an outline script for one episode. He also wrote scripts for professionals (including doctors) to read rather than giving them the opportunity to express their own views, and would think nothing of drafting in his own relatives and contacts to ensure "correct" responses. For a journalist as charismatic as Byford-Jones, it would not have been difficult to persuade the company to make the programme (the case then being as compelling as it is now), and there would have been little or no editorial interference. Professor Webster – as with most people in the 1950s – would have had little

---

[233] *Nobody Hurt in Small Earthquake (William Heinemann Ltd, 1990).*

experience of the medium of television, particularly in front of the camera. Moreover, by this time, his increasingly erratic behaviour had resulted in his employment being terminated early. This meant that he would have had no ongoing official dialogue with the police. If Byford-Jones had told him that the case had been solved and asked him to say a few kind words about Tommy Williams' investigative skills, there would have been little reason for him not to comply.

The *Wolverhampton Express & Star* eagerly reported the ITV broadcast, with *Quaestor* himself quoting Webster's "classic piece of deduction" remark. Later in the same article, he repeats the same words – arguably in a bid to demonstrate that this was the finding of an independent and credible person, reinforcing the notion that it must be true. In the days after the broadcast, he was quoted by his own newspaper (in his capacity of "case expert") as saying: [234]

> Up to 1954, neither the identity of Bella had been discovered, nor the mode of death. This I can say after taking part in conferences with detectives engaged on the case.
>
> Information was passed to the officer in charge as a result of investigations carried out, and this was followed up.
>
> Visits were paid to Holland, and at least one important "witness" was questioned. If the identity of Bella has been discovered, then the discovery must have been made within the last year and no public statement has been made.

There is absolutely nothing to back up Byford-Jones's claim that the police had visited Holland; this was presumably an attempt to shore-up the story concocted by himself and Una Hainsworth (and probably also planted with Zita Boyden). It is likely that this TV programme and its aftermath caused more negative reaction towards Byford-Jones than he had anticipated: James Webster would have been very unhappy at being duped in this way, and the reaction of Tommy Williams – probably still seething from Byford-Jones's earlier actions – can only be imagined.

It is puzzling that the *Express & Star* and its editor were prepared to

---

[234] On 23/05/1956.

keep indulging Byford-Jones, but perhaps circulation figures talked. It may have been their and Tommy Williams' deeper concerns that resulted in it taking four years from the meeting at the Whittington Inn and 20 months from the ITV broadcast for *Quaestor* to pen the story that he had been itching to tell: the article *Kinver Inn Meeting sheds light on Mystery of Bella* not being published until 16 January 1958. This unconvincingly claimed that it was the "Professor's" statement within the ITV programme that allowed *Quaestor* to now divulge further information about the December 1953 meeting:

> So now a pledge I made to keep further facts of the death of Bella of the Wych Elm is purged, I can tell of my dramatic meeting with a woman who claimed to know how Bella died.

Even by Byford-Jones's own standards, this article was pretty preposterous. It starts by setting the scene with a very theatrical account of the evening at the inn, where he, Tommy Williams and two other members of CID staff had arranged to meet "Anna". This inn was (and remains) a very striking building and, although the location was ostensibly chosen by Una Hainsworth, it is difficult to conclude other than that this was all part of Byford-Jones's careful stage management.[235] He maintains the deception that, at the outset, he was as unaware as the detectives as to just who they were expecting to meet. Looking at all the women entering the pub, they had to decide which might be "Anna". Byford-Jones claims to have used his professionalism to identify the likely target and, in a bid to presumably impress his readers, contends that he confronted her with the dramatic words: "Anna, I believe?" This is as outrageous as it is dishonest.

Byford-Jones is careful to reinforce that "no one else would ever have heard of it [Una's story], but for the fact that *I* [author's italics] had reopened the case", and he does treat it very much as *his* story. He did, of course, have a duty as a journalist to protect his source, so – in other circumstances – an element of deception might have been legitimate,

---

[235] Within her letter arranging the meeting, Una initially refers to the inn as the "Dick Whittington" rather than the "Whittington Inn", suggesting that she may not have been as familiar with it as she claimed.

particularly "Anna's" connection to the alleged protagonists. There are many "facts" that appear in this article which do not accord with police records of the meeting, yet have nevertheless made it into the public consciousness. But the police were witnesses to everything that took place between Una Hainsworth and Byford-Jones during the half-hour that they talked, as well as having the more formal interview with her subsequently. Accordingly, if any of the more outlandish claims made by Byford-Jones had substance, they would surely have followed them up.

These claims included the detail that one of van Ralt's associates was a trapeze artist. Whilst Una Hainsworth had seemingly spoken of a show-business (ice skating) connection, there had been no previous mention of a trapeze artist. Neither Una's police statement nor letters make any direct reference to there being a fourth person in the car, but Byford-Jones now (within this article) places the trapeze artist in the car with Jack Mossop, van Ralt and the victim. Next, although Una had earlier said that she had no firm evidence of van Ralt being a spy, Byford-Jones's article also "reveals" that Mossop had been asked by the trapeze artist to identify munitions factories and that, as a result, one of these had subsequently been heavily bombed. He then goes on to relate that Una spoke to "the officer" (Jack Mossop) on two consecutive nights: firstly, on that of the murder; and the following night, after he had revisited the wood to confirm that he had not been hallucinating. This, once again, is information lacking in both the *Anna of Claverley* letters and police interview records. Byford-Jones yet again gets his dates wrong (saying that Mossop "confessed" to Una in April 1943, whereas this was the date of the discovery of the body). Finally, this is where he states categorically that MI5 "was brought into the case".

The fact that police documents are now in the public domain means that all these inconsistencies are quite clear to see. It could be argued that Una had maintained a separate dialogue with Byford-Jones, but her police statement must be taken as a more reliable source, as Una would have been aware of the risks of lying to the authorities. Hence, there is little real detail within this statement: Una refers vaguely to her suspicions, and qualifies some claims by stating that they had only been told to her by her former husband. In this way, the police would be unlikely to be able to disprove anything; even if they did, then Una

Analysis

would be able to reasonably counter that she had never been told the truth and was just resorting to guesswork – or that she must have been lied to. So, there is no mention of specifics, such as details of the munitions factories allegedly targeted, within these interview records. Byford-Jones was not so constrained of course, and it is difficult to draw any realistic conclusions other than that he was becoming lazy; couldn't be bothered to cross-check to his previous articles; was making things up to better present his point of view; and complacently felt that nobody would take issue with him.

Found out at last

Perhaps the most valid questions to ask are how Byford-Jones thought that he could get away with all this and, indeed, how he managed to do so for so long. The answers may lie within the military assessment of his intelligence. Byford-Jones comes across as something of a sociopath, and one of the traits of sociopaths is that they feel that they are more intelligent and better than others. His lack of attention to detail and mistakes in his work are easy to find, but he had a charisma which allowed him to get away with things, certainly in an era when journalists held more sway.

Whatever one's opinion of the way that the police handled the whole inquiry, they were far from stupid, and Byford-Jones's duplicity increasingly became clear for most to see. What is more surprising is that at no time do they seem to have taken any action against him. But because the dynamics were somewhat different then, and Byford-Jones had a high standing in the community, he was able to get away with it for a long time. It would appear, however, that Byford-Jones did not get off totally scot-free: very soon after his January 1958 *Kinver Inn Meeting* article, he seems to have been abruptly "dropped" by the *Express & Star*. Whether the senior management of this newspaper were already wise to his deceptions, or Tommy Williams made them finally see sense is open to question – but the practices of the time meant that their star journalist could be sidelined without too many questions being asked in public. It is against this background that Byford-Jones went into exile and, by the time that he died in 1977, his name was no longer being mentioned in despatches. Obituaries referenced his war and foreign correspondent roles, but not his involvement in reporting one of the great murder mysteries of its time, and this seems to have been airbrushed from much newspaper history in the intervening years.

CHAPTER 17

Other Sources of Confusion

Whilst it would be natural to cast Wilfred Byford-Jones as the villain of the piece in all this, he – as others before and since – would have been under pressure to provide content and sell newspapers. And it would be wrong to suggest he was the only locally based journalist to manipulate the facts.

The *Black Country Bugle* / Harry Taylor

The *Black Country Bugle* editor Harry Taylor found, as Byford-Jones, that the "Bella" case was a gift to journalism which just kept giving. Taylor identified that there was sufficient interest to reprise the case in 1973, and to then revisit it five years later. Unfortunately, the *Bugle*'s reporting of the case and lack of attention to detail was very much in the same mould as Byford-Jones's. Taylor even – as his illustrious predecessor – used a pseudonym.[236] It is as a result of Taylor's articles that the four individuals came forward with what was claimed to be new information. Their credibility and the value of their insights are discussed below.

The policeman's tale

It was Richard Skerratt who related his former colleague Jack Pound's assertion that the killer was from the services ("I reckon as the chap we'm [*sic*] looking for is now helping to drive Rommel out of North Africa").[237] Wilfred Byford-Jones, of course, had served in North Africa, and the dates of his service are by no means set in stone. Pound's comments *could* point to Byford-Jones, but they were almost certainly based on some

---

[236] Aristotle Tump, as referenced within Chapter 9.
[237] Another "reading" of this could be that Skerratt had heard that one of the Gatacre family, based in Africa at the time, could have been involved – see later in this chapter.

widely held early perceptions (reflecting the transient nature of the population and some other murder cases) rather than any official intelligence. However, both Pound and Skerratt were junior officers at the time so would not have been party to full details of the investigation; but they may have heard rumours that CID were examining the role that Byford-Jones had played and put a wrong interpretation upon them. Whilst concluding that it would be ludicrous to attribute the murder to Byford-Jones (there are examples to be found of a killer inserting himself centre stage into an investigation), such a scenario would be scarcely less believable than many of the other ridiculous theories which have gained currency – some of which the journalist himself was behind.

The Home Guards' tale

It will be recalled that Geoffrey Grove and Harry Basterfield were the two Home Guards that Harry Taylor persuaded to come forward. Grove's claim that witches were regularly meeting in the Wood for black magic purposes was contrary to just about all the evidence gathered at the time and since by local historians and experts in the field. His contention that the Home Guard knew that two spies had been parachuted into the area, and that one was a woman, may reflect some popular rumours, but it flies in the face of everything that is known to be true about the case.

Basterfield's account is quite absurd on just about every level, but bears the mark of a story designed to fit in with some of the wilder conspiracy theories already doing the rounds. Basterfield's daughter (Irene Oliver) said that her father had told her that it had been very unusual to see cars parked in Hagley Wood Lane, but this does not fully correlate with other reports of the time. Clearly car ownership was restricted, but some witnesses have said that it wasn't uncommon to see vehicles in the lane, as it was a favoured venue for courting couples. And RAF or other service officers would be more likely than most to be able to afford a vehicle and obtain the necessary petrol coupons. It is quite likely that there were numerous occasions when Home Guard patrols came across courting couples in cars, so there was plenty of scope for confusion over dates and venues.

Just to run with this, if it had been Mossop in the front seat of the car

Analysis

seen by Basterfield, then the other occupant(s) – fortuitously for them – would have presumably been reconnoitring the wood for a suitable hiding place when the Home Guard knocked on the window. And, if true, it would have been the first indication that Mossop was using false ID papers. It is quite a step from wearing a uniform to which you are no longer entitled, to carrying fraudulent identification. Of course, there is the possibility that the Home Guard officers did not ask to see ID: there is plenty of anecdotal evidence of the Home Guard not always being assiduous in carrying out such duties, and if this had been overlooked, the officers would have been unlikely to admit it.

What undermines both witnesses, of course, is the timing of their coming forward. Grove does not appear to give any reason why he had remained silent for nearly 30 years, whilst Basterfield contends that he was unaware of the finding of the body at the time. Even if had he moved away for a period, he had grown up in Halesowen and later returned there, and it seems highly unlikely that it would take so long for him to tie up the two incidents. And, if this were the case, would his colleagues have also each failed to spot the significance? The police had interviewed members of the Home Guard at the time of the Ann Forrest missing person enquiry, so they would surely have been told of such an incident if it had occurred – and particularly if it had been a memorable event. The account does seem to be based upon the fiction spun by Una Hainsworth and Byford-Jones that Jack Mossop was involved in the murder. The fact that Harry Basterfield was related to one of the families that lived in the properties in Hagley Road and identified in some of the wall messages also needs to be taken into consideration.

The cobbler's tale

There are also a number of highly significant anomalies within Leonard Cogzell's account. For one thing, Cogzell was adamant that the programme that he watched, which allegedly showed a close-up of the shoes, was broadcast around 1970, but could not provide anything more detailed. He claimed that the *Black Country Bugle* article reminded him of the broadcast, and that the reason for not coming forward earlier was that he was nursing his seriously ill wife. Given this, it would seem reasonable that he should have been able to pinpoint the date of the programme with some accuracy. Nevertheless, the information that he provided on the programme strongly suggests that the broadcast in question was that of 1956, in which Professor Webster had allegedly claimed that the case had been solved. The logical explanation would be that Cogzell had seen a repeat, but it was unusual for programmes to be repeated at this time, and very rare for a copy of a programme made in 1956 to be even retained, let alone repeated 14 years later. Further, there is no record of a broadcast in 1970, and nobody else with an interest in the case has come across it.[238] Even if such a broadcast taken place, there is no guarantee that the makers would have taken care to ensure that the shoes shown were the ones from the police archives: it would have been far easier just to use props for display purposes.[239] And why should Dr Davies have been compliant with a cobbler and / or journalist demanding to see items from a "cold case" when he had more important issues to deal with? Dr Davies's colleagues advised that his being "obstructive" did not fit with their perceptions of him, and one does wonder whether his patience was being tried to the limit. Above all else, though, the police had established beyond reasonable doubt that the shoes in question had not been manufactured prior to April 1940 – yet Cogzell claimed that the distinctive stitching he recognised was from seven years earlier.

In the end, the *Bugle* seemed far more interested than the police in taking this forward. Cogzell comes across as somewhat obsessive, but not necessarily a fantasist: he appeared to be firmly of the view that he was right. In terms of the wrong shoes being shown he may have been correct, but there was really no story here until the *Bugle* decided to make it one. The quality of their journalism was poor, containing contradictory statements.

---

[238] It is possible that Cogzell was referring to a programme that he saw in 1956 and that the newspaper misrepresented him; if so, though, it is still extraordinary that he had allowed so much time to elapse before coming forward.

[239] Indeed, one of the photos within the police archives is identified as showing a similar shoe rather than one of the pair in question.

Analysis

More parallels

Yet another illustration of Harry Taylor's work reflecting that of Byford-Jones was the individual(s) drawn out by his articles who would send the two anonymous letters. The first of these – which purported to have been sent from Canada in September 1973 – posed a series of questions, as detailed in Chapter 9. Yet all these were based quite obviously on the work of others (including Byford-Jones and Farago), and appear to have come straight from the pages of McCormick's *Murder by Witchcraft*. There is certainly nothing within this letter by way of new suggestions or leads. The inescapable conclusion is that this was penned by either somebody very familiar with the case, or close to Farago, McCormick or Byford-Jones. In fact, it has to be considered whether the author could have been one of these, possibly in league with Taylor. If so, Byford-Jones would have to be favourite, given that the two men were both journalists who had plied their trade in the Midlands. The phrase in the letter that: "there is an eternal justice beyond earthly laws" is lifted directly from one of Una Hainsworth's letters which was, in all probability, drafted by Byford-Jones.

In the 20–25 years between Byford-Jones's articles and those of Harry Taylor, journalism had changed quite considerably. There was now even more emphasis on sensationalism, and some of that then displayed by the *Bugle* – such as the tacky use of a medical skeleton in a posed photograph – hardly covered the profession in glory. Taylor's articles seem to contain as many errors of fact and inconsistency as Byford-Jones's.[240] It is worthy of note that the police – whose inquiry was still officially open at the time – didn't see fit to take copies of any of the *Bugle*'s articles for their files.

Gatacre and the Canadian connection

Given that Canadian connections continued to surface into the 1970s (with the response to the *Black Country Bugle* article), it is worth looking in more detail at the circumstances surrounding the Gatacres.

---

[240] In fairness to Taylor, a lot was still outside the public domain at this time, and he would not have been aware of some of the glaring errors within Byford-Jones's accounts.

Other Sources of Confusion

The story circulating was that the individual who allegedly made a serving girl pregnant, undertook a moonlight flit and allowed the Hall to fall into disrepair was the second son of a former squire. From this information, this would appear to be Galfry William Gatacre (1886 – 1973). He served with the Canadian Expeditionary Force in the First World War, and, when his elder brother Captain Edward George Gatacre was killed in 1916, he became the next in line to the title. He married Zoe (née Scott-Camus) and had three children by her: two girls and a boy, Rex Arnold, born in 1915. By 1924, the family had returned from Canada. We know this because, that year, there was an (unsuccessful) prosecution taken out against Major Charles Thomas[241] for assaulting Zoe. During the trial, it emerged that the pair were living together,[242] but that Galfry (installed at Gatacre Hall) had tracked them down and an argument had ensued when he tried to take back his children. The 1939 Register shows that Gatacre Hall was still then occupied by Galfry Gatacre (along with his third wife), and there is also evidence that, during the 1940s and 1950s, he spent considerable time back in Canada.

Whether Galfry did subsequently leave the Hall in the circumstances described is open to conjecture, although the limited amount we know of him would suggest that he may have fitted the profile of a womaniser. He was 26 years older than Jack Mossop, but this would not have precluded him from moving in the same drinking circles. However, given the number of times that stories and accounts have been conflated during this saga, it may be that his son, Rex, was the one who was part of the same clique as Mossop – although there is little in his background that would put him in a possible murder scenario. He was only two years or so younger than Jack Mossop, and the pair would have had a lot in common – not least a dysfunctional upbringing. Rex appears to have joined the army and travelled widely – although mainly within Africa (Nigeria, Ghana and Sierra Leone),[243] before coming back to the UK. He lived in Farnham (Surrey) for a time, before returning to live on the Gatacre

---

[241] Thomas was Galfry's brother-in-law.
[242] At this time, in a private hotel in Cheltenham.
[243] On which basis, a case could just be argued that this was the murder suspect "now helping to drive Rommel out of North Africa" as commented upon by PC Jack Pound.

estate – where he died in 1976. It could, alternatively, be that it was his absence(s) that were construed – or misconstrued– by local people, both at the time and subsequently.

The reasons why the squire has been linked to the case have not been widely articulated, although if we are to take Byford-Jones's reporting at face value and accept what he claims Mossop had told Una – and this is a huge leap of faith – there may be an interpretation that would shed some light. This would be the possibility that the squire / one of the Gatacres may have been a fourth occupant of the car (along with Mossop, van Ralt and the victim) on that alleged fateful night in 1941.[244] It might even alternatively be argued that the squire could have killed his wife or the mother of his illegitimate child, and that one of these could be the body found in the tree. More realistically, this rather provides yet further illustration of just how easy it is to develop a conspiracy theory. If Jack Mossop had been part of a regular Claverley drinking school with van Ralt and one or more of the Gatacres, then police enquiries would surely have established this – and thus identified and traced the elusive van Ralt.

What does seem of more significance is that, in addition to the commonly held view that Jack Mossop was friendly with the Gatacre family and spent time in the local pubs with at least one of their number:

(i) Galfry Gatacre's First World War military papers show the family were then resident in Toronto; and

(ii) Galfry Gatacre was born in Barnstaple in Devon, and had spent his early years in the same county (where the family had roots).

This all brings us back to the *Bugle* articles and their responses – one posted from Toronto and the other bearing an unspecified Devon postmark. It really does seem too coincidental for these not to have involved members of the Gatacre family, or sources close to them in some way. It could be construed that the family was trying to cover up for the misdeeds of a forefather, but a far more realistic scenario is a

---

[244] Even then, Byford-Jones's version of events has the mysterious "trapeze artist" as the additional occupant.

Other Sources of Confusion

journalistic contact pulling a few strings. If any one of the Gatacres was a drinking partner of Jack Mossop, then he would almost certainly have been known to Byford-Jones. We know that Byford-Jones was still alive when the Toronto letter (which was stylistically so in keeping with him) was sent, although the Devon letter (1978) post-dated him.[245] It is also worth pointing out that, within these letters, the *Bugle* is twice implored to let the case rest. The sign of a journalist with a guilty conscience, or possibly one who was concerned about being exposed?

TV and radio inaccuracies

The nature of the medium is such that what appears on television is often remembered more vividly than the written word, and more readily perceived by the public to be true. Another of many disappointing aspects of this case is the number of obvious errors which have become widely accepted as fact, in addition to what one might categorise as deliberate falsification. TV programme makers appear to be particularly culpable in this regard.

The majority of broadcasts on the case have been very unsatisfactory both in terms of factual accuracy and the conclusions that they have drawn. In some cases, of course, this is the result of some of Wilfred-Jones's more outrageous claims being unchallenged and presented as truth. Of those from the more modern era, the *Crime Stalker* programme was particularly poor. John Stalker was formerly a very senior and well-respected police officer, but after he retired was searching for a vehicle for his talents. *Crime Stalker*, although running for six years, was not a particularly suitable outlet for him: of insufficient length to allow detailed analysis of cases, the episodes were sensationalist rather than enlightening, and the quality of the journalism was poor. An illustration of this was the filming of the episode in question in Wychbury Wood (near to the obelisk) rather than Hagley Wood. Further, an *Express & Star* reporter who was interviewed states that one of the alleged protagonists was Una Hainsworth's brother rather than husband; with full access to the newspaper's archives, he should have been in a

---

[245] For reference, Ladislas Farago died in 1980, whilst Donald McCormick lived until 1998.

Analysis

position to know that it was Jack Mossop who was in the frame. Certain other "facts" presented – such as that "Bella" had been parachuted into the area – were also from outside either the police or his own newspaper's files. By interviewing Bob Farmer, one of the teenagers who found the body, the programme was able to refute that the clothing found within the mouth cavity was the likely cause of death, but it went on to state that this proved that asphyxiation was not responsible. It also strongly implied that, had this item been used in that way, it would have been proof that the police were dealing with a crime of passion. That might be the case, but is far from an inevitable conclusion.

The September 2005, BBC West Midlands *Inside Out* programme perpetuated the same location error,[246] although little more is known about that episode. Of all the still-accessible broadcasts, however, it is the 2018 UKTV *Nazi Murder Mysteries* episode that is arguably the most factually accurate and interesting; nevertheless, the programme's conclusions are still troubling in that they are again sensationalist, and fixate on the spy ring theories. Given that it is light-hearted and quite tongue-in-cheek, the *Punt PI* radio episode offers a surprisingly good and balanced insight into the case. It is not, however immune from errors – although these often come from the interviewees themselves rather than the researchers.

---

[246] It seems that, in both cases, a retired Hagley Estate manager was responsible, but it is puzzling why he contradicted police and other evidence by insisting that this was the deposition site – unless this was a deliberate attempt to keep trespassers away.

CHAPTER 18

Loose Ends

Not all the sources of confusion surrounding this case can be attributed to journalists or publicity seekers. The names of some of the potential victims or suspects were put forward by people who had genuine concerns, but have nonetheless clouded some aspects of the investigation. Most – but not all – of these "candidates" have been considered elsewhere within this book.

Other possible victims

"Billy" Gibson

The one name in the police files that probably deserved more attention in this regard is that of "Billy" Gibson. Leon Hughes had little to gain by raising a missing person report, and comes across as a genuine individual who was registering a real concern. The police don't appear to have given the matter the level of consideration it warranted (even though the reasons may be understandable), so some degree of analysis is called for. In particular, it is once more the family dynamic that provides the greatest insight.

To revisit this angle of the case, the obvious starting point is Oswald Gibson who, according to his former work colleague at S&L Ltd, lived at the Manor House, Hagley – which immediately conjures up images of Hagley Hall, and a tie-in to the tree murder. Except, there was no Hagley Manor House and there wasn't even an Oswald Gibson. There was, however, an Osborne[247] Gibson, who had lived at The Manor, Kidderminster Road, West Hagley, and who had worked at S&L. Undoubtedly this is the individual referred to by both Leonard Whyley and Leon Hughes. This inaccurate information does beg the question as

---

[247] Incorrectly spelt "Osborn" in some official records.

Analysis

to how well they knew him, although there may have been a slip of the pen arising from the fact that the headquarters of the S&L factory was located in Glasgow's Oswald Street. Further, the formality of the day demanded that junior employees would refer to their senior colleagues only by surname (prefaced by "Mr"); and salary records show that Hughes was subordinate to Gibson.[248]

Osborne Gibson – "Billy's" husband – was born in Bucklow, Cheshire, on 25 December 1906, to Arnold Howard Gibson (a physicist) and Amy (née Quarmby). His father had grown up in Manchester, attending both the grammar school and university there; after graduation, he taught mathematics at Salford Technical Institute, and also lectured in engineering and hydraulics at the same university that he had attended. As a young man, Osborne travelled quite extensively, even spending three months as a student in the US in 1927. He lived for a time in the Wirral (Cheshire) and then, in April 1935, joined steel tube manufacturers S&L at their Coombs Wood (Halesowen) site, working in the steam mains department. S&L was a significant employer in the West Midlands, part of a company that had been created by the amalgamation of two of the largest iron and steel makers in Britain. He left the site in 1938 to take up a post in an ordnance factory in Calcutta (most probably with a subsidiary of S&L).

Full details of Osborne Gibson's war service are not to hand, but, in a letter that he wrote to Leon Hughes in January 1943, he advises that he had just been posted back to GHQ after three months' active service "in the Burma Border". In 1946, he was a temporary lieutenant in the Indian and Electrical Mechanical Engineers, by which time he had taken a bride. This was Hilda Louis Paynter, a member of the Territorial Army Nursing Service and two years his senior; the couple had presumably met through the war, and married in Calcutta in 1945. There is no indication that Gibson had married before, although Indian marriage details are not easy to research. Both the marriage and Gibson's military service seem to have lasted, as an army record shows the pair returning to the UK from a posting in Basrah (Iraq) in 1957. From the one letter from

---

[248] Alternatively, it may be that the police had wrongly transcribed these details from correspondence. There is obviously at least one letter missing from the police folder on this line of enquiry.

Gibson that appears on police records, we know that he was fond of hunting. This letter suggests that he was quite bloodthirsty, with a real enjoyment of shooting animals, although this attitude was probably not uncommon at the time – particularly amongst those who had spent time in India.

What the above synopsis omits, however, is that, in 1935, there is a record of a Millicent Evelyne Orrell marrying an Osborne Gibson at Woodchurch, the Wirral. That this was the same Osborne Gibson is confirmed by electoral register records which show the couple resident at the same Manor address, from 1936 up to October 1937.[249] And it is easy to see how the bride's forename Millicent – typically shortened to "Millie" – may have been corrupted to "Billy". Osborne Gibson's former work colleagues estimated that "Billy" would have been no more than 29 years of age in 1941. This would be very much at the lower end of Webster's spectrum, but would not necessarily preclude her from being the Hagley Wood victim. More importantly, research into Millicent Evelyne Orrell's background shows that she was actually born in 1907, which would have made her 34 years of age at Webster's attributed time of the murder. The dates of her husband's Indian travels do not fit well, however – although Professor Webster's estimate of time of death could – as already established – be significantly out. There is also the possibility that Gibson could have

The photo provided to police showing "Billy" Gibson. The man to her left would appear (judging from a Royal Aero Club photo of him in 1933 which displays similarities) to be Osborne Gibson. The identity of the other man is unknown (but possibly the father of one of them).
(Photo courtesy West Mercia Police)

---

[249] This is fully consistent with Osborne Gibson relocating to India in 1938.

returned home at some point, or arranged for a third party to undertake her killing. The fact that "Billy" had a gold tooth is worthy of note, although one of the witnesses suggested (without being sure) that this may have been in her upper rather than lower jaw.[250]

Very much in keeping with most of the individuals featured, Millicent's background was quite chaotic. One of five children born to Edward Orrell and Jessie Constance Hughes Roberts, her parents did not actually marry until 1913 – some six years after Millicent's birth.[251] Her mother used a variety of surnames: not just Roberts and Orrell, which she called herself even before her marriage, but also Mortimer. At the time, she was claiming to be a widow, and there is no reason to doubt this. Additionally, Millicent, too, was going by the surname Mortimer, and the name of her father is not recorded in many official documents. He was apparently killed in action in 1917, whilst Jessie lived until 1945.

Jessie's mother's will, written in January 1945 – only a few months before her death – is quite enlightening. Within this, she splits her estate between her three children (the implication being that the others had pre-deceased her, or were estranged). One of these three is listed as Millicent Evelyn King. Despite the slightly different spelling of her middle name, this must surely have been Millicent – i.e. the person otherwise known as "Billy" Gibson. Being still alive in 1945, hers cannot, therefore, have been the body in the tree. Although it's not been possible to trace a marriage certificate, it seems that Millicent married David Halford King, and died in West Kirby, Merseyside, in August 1983. The fact that her siblings were named within the probate notice following Jessie's death (in all likelihood as executors) whilst Millicent was not, would lend weight to the view that she may have remained in India – and possibly married King out there. If she had run off with another man, it would also explain why Osborne Gibson (clearly a proud man) was reluctant to enter into correspondence about her whereabouts.

This line of enquiry has also thrown up yet more coincidences of the

---

[250] The wording used was "high tooth" and the meaning is not clear. This could alternatively be interpreted as being at the front of the mouth, or could even be an eye tooth (which would suggest the upper jaw).

[251] As with others in this saga, there are numerous different dates of birth attributed to Millicent. On one document, this is recorded as the date of her parents' marriage.

type which have come to characterise the case. For Leon Hughes, Osborne Gibson's one-time work colleague, was a resident of Albert Road in Hasbury – a stone's throw from the Rose & Crown and the houses that were the subject of some of the wall messages. Just two doors down (at No. 19 Albert Road), an Albert and Edith M. Allsop are listed in the 1939 Register. This would not appear to be the same Albert Allsop as was living in Hagley Road in 1944, but it is yet another link to the family of that name. And where there was an Allsop, inevitably there was a Willetts: a female living at the same address as Whyley (presumably a sister) in 1939, went on to marry one of the Willetts family; whilst an E. T. Willetts was also listed amongst S&L employees at the time. Certainly S&L was a large employer, but it is nevertheless noteworthy that their staff also included individuals with the surnames Plant, Edgington and Basterfield – all of which feature elsewhere within this account. More tenuously, Osborne Gibson was one of the many falling under suspicion with links to Manchester (through his father).

Police suspects

Whilst "Billy" Gibson was just one of several missing women on the police radar who were considered at various times as potential victims, the number of identified viable murder suspects was negligible. The very few names that were aired under this category include Arthur Edgington and Harry Truman, who could be quickly and easily dismissed. Even Jack Mossop, for the brief time that he may have been "in the frame", was there more as an accessory than a likely perpetrator. Swaley Forrest and Osborne Gibson were briefly considered and eliminated, and van Ralt was almost certainly the figment of vivid imaginations. That left just one name.

Victor Crumpton
After his encounter with PC Horrobin, Victor Crumpton entered into a chain of correspondence with the police, and Williams paid a lot of attention to him thereafter. Amongst his ramblings, it is difficult to identify what might be of significance, and what is not. Crumpton's letters show him in 1953 residing with a Mrs Blest, at 35 Harcourt Road,

Analysis

Old Hill. Within them, he tells of an intention to marry Mrs Blest, at least in part to satisfy his late mother's last request.[252] It would seem highly likely from this that Mrs Blest was Crumpton's nurse or carer.[253] Whether Crumpton's mental frailties did derive from a wartime injury and subsequent electric shock treatment, as he claimed, is open to question. If so, it would be helpful to identify when this occurred, in relation to the Hagley Wood murder. Using Webster's timings, Crumpton would have been around 32 or 33 at the time of the murder.

Crumpton's behaviour on 7 December 1953 (as divulged to PC Davies) was typically bizarre. It would be most unlikely that his night-time visit to Hagley Wood was the result of a wager, as he claimed. It seems that this particular manifestation of Crumpton's mental instability stemmed at least in part from his being required to lay out the body of a female neighbour (who had died from natural causes), which caused him great agitation. PC Davies wrote:

> it is difficult to understand what actuated CRUMPTON [sic] to visit the scene of this CRIME [sic] at the alleged time stated, although it is possible that the sight of the body of the female neighbour may have revived a certain impulse of some past action of his.

Something else that is certainly intriguing appears within a further letter of Crumpton's, dated 15 December 1953. Addressed to Tommy Williams, it reads: "I wish to dispose of (a) souvenir so would you accept same it will interest you." Williams in turn thanks him, without their exchanges of correspondence indicating the nature of this gift. He later also thanks Crumpton for taking the trouble to bake a cake for him and then patiently explains why the candidates put forward by Crumpton do not match the characteristics of the murdered woman. In other pieces of correspondence, there is confirmation that the constituency that Crumpton served as a councillor was Rowley Regis; in another, the revelation that he was in the habit of regularly attending police balls. On

---

[252] He would also relate that he intended the marriage to take place at St Kenelm's Church, on part of the estate formerly owned by his own family.

[253] There are other inferences that may be drawn from this. Crumpton seems to have been very close to his mother, and may have been traumatised by her death. Further, he seems to have made unwanted proposals of marriage to other women.

the face of it, Williams' correspondence demonstrates a very compassionate and admirable treatment of a man who, for whatever reason, struggled to fit in with society. It is likely, reading between the lines, that Tommy Williams knew him through the family business (through which the family became prominent in local society), and via Crumpton's own council work, when he was not so mentally impaired. There is an interesting comment made by Williams within one of his letters, which is open to different interpretations. Replying to an earlier letter from Crumpton, Williams wrote (on 28 December 1953) about Crumpton's desire to marry Mrs Blest:

> ... all the best to you if you marry Mrs Blest (you know you really need somebody to keep you under control)

PC Davies was clearly of the view that Crumpton knew more about the crime than he was admitting. He further opined that: "if he [Crumpton] is eventually certified, it would be very interesting to know what his reactions will be under the Modern Science treatment given to subjects such as he, with the "truth drug" injections, as applied in mental institutions". Early on, it would appear that Williams himself also entertained concerns that Crumpton may have had an involvement, writing:

> the possibility of him [Crumpton] having committed this crime could not be ruled out, as he was resident in ROMSLEY [sic] Area during the material dates when this CRIME [sic] is alleged to have occurred.

The implication that Crumpton could have been responsible for the murder is an intriguing one. But the fact that his visit to Hagley Wood resulted in such emotion that he evacuated his bowels suggests that he would have lacked the constitution to have killed a woman and placed her body inside a tree. The police opinion (as to whether he could have committed the crime) changed over time, and the most powerful reason for Crumpton not being higher up the list of suspects is a further manuscript note made by Tommy Williams on an official police record. This is dated 9 December 1953, and reads:

Analysis

Crumpton is a queer type and made a special journey to Hindlip[254] to see the ACC and myself. I questioned him closely but am satisfied that he does not know anything of value in this enquiry and is not himself responsible for it.

This, of course, is not proof of Crumpton's innocence. Williams could have been wrong, or – for reasons of altruism – protecting Crumpton, who would soon (due to readmission to the Barnsley Hall mental institution)[255] no longer be in a position to harm anybody (else?). There is a postscript to one of Crumpton's letters (dated 13 January 1954) which makes for slightly alarming reading:

> No man is wholly bad, and in all lives some moments come where the vision presents itself of a worthier and happier life which might be lived. What is needed is courage to make the start, form while life lasts, it is never too late.

The work of a disturbed man, or a confession to murder? It transpires that this is a quotation from a piece of prose by the writer and philosopher E. C. Burke, but its choice remains troubling. A further letter contained an epitaph from a tombstone:

> Here lies the body of Thaddeus Gray
> He died defending his right of way
> He was right, dead right, as he sped along
> But he's just as dead as if he was wrong.

---

[254] This is a reference to Hindlip Hall, Worcestershire CID HQ (and now home to West Mercia Police).

[255] Barnsley Hall Hospital was opened in 1907, to supplement Worcestershire's only existing asylum at Powick Hospital (near Malvern). At this time known as Worcestershire Mental Hospital, it was later used as a military hospital during both world wars. In 1948 it was absorbed into the National Health Service, being renamed Barnsley Hall Mental Hospital. The following year it became Barnsley Hall Hospital for Nervous and Mental Diseases, and at its height had a capacity of 1,200 patients. Victor Crumpton was readmitted there on 4 January 1954; it is not known whether police were instrumental in this action.

Loose Ends

This is again unoriginal, although folklore has numerous variations, with the gentleman's name more commonly identified as Henry Gray or William Jay. The context is unclear but, nevertheless, puzzling. On balance, Victor Crumpton is a person of interest, but the limited police file detail points more to him being a harmless eccentric rather than homicidal maniac; and Tommy Williams' continued interest in him probably was more for humanitarian than professional reasons. He only came to police attention after the publication of the *Quaestor* articles, which might again suggest that his actions in visiting the crime scene reflected prurient interest rather than direct involvement. Against this, his forwarding of the unidentified "souvenir" to Williams is intriguing.

PART III:

In Conclusion

CHAPTER 19

Summing Up

So much that is sensational has been has been written about this case that it is difficult to know just what is fact and what is fiction. Much, however, is palpably untrue.

The police files do not greatly help in unravelling the mystery, and it has to be acknowledged that they are disappointing. By modern standards, the overall police investigation was poorly recorded. It would be interesting to know whether other murder case files of the time were equally shambolic and, within *Under the Shadow of Meon Hill*, author Paul Newman makes some thought-provoking comparisons between this case and the way that the neighbouring Warwickshire Police force handled the Charles Walton investigation. He advises that he received much greater cooperation from the Warwickshire Police, and implies that this could suggest that the Worcestershire force were hiding something. There are other factors, however, that could explain this state of affairs – principally that, for the murder of Charles Walton, there was a prime suspect as well as an identified victim. This meant that, in addition to the involvement of Robert Fabian (whom there would have been a desire to impress), there was a structure to the inquiry from the outset. If the Worcestershire Police were more defensive, it may well have been because they realised the limitations of their records. Missing files can be a fact of office life, and major reorganisation and rationalisation of several local police forces did take place soon after the body in the tree was discovered. Accordingly, files will have been moved and not always accounted for – and it is difficult to read too much into this. It was also the case that some lines of investigation (such as those surrounding the fruit market wall messages) were initiated by other forces. Having thoroughly reviewed the archived police files and other evidence, it appears that the police failings in this regard are arguably more down to cock-up than

In Conclusion

conspiracy; but the possibility that some papers may have been deliberately removed cannot be dismissed.

Great care has to be taken with the second- or even first-hand accounts which surfaced years (in some cases very many years) after the event. Some were undoubtedly fuelled by a wish for publicity, and, in these cases, the journalists involved in the reporting were often very amenable, encouraging witnesses to embellish their stories. In fact, the journalists are of far greater concern in terms of their conduct than any police officer. Of these, Wilfred Byford-Jones's behaviour was quite extraordinary, even drawing in an accomplice to destroy the reputation of a dead man. It is puzzling how his own newspaper bosses either failed to see what their star reporter was up to, or turned a blind eye to it for so long. In a more modern age, Byford-Jones surely would have been prosecuted for wasting police time, or even perverting the course of justice. W. Stewart-Turner (of *The British Jeweller*) and Ladislas Farago were no better, badly damaging the reputation of a Midlands-based jeweller for misplaced reasons of patriotism; whilst Donald McCormick seemed to write the first thing that came into his head.

Overall, many of the popular theories that have been put forward owe far more to the need to maintain circulation figures and sell books rather than to objectivity, and some are almost too ludicrous to be worthy of consideration. Others unravel in the light of obvious journalistic involvement. Circumstantial evidence also points to at least some of the wall messages being attributable to or sponsored by a journalist, and the locations even more firmly point to *Quaestor's* involvement (whether directly or indirectly) at some point. Regardless of their source, it is quite ironic that Byford-Jones chose a byline for his column which translates as "seeker of truth"; it is often said that truth is the first casualty of war, and the sentiment certainly seems to extend to this wartime incident. In the absence of fact, speculation flourished, and the police were persuaded to effectively reopen the investigation (whilst denying that it had ever been officially closed). The fact that society at this time was generally respectful of journalists – particularly those who had distinguished war service behind them – made the situation ripe for exploitation. The public, bored and cowed by years of wartime deprivation and rationing, were keen for anything approaching excitement, and salacious details of a murder often fulfilled such a need. Notably, though, interest in the case has continued to the present day.

Nevertheless, whilst so many of the unlikely theories can be readily dismissed, one that continues to persist is that of the spy ring. This is probably because it contains all the elements of public interest that Byford-Jones and others targeted so well, and a recent television documentary has provided a veneer of authenticity. But it has to be said that other, more reliable and objective, sources have become hoodwinked, too, by these arguments. And, whilst Una Hainsworth may have been a pathological liar, she was being used by Byford-Jones. The evidence that she and Byford-Jones were well acquainted, however, is not in itself a reason to completely reject the spying angle. It is just possible that there was either a kernel of truth in what she said, or that she was relaying what Mossop had told her – and that she was using Byford-Jones to draw out the story (with his obvious blessing). But this would be a very generous interpretation, and both the role allegedly played by Jack Mossop and the existence of van Ralt depend solely on the "testimony" of the unreliable Hainsworth.

The reality

If we take out everything that links journalists and those fantasists and attention-seekers drawn out by their articles, we are left with the original police inquiry. This revealed that even the disappearance of known prostitutes from their patch, and those who had moved away from home due to the war effort, were identified and investigated early on. All the (recorded) missing persons enquiries drew a blank and, whilst the Midlands certainly had its fair share of displaced and foreign women (including Dutch refugees) living within its towns and cities at this time, this was not London. Even the overseas contingent lived in quite tight communities which would have alerted authorities to any sudden and unexplained disappearance.

Before being diverted by other "developments", the police started to concentrate their enquiries on the travelling community, and there is every indication that they were right to do so. In short, the inescapable conclusion is that the protagonists were very probably both (or all) from

In Conclusion

the travelling community – people whose movements would not be viewed as unusual, and who would be most unlikely to cooperate with the police, even if one of their own had been murdered. It is the sad reality that spousal and other abuse against women was fairly rife in this hard-living sector of society, particularly in wartime when deprivation was even greater. The clothing – whether worn by the victim or deposited previously – and cheap unhallmarked ring were consistent with what would have been by Travellers. The relatively expensive and over-sized shoes (found / donated / stolen) discovered in the vicinity of the skeleton would also sit comfortably with such an interpretation of events – as, additionally, the story that one pair of these distinctive crepe-soled shoes had been given to a Traveller in exchange for a cup and saucer. Finally, the victim's dentition would be a good "fit", too: it would be likely that a Traveller would shun regular dental checks but pay for an extraction when in great pain. And, if the victim were a Traveller, her death is unlikely to have been a natural one, as (to generalise) this community has traditionally honoured its dead in lavish style. Travellers, too, (particularly those who regularly visited Hagley Wood) would have been more aware than most of places to secrete a body there; their presence in Hagley Wood Lane was less likely to be noted; and they would have had the opportunity to bide their time before hiding a corpse. If the death was the result of either a domestic or territorial dispute, even those related to the victim would be more likely to help cover it up rather than involve the police. Accordingly, the perpetrator may well have had help in moving the body – either soon after death or after rigor mortis had set in.

It is also a reality that, had the police come to the conclusion that the murderer and victim were both Travellers, they would not have diverted too many resources to identifying and bringing the culprit to justice. This is not necessarily a criticism, it just reflects the mores of the time (and the community would not have wanted it any other way, either). Even the lack of evidence found by the police – and accepting the constraints imposed by war – would point to them perhaps not having pursued this in the same way that they would if they felt that members of the "regular" public were involved. The discovery of Dr Markham's empty handbag in 1944 offers some insight: less than 200 yards from the site, it

Summing Up

appears to have lain unfound by the public or the authorities for nearly five years. And the tree by which it was found had a very distinctive carving on the bark. It does not seem that likely that this was some lovers' symbol (in the way, for example, that a heart might be): the tree clearly meant something to someone, suggesting that this part of the wood may have been familiar to particular individuals. The fact that relatively few people regularly used Hagley Wood Lane also leads one to question who would have been most likely to have broken into Dr Markham's car in the first place. An opportunist, probably, and most likely a Traveller who may have noticed the car entering and parking in the lane; someone who would have developed a familiarity with the wood after regular visits, and perhaps known where to hide evidence without any great likelihood of discovery. Also worthy of consideration is that, whilst anyone could have parked in Hagley Wood Lane and taken a body into the wood, for most this would have carried a real risk of discovery. For Travellers camped alongside, it would have been easy to choose their time, and dispose of it when nobody else was about.

Most persuasive is the numerous stories circulating of a female missing from a travelling group that were regular users of Hagley Wood and its environs. Joyce Coley reported that these beliefs were still prevalent some 70 years after the event. Coley was not a self-publicist bent on making a name for herself, and those who were feeding her the information were similarly not seeking attention; indeed, they were not identified – they were just disseminating what had been passed down to them over the years. Given what we now know about the families named by them – the Lees and the Smiths in particular – their involvement becomes highly plausible. When questions were asked, however, they were told that the individual had "gone off" to have a baby. Given that some of these witnesses were from Traveller stock themselves, or derived an income from their patronage, it is not surprising that they didn't consider too closely whether they were being fobbed off with the pregnancy story. Further, given the violent background of the families concerned, few witnesses would have been keen to voice any concerns to the police – for fear of retribution. The domestic violence that was known to have been inflicted by a number of these particular families on their own womenfolk has been well-documented.

In Conclusion

In all of this, it is the dates that cause the most concern, as not all are consistent with any logical interpretation of events. But it would seem reasonable to believe that the killing would have taken place soon after the closure of the Illey Farm Traveller site in 1940. It would also seem logical, given the state of decomposition, that the victim's death took place significantly before the end of 1942, at which time there was heightened activity in the vicinity of Hagley Wood Lane. The fact that stories of the disappearance of one of the Travellers did not start to circulate amongst the gorger community until 1942 – clearly after the poor woman's demise – should not necessarily be seen as important. Rumours take time to become established, particularly where groups of itinerant workers may not be seen from one season to the next, and are not keen to share domestic details with outsiders.

Significant, too, may well be the behaviour of Bill Fletcher. His background meant that he would almost certainly have heard the tales of a missing woman in advance of the general public, but still not necessarily at the time that she disappeared. Fletcher had been called up to the army in February 1940, but his own testimony (which must, admittedly, be treated with great caution) states that he had not seen Mary Wenman (Lee) since December 1939, when he believed her to "probably" be pregnant. That Mary was by all accounts alive and well does not alter the fact that Fletcher was unaware of this; nor does it detract from his having heard that a woman had gone missing. Fletcher's ethical code meant that he would only have contacted the police in exceptional circumstances. It is implausible – as he would later claim – that he was concerned about Wenman's mental state or that he was trying to trace her so that he could rekindle their relationship (there would have been far more suitable avenues for pursuing that). In a situation where he felt that the mother of his child might be a murder victim, he might still have some reluctance to involve the police himself; but to send a letter allegedly from a third party would make a lot of sense. Fletcher's subsequent actions, and his loose tongue when drinking, further demonstrate that he had great knowledge of events, knowledge which was garnered at different times. Fletcher warranted a great deal more attention than he was afforded by the police. His brother-in-law freely admitted to having been in the vicinity of the interment site after

Summing Up

the event (when he claimed to have found a shoe), and both were part of a group drinking in the Star Hotel and overheard claiming that one of the party knew the details surrounding the victim's death. Fletcher and Shearwood were regulars in the Star – a known haunt of Travellers – and many rumours about the case emanated from there. Fletcher himself seems to have been overly troubled and annoyed by the actions of Shearwood in going to the police, even asking the landlord of the Lyttelton Arms to tell the police that Shearwood was unreliable. This seems to be something over and above the usual Traveller policy of not assisting the police – and suggests that there may have been something specific that he wanted to hide.

Why, then, if the murder took place significantly before, has so much attention been concentrated on the events of late 1942? This is when the police were able to confirm that the Smith family was camping in Nimmings Wood, and when a fight broke out between two rival Traveller families. It is also the time of Kenneth Patten's strange behaviour. For the body to have been placed in the tree sometime after the murder would make a lot of sense; and it may be that the dispute between the warring factions over how the body would be laid to rest was responsible for a fresh outburst of violence. It is far from inconceivable that the body would have been kept with one of the travelling families and then, later, interred in a spot close to where the murder took place. The rumours reported by Joyce Coley certainly suggest something along these lines. Whilst it may be that the missing woman was associated with the Forrest clan (given their rather disturbing actions and the fact that they had also been displaced from one of their regular "pitches"), it would seem most likely that she would have been amongst those who were previously regulars at Illey Farm – the extended Smith / Butler families. Just to spell out the problems of identifying any one individual who may have gone missing from this group, this entourage included those with the names Lee, Beaver, Button (Botton), Brazil, Buckland, Bull, Day, Dickson (Dixon), Drummond, Franklin, Gurney, Lin(d)say, Loveridge, Mellis, Nunn, Oldham, Sherriff, Wenman and Williams – to name just a few. And, as established, the frequent name changes and swapping of identity cards makes any search akin to that for a needle in the proverbial haystack.

In Conclusion

Whilst the evidence that exists to back this up is largely circumstantial, there is plenty of it. And there is still more – some of which is quite compelling. As also established, whilst dismissing most of the wall messages as misleading or meaningless, those identifying specific addresses in Hagley Road may be the exception. The obvious person of interest here would be the occupier of No. 404 – Samuel Allsop senior, who withheld details which he knew would have been of great interest to the police. The likely (albeit distant) family link to Alfred James (owner of the Illey Farm site), allied to serial lying to the police, also raises some red flags. But other of these messages referred more generally to properties opposite the Rose & Crown. Within these parameters, two houses were occupied by members of the Willetts family, including the owner of the timber yard which had the Hagley Wood timber concession. Even if Harry Willetts, the tenant of Nimmings Field, was not closely related to Walter, they would anyway have been known to each other through their respective occupations. Whilst Harry would not be entitled to officially sublet any part of Nimmings Field, the reality would have been different, and he would certainly have known the movements of anyone using it. In these circumstances, he would have been understandably reluctant to disclose that any party had been camping there when not sanctioned to do so. It may also be relevant that Walter Willetts advised Tommy Williams that the person hiding the body must have either got lucky or been familiar with the properties of the wood.

Moreover, Walter Willetts was married to Lily Lea, seemingly once part of the same Traveller group which is of such interest in this context. It appears, then, that somebody may have been pointing the finger at Willetts in terms of an involvement in the disappearance of one of the group, in conjunction with others. These others may even have included their next-door neighbours; after all, this was a very close-knit community. It would seem unlikely that any of the Willetts would have taken part in the killing, but they would certainly have been able to help or offer advice in terms of opportunities to hide a body. Through his business, Walter Willetts also had legitimate reason to be in Hagley Wood without being challenged, and it would further appear that somebody may have had knowledge (or believed they had knowledge) of people living here being linked to the crime. At this point, the graffiti near to

Summing Up

Palmer's timber yard becomes of greater interest. There were not that many timber merchants in the area, and the Willetts and Palmer families would certainly have been known to each other. The Palmers were very mixed up with numerous activities in or close to Hagley Wood, and there was also a further link – through employment – to Bill Fletcher's brother-in-law Eddie Shearwood. It is doubtful that the police wouldn't have recognised the significance of these particular daubings; whilst it would be one thing to ignore an internecine murder in a community that had no time for the police, the involvement of a "civilian" – albeit as an accessory after the event – would have been a different matter. Williams' acknowledged friendship with the Willetts family could have placed him in a difficult position, and he would have been open to disciplinary action if he had been found to have suppressed evidence. It is in these circumstances that it is possible that some of the case files could – conceivably – have been interfered with.

Where the Willetts family is concerned, there is another potential connection here that, strangely, has not been discussed by other commentators on the case. For not only were Walter Willetts and his son linked to the tenant of Nimmings Field, there was a further Willetts who had played a key role in the whole drama. This was, of course, Thomas Willetts, one of the lads who discovered the victim in the tree. Although the surname is hardly common across the country, it was quite prominent in this part of the West Midlands at the time, and it has not been possible to find any obvious direct link between Thomas on the one hand and either Walter or Harry on the other. Once again, though, there are some reasons for believing that there may have been a distant relationship. It cannot be beyond the bounds of possibility that one of the older Willetts had become aware of the murder and the body in the tree and, rather than risk the wrath of the travelling community by going to the police themselves, "used" a younger relative to draw the story out. Against this, there would have been a high risk of the youngster inadvertently giving the game away. But, in such a scenario, Walter Willetts could then have confessed the full background when spoken to by Tommy Williams – who would have tried to keep his name out of things.

Within any objective analysis of the case, the Lavins should also not be discounted. Both Jack and Mary Lavin lied to the police, and were

In Conclusion

additionally very selective in terms what they did tell them. The police were clearly convinced that Jack Lavin was working in the area in the spring and / or summer of 1941 – a critical time in terms of their investigation and, whilst there is much evidence to support that Lavin *was* there then, he vehemently denied it. Although for the most part having semi-permanent homes, the Lavins and their extended family espoused the values of the travelling community, so could have had an oblique, if not central, involvement in what happened in Hagley Wood.

Although it can't be completely discounted, it's probably a step too far to suggest that Bill Fletcher's army service in Nottingham would have resulted in a link to Kenneth Patten.[256] Patten remains of interest, however, and his background and associations may have meant that he was acquainted with the Lavins. His actions were certainly suspicious, and Vivienne Coss's testimony should not be ruled out. Coss has largely gone "under the radar" to date, but she comes across as a much more reliable witness than many who came forward after the event; and she did not have a journalist championing her legitimacy. The evidence against her statement is the timing, but again, this should not necessarily be used as reason to completely reject it. It is actually in Coss's favour that she was aware of the discrepancies in timings, but did not try to change her account to better fit the dates. Unlike others, she had not sought publicity (being persuaded to come forward by a third party) and was not obviously seeking financial benefit (the newspaper "reward" only being offered subsequently). Coss also gave a believable reason for not coming forward sooner. Also relevant, was that, whereas Hainsworth and Plant told stories which carried little risk of being disproved, Coss named a suspect who was very much alive and who could be (and was) interviewed by police. If we take her statement at face value, Patten appears to have had the means to have stored and moved a body. Coss's contention that, when challenged as to why he wanted to be taken to Hagley Wood, Patten told her "[that] he could not possibly tell me, but that one day [she] might know" is quite chilling from a position of hindsight. It could be that Patten's presence in Hagley Wood in November 1942 was at the request of another, and aimed at either

---

[256] Similarly, although the Lavins and the Lees both had strong links to Wales, there are no real grounds for suggesting a connection.

Summing Up

confirming that the deposition site was undisturbed, or seeking a better hiding place. One wonders, too, whether the Garretts had any ulterior motive in persuading Coss to come forward. It is possible that Coss was wildly exaggerating when speaking to Mrs Garrett, but, when the police became involved, felt compelled to give them something more tangible. It is disappointing that the police considered there was little merit in her story, but this may have been because they could not identify a potential victim of Patten. They also expressed the view that Patten's claimed lack of knowledge of the area made him an unlikely candidate. But Patten was another who was clearly lying about this and numerous other issues.

Of course, narrowing down the protagonists to a few travelling families does not tie down the individuals concerned – but it does reduce the field significantly. The missing part of the victim's hyoid bone would suggest that the woman died from manual strangulation and, in turn, increases the likelihood that the victim and perpetrator were known to each other. The explanation of the crime being the result of a domestic or "tribal" dispute is not one that is particularly "sexy", and the need to fill media space with more exciting stories means that there will continue to be articles and programmes that insist that the answer to the question "Who put Bella in the wych elm?" is to be found within something more "glamorous" or exotic. Somebody will no doubt "discover" a new and tenuous link between a German spy and somebody from the West Midlands, and a new conspiracy theory will be born.

The interest in this case is likely to continue as long as it remains unsolved. Although unlikely, it is not necessarily unsolvable: new evidence of old cases emerges from time to time, particularly as the world wide web becomes more populated with uploads of historic data. The Jack the Ripper case pre-dates the Hagley Wood murder by more than 50 years, yet new facts and plausible fresh theories appear on a very regular basis. It is still possible that some of the missing Hagley Wood murder police files and papers will surface (possibly amongst other case files), or that newly discovered family links may provide fresh clues. Some files which are due to be released in the next few years may also be illuminating. Less likely is that the skeletal remains, which could harness modern techniques to provide details of the victim's background or even DNA, will ever be located. Against this, the strong likelihood of both

In Conclusion

victim and killer being from the transient community does significantly reduce the chances of successful resolution. Even if names do come to light, the way that these members of society conducted their business means that there can be little reliance that they correspond to a birth certificate in the same name. The poor victim really does deserve a better and more fitting epitaph.

CHAPTER 20
The Area Today

Aside from the positions of those who may have been involved and the circumstances of their demise, cases such as this also provide a fascinating insight into how social, economic and geographical changes have impacted over time. There are few younger people today, for example, who would understand that there was once an army of domestic crop pickers who spent half the year travelling from farm to farm. Where not specifically referenced elsewhere, this chapter updates what has happened to some of the sites and buildings featured.

Hagley Wood and the surrounding area

It is hardly surprising that, after some 80 years, most of those mentioned within this narrative have passed on. But many of the sites mentioned have not fared well either, particularly those in West Hagley. Spout Farm, where the Forrest family camped, (and then entered from Worcester Road) is long gone, as is the nearby Vaughan Nurseries – which closed in the 1970s. The current Spring Close passes through the former farm land, whilst Nursery Close commemorates Vaughan's. Similarly, Holliers Farm – once tenanted by Felix Tate – is no more. This suffered badly in the 1960s, due to "progress" – i.e. the impact of road widening and improvements. By the mid-1980s, the farm had fallen into disuse, although some of the land was rented out for the grazing of horses. A housing estate was built on the site in 2000.

In terms of the deposition site, as indicated within Chapter 1, some road layout changes have impacted upon the approach to Hagley Wood from the northern end. Evolving woodland management techniques and coppicing also mean that the appearance of the wood itself has changed, but at the southern end, the border with Nimmings Field (no longer referred to by that name on modern maps) is pretty much in the same place.

In Conclusion

The border between Nimmings Field and Hagley Wood, as it is now (left) and trees close to the scene where the body was discovered. The vegetation now appears much less dense, with few opportunities to secrete a body (both pictures 2018).

Contemporary accounts of the deposition site frequently mention the proximity to the Birmingham Water Track. More correctly known as the Elan Aqueduct, this continues to be an important pipeline which carries drinking water from the Elan Valley in mid-Wales to Frankley Reservoir, from where it serves the Birmingham conurbation. It was completed in 1906, with extra pipes being added between 1919 and 1961. More to the point, its route is now much more difficult to locate, it having more recently been re-sited underground.

Two views of the Hayley Green supply tap to the Elan pipeline, pictured in 2019. This is just to the east of Hagley Wood Lane (with the entrance facing north).

The Area Today

Mental health institutions

County mental hospital

The county mental hospital, where Jack Mossop spent his last days, is also long closed. Opened as the Stafford General Asylum in 1818, it originally housed 120 patients. Extended in 1850, 1879 and 1884 it was renamed the Stafford Mental Hospital in the 1920s, by which time it could accommodate nearly 1,000. When Mossop was admitted, it was a bleak, austere institution which reflected societal attitudes to the mentally ill, with the emphasis on keeping patients (or "inmates" in the language of the day) away from the public rather than on rehabilitation. Restraints used included "the leather muff" (by which individuals were tied to beds with straps passed through iron loops), iron handcuffs and the restraint chair, whilst suicide cages were present in the stairwells. At times, dysentery and syphilis were prevalent. Mossop must have suffered mental torture when he was here and, whatever had gone wrong in their marriage, it does not reflect well on Una Hainsworth that she sought to make capital out of his anguish. With the advent of the National Health Service in 1948, Stafford Mental Hospital became St George's Hospital, which incorporated more general facilities. After further NHS reforms, the inpatients' psychiatric unit was moved to another block, with more modern facilities, in the 1980s. The old building was closed in 1995, and few tears would have been shed at its passing. It was subject to vandalism

St George's Hospital, Stafford: old and new. The site of the old asylum in 2014, with water tower still in place but now surrounded by new apartments.
(CC-BY-SA/2.0 - © Jonathan Hutchins - geograph.org.uk/p/4312441)

and arson for a number of years, before being purchased by a development company. The site now houses 102 private housing units, known as St George's Apartments.

Barnsley Hall Hospital

Barnsley Hall Hospital, where Victor Crumpton spent at least two spells, closed in 1996, and most of the buildings have now been replaced by domestic housing.

Barnsley Hall Hospital – the site in 1998, two years after closure. (CC-BY-SA/2.0 - © James Pratt - geograph.org.uk/p/1863309)

Public houses

Of the pubs that are mentioned in this narrative, the Cross Keys at West Hagley was converted into residential accommodation in 1995 and the Shelton at Belle Vale has since (in the second decade of the 21st century)

The Area Today

gone the same way. The Star at Halesowen is another victim of progress, and the George at Halesowen is closed at the time of writing, with its future uncertain. All that remains of the Ivy House Hotel at Coseley, a sizeable pub that at various times was managed by Mary Ann Crump (Stanford) and Louis Mossop, is the road that bears its name – Ivy House Lane. On the junction with Birmingham Road (and with a postal address sometimes given as Sedgely), it became a restaurant before being demolished. A takeaway food establishment now occupies its site. The other eleven pubs referenced are still operating, however, quite a survival rate in comparison with the national picture. These include the two in close proximity to Hagley Wood that feature prominently in the case. The first of these is the Lyttelton Arms,[257] on the Bromsgrove Road. At the time of the murder, this was part of the main A456 Kidderminster–Bromsgrove Road. The other is the Badger's Sett (formerly the Gipsy's Tent), which has undergone significant change. The main road here was widened significantly post-war, although the setting remains quite rural (notwithstanding the spreading urban enclave of Birmingham).

The Waggon & Horses at Wombourne, which was known to so many characters within the narrative, seems no longer to be referred to by its informal name of the Brick Bridge, and is now part of a pub restaurant chain. The pub in Halesowen that Bill Fletcher referred to as the (Old) Lyttelton Arms now trades as Pick's.

Pick's, Halesowen, pictured in 2014.

(CC-BY-SA/2.0 - © CHRIS WHIPPET - geograph.org.uk/p/4100130)

---

[257] Named after the British aristocratic family who hold hereditary titles including that of Viscount of Cobham, Hagley Hall is an ancestral home of the family, which also own Hagley Wood.

In Conclusion

Other locations

Coventry Hippodrome

The once-impressive Coventry Hippodrome, which featured in Una Hainsworth and Wilfred Byford-Jones's fantasy, and which prompted enquiries that diverted police resources, is also no more – demolished in 2002. The site is now occupied by Millennium Place and the Coventry Transport Museum, which has been extended and provided with a new frontage.

Millennium Place, 2021, dominated by the Coventry Transport Museum's Whittle Arch – commemorating the inventor of the jet engine.
(CC-BY-SA/2.0 - © Gerald England - geograph.org.uk/p/6977066)

Market Street

Market Street in Birmingham, the proposed venue of the meeting between the police and the mysterious Mr Wood, is also now only an historical footnote – another victim of post-war redevelopment. Its former site today corresponds (roughly) to a walkway which passes under Jennens Road leading towards Coleshill Street.

The Area Today

The Hagley Obelisk

Although the wall message posted in October 1944 was probably the last of any arguable relevance to the case, similar graffiti has continued to appear to this day. A regular target has been the Hagley Obelisk (also locally known as both the Wychbury Obelisk and Wychbury Monument), where a popular footpath to the summit of Wychbury Hill passes close by. The popular perception is that this has been a target of the graffiti since the 1970s, although press reports seem to date it only from 1993, following yet another resurrection of the case by the *Express & Star*. An older documented example was graffiti scrawled on a car park wall at the rear of Hagley village library in August 1984. The bulk has been the work of bored youths – presumably penned by individuals whose knowledge of the case has been gleaned only from parents and grandparents; opportunists; or, possibly, by more journalists looking to keep the story alive.

The Hagley Obelisk, originally built c.1750 and renovated many times since (pictured in 2018).

In Conclusion

This is much to the annoyance of the current Lord Cobham, who has the expense of maintaining and cleaning the obelisk brickwork. Over the years, his patience has worn thin. Removing such paintwork from a listed monument is not cheap, and at one time the structure had deteriorated to such a state that the Hagley estate felt that it would no longer be able to withstand yet more cleansing – so the extant message was allowed to remain *in situ*. Following funding provided by English Heritage, however, the crumbling obelisk was deconstructed and rebuilt – with this work being completed in 2011. Unfortunately, but understandably, it is now protected by unsightly fencing. The graffiti has returned, however, and, should it be removed again, will no doubt reappear. For the police, it has become a bit of a nuisance, in the way of other low-level vandalism, with Carl Baldacchino of West Mercia Police saying (of the graffiti): "It's just a joke ... it doesn't mean anything [any more]". It is ironic that the obelisk, which has no bearing whatsoever on the case, has become so symbolic of it.

The story lives on

In music a Coventry-based indie band, The Pristines, released an album called *Who Put Bella in the Wych Elm?* which depicted the obelisk on its cover, in 2003.[258] And songwriter Owen Tromans recorded a song called "Bella in the Witch Elm" on his 2013 EP *For Haden*. The American group Self Defense Family included on their 2014 album *Try Me*, the track "Nail House Music", which relates the tale of the body in the Hagley Wood tree. More cynically, the motivation behind some of the recent graffiti has been to promote a track by a local band that draws on the "Bella" legend.

---

[258] Image reproduced courtesy of The Pristines.

The Area Today

The legend of Bella has also spawned an opera, by classical musician and composer Simon Holt. He was inspired by one of a number of articles on the subject appearing in *The Independent* newspaper.[259] The central theme has the ghost of Bella appearing to two of the boys (depicted as grown-up) who found her, and recounts her grisly death. Holt neatly summed up the fascination that people have for the mystery: "You can put on your own angle on this story it's so open ended – that's why everyone likes it." His opera premiered in 2003 to a number of good reviews. And, in 2007, local amateur dramatics society, The Stourbridge Theatre Company, marked its 75th anniversary with a specially commissioned play about the murder by Stourbridge playwright and historian David Morris. Both these productions were, predictably, entitled: *Who put Bella in the Wych-elm?* In 2017, indie film-maker Thomas Lee Rutter wrote and directed a film of the same name, a 36-minute "folk mystery phantasmagoria ... an exploration of the true-life Hagley Wood Mystery". It is shot in black and white without dialogue between the cast, and is narrated by a local man, "Tatty" Dave Jones, whose Black Country accent adds a degree of authenticity. The film does not add any fresh insight, though, and draws largely on the events as outlined by Andrew Sparke in his book. It premiered locally, and has subsequently been released on DVD.

In March 2018, the Pregnant Fish Theatre company staged a 60-minute performance of *Who Put Bella in the Wych Elm?* at The Space in London. This comprised narration from published documents and sources, by a cast dressed in plain navy overalls (to facilitate the audience's attention being focussed on the evidence). Whilst this did bring the case to a wider audience outside the Midlands, it suffered from concluding that Clara Bauerle was the victim. In similar vein, The True Crime Museum – a relatively new venture in Hastings which claims to hold the largest collection of crime artefacts in the UK – has hosted an exhibit relating to the case which is described as possibly holding "the key to unravelling one of the most compelling murder mysteries of wartime Britain". Except that it doesn't! For it is a gramophone record purporting to be Clara Bauerle's final recording prior to meeting a sticky end in a West Midlands' wood.

---

[259] This particular article, by journalist Richard Askwith, appeared in 1999.

In Conclusion

A number of podcasts dedicated to (or including articles about) the case have also started appearing over the last few years. These are too numerous to detail and, whilst some are better informed than others, none (as at the time of writing) offers any new insight. The genre is probably best summed up by an independent review which describes a particular podcast as being "more entertainment than documentary". The national media has not ignored the story, either. As recently as November 2016, *The Sun* newspaper ran an article on the case. Although this inevitably contained many errors (including the assertion that Jack Mossop was Una's cousin) it also suggested that a Reddit user had claimed to have found an old diary of their grandfather's which contained the entry: "I put Bella in the Wych Elm". Almost certainly too good to be true – and with many similarities to the "discovery" of the Jack the Ripper and Hitler diaries – it is proof, nevertheless, of the enduring interest in the case.

Writers have also latched on to the plight of "Bella", clearly appreciating the old adage that truth is often stranger than fiction. One such is James Brogden whose book *The Hollow Tree* was published in 2018. This pursues some very familiar themes, including spying, prostitution, witchcraft and Gipsy activity. Some background details have been slightly changed, such as the central character becoming Mary, and the scene being the wider Lickey Hills rather than Hagley Wood – but the author does fully acknowledge the source of his inspiration.

The Ghost of Bella?

Simon Holt's opera was based in no small part on the alleged paranormal activity at the Badger's Sett, the pub opposite Hagley Wood. Down the years, many wild claims have been made about hauntings at the pub, ranging from spectral figures to doors opening on their own and the presence of cold spots. It is inevitable that its proximity to Hagley Wood, as well as its licence to sell alcohol, would result in claims that "Bella" might be lurking on the premises, and the unfounded / unsupportable speculation that the poor woman may have once worked behind the bar has helped that notion to take hold. For those who buy into the idea that the spot is haunted, in 2007 a witness came forward in the shape of a retired police officer. Former Detective Constable Roger

Ryder reported his own supernatural sighting from 30 years previously:

> As I drew closer to the pub, suddenly the figure of a man ran out of the car park. He was dressed like one of the old Cavalier soldiers – the big hat, boots, red uniform and sword. My initial thought was that the pub was holding a fancy dress party and some drunk was larking about. He ran straight across the first two lanes of the carriageway and stopped right in the middle of the central reservation. As I approached, our eyes met. It all happened so fast but I remember thinking that if he starts running again, I'll never be able to stop in time. Suddenly he sprinted out diagonally across the road in front of me towards Hagley Hall. I slammed my brakes on but knew, at 60 mph, it was too late. I went straight into him and swung the steering wheel right round.
>
> I got out and looked for the body on the road. Nothing. I checked the field next to the car, the hedge and finally under the car itself. Nothing. It was deadly quiet. I looked across at the pub – it was in total darkness.

Other sightings of spectral Cavaliers have also been reported, and a local paranormal group claims to have uncovered further witnesses to unnerving experiences along the same stretch of road between Hagley Wood and the nearby Iron Age hill fort of Wychbury. It is anyone's guess what all this means, but if you believe in ghosts, hauntings in this part of the country may be down to some rather more significant national events than the murder of an unknown woman in a wood a few hundred yards away. There are also locals who will tell you that the road between the pub and Hagley Road was cursed by a Gipsy woman, whose child was killed when running out of her family's camp.

History repeating itself?

Of course, any similar crime in the vicinity instantly becomes highly newsworthy, and some interesting more subsequent findings / incidents have been reported. The first of these was in June 1964, when forestry workers discovered a freshly dug grave close to the site of the witch hazel in Hagley Wood. But, when the fuss had all died down, it was revealed that this contained only the body of a pet dog.

On Christmas Day 2004, the body of a 38-year-old local man was

In Conclusion

found by a passer-by in his car at the Nimmings Wood visitor car park, in the Clent Hills. This transpired to be a suicide, with a typically sad backstory of marital breakdown. Of far more significance in terms of a parallel with "Bella", however, was the discovery of a human skeleton in deep undergrowth near the same visitor centre just a few months later on 6 June 2005. In a chilling echo of events of more than 60 years previously, the find was made by two teenage boys. This was identified as being that of a man, although a post-mortem was unable to confirm the cause of death. It was estimated that the body had there for at least three years. Strangely, the media trail then goes cold. Local opinion was that this was the body of a vagrant, whose disappearance was sadly neither noticed nor mourned. In August 2009, the body of a 57-year-old grandmother from Kingswinford was found in woodland at Nimmings Wood. A post-mortem failed to identify a cause of death and returned an open verdict, although the woman had been drinking alcohol and had left two notes, alluding to problems at work.

Appendices

Appendix

APPENDIX A

Timeline

1886
Galfry William Gatacre (future Squire of Gatacre) born.

1891
Charlotte Crump (Jack Mossop's mother) born.

1905
Wilfred ("Bill") Jones (later Byford-Jones) born. Ann Forrest (née Hibbs) born.

1906
Clara Bauerle born in Stuttgart, Germany.
Birmingham Water Track completed, across Hagley Wood.
Amy Isabel Shemwell born in Cannock (6 January).
Osborne Gibson born (25 December).
Bella Evans born (19 February).

1907
Millicent Evelyne Orrell born (27 February).
Alfred Hainsworth (senior) marries Nellie Spencer at Coventry (June).

1909
Frederick Victor Crumpton born in Old Hill, to Frederick and Laura Crumpton.

1912
Warwick Daniel Aston Plant born (5 July).
Jack Mossop born (29 August).

Appendix A

1913
Louis Mossop born.

Una Ellen Abel born (14 November).

1915
Rex Arnold Gatacre born.

1916
John Edward ("Jack") Lavin born in County Mayo, Eire.

1918
Charlotte Mossop (née Crump) dies in Spanish flu epidemic. Sons Jack and Louis sent to live with different aunts.
Alfred James Spencer Hainsworth born in Coventry.

1921
Samuel Allsop (junior) born.

1924
Mervyn Phippen ("M.P.") Pugh appointed Agent for the Director of Public Prosecutions.

1927
Lucy Stephens marries older man named Macefield. Amy Isabel Shemwell marries Frank Lawley.

1930
Wilfred Byford-Jones marries Winifred L. Dawson (September).
Louis Mellor convicted of murdering his landlady with a hatchet (but found insane) at Stoke-on-Trent.

1932
Julian Mossop born at Wolverhampton (3 August).
Jack Mossop and Una Hainsworth marry in Wolverhampton district (September).

Timeline

1934
Jack Mossop (shown as a dairyman of the Bridge House, Wombourne, Wolverhampton), declared bankrupt.

1935
Millicent Orrell marries Osborne Gibson, in the Wirral.
May Truman obtains separation order from her husband Harry – and takes custody of their children (18 June).

1936
(Edward) Percy Mossop (Jack's father) dies. Jack Mossop now working at Lockheed in Leamington.

1937
Jack Mossop joins Airwork Service Training Corps and is posted to Hampshire.

1938
Jack Mossop working at Armstrong Siddeley, Coventry.
Harry and May Truman become reconciled.
Osborne Gibson leaves S&L to take up a post in India.
Ice performers Frick and Frack appear at Coventry Hippodrome.

1939
Birmingham Road widened, reducing extent of Hagley Wood – and bringing an influx of temporary labour (February).
Lallie Smith (daughter of Lennie) gives birth (estimated date).
Jack Mossop begins work as fitter at the Standard Aero Works No. 1 Factory, (3 November).
Dr Dorothy Markham reports theft of handbag from car parked in Hagley Wood Lane.
Crumpton family forced to sell St Kenelm's Hall.

1940
Bill Fletcher conscripted into army (2 February).
Jack Mossop convicted of a number of motoring offences (April).

Appendix A

Earliest time that the particular crepe-soled shoe of type found in tree could have been manufactured (April).
Occult "Operation Cone of Power", designed to protect the UK from Nazi invasion (May–August).
Laura van Raalte holidays at Beauchamp Hotel, Malvern, with a Miss M. Chapman (17–24 August).
Alfred Hainsworth junior joins Standard Aero Works, Banner Lane (September).
Jack Mossop transfers to No. 2 Factory, Banner Lane – taking up duties in the assembly shop (November).
Una Hainsworth alleges to have been introduced to the mysterious van Ralt (exact date unknown).
Illey House Farm closes as Traveller site (likely date).

1941
Josef Jakobs captured by Home Guard after parachuting into Ramsey, Cambridgeshire (31 January).
Claimed by Donald McCormick that a woman (codenamed "Clara") was parachuted from a plane over the Birmingham area during an air raid. Una Hainsworth claims that Mossop confessed to her his involvement in the murder of "the Dutch piece" (March / April).
Date that Donald McCormick later claims that Abwehr records show five agents from Holland were sent to the UK; one of whom was parachuted in during an air raid on the West Midlands (April).
Most likely time of death of victim ("Bella") found inside witch hazel tree, Hagley Wood, as determined by Professor Webster (April–October).
Dinah Curley (aka O'Grady) reported as a missing person to the Birmingham Citizens' Society. Informant is (allegedly) a Mrs M. Lavin. Jack Lavin at this time registered at Cannock (May).
Manager from a local industrial company phones police regarding screams from Hagley Wood. Schoolteacher walking nearby also hears them, and the wood is searched (July).
Police called to investigate domestic incident (assault) involving the Forrest family at Spout Farm (run by Percy Cutler) – some 3 miles from Hagley Wood (6 July).
Josef Jakobs executed as Nazi agent at the Tower of London (15 August).

Timeline

Jill Kyra Mossop born (19 November).
Una Mossop leaves her husband and vacates Barrow Road address, to live with Alfred Hainsworth (13 December).
Jack Lavin marries Mary Ann Dowling (21 December).
Home Guard officer Basterfield allegedly speaks to driver of car parked in Hagley Wood Lane (date unknown).
Squire of Gatacre disappears from Gatacre Hall (date unknown).

1942
Frankley Police Station receives a letter (allegedly from a Private Haywood stationed at Ilfracombe) asking them to investigate apparent disappearance of a Mary Lee (6 January).
Jill Mossop dies at her "parents'" house, Nuthurst, Shrewley (7 January).
Inquest into Jill Mossop's death held (9 January).
Alfred Hainsworth registers the death of Jill Mossop (12 January).
Police receive first letter regarding "missing person" Mary Wenman (January).
Bella Luer goes missing (4 February).
Jack Mossop reports car and driver missing, to Coventry Police (February).
Jack Mossop admitted to the county mental hospital, St George's, Stafford (6 June).
John Swindon sees soldier and woman enter Hagley Wood – in a statement issued seven years later (16 June).
Last reported sighting of Bella Luer, in London (June).
Letter from Private W. (Bill) Fletcher to Halesowen Police asking if they could trace whereabouts of Mary Lea / Lee / Wenman, as a matter of some urgency (19 July).
Rev. A. G. Harper (chaplain attached to 2nd Battalion Oxford & Bucks Light Infantry) requests Worcestershire Police for assistance in tracing the whereabouts of Mary Lee / Wenman (3 August).
Jack Mossop dies in St George's Hospital (15 August).
John H. Jones claims to have had premonition that "something was going to happen" as he passed Hagley Wood (August).
Kenneth Patten (according to his own testimony) takes up residence in Stourbridge (October).

Appendix A

Strange events surrounding actions of Kenneth Patten, as later claimed by Vivienne Coss (October / November).
Dutch national Johannes Marinus Dronkers executed as a spy at Wandsworth prison.
Clara Bauerle dies in Berlin (December).
Time that police report shows that Smith / Butler families were camping in Nimmings Field, when they left some old clothing behind (December).
Dead horse collected by Messrs Spalding, from Hagley Wood Lane.
Kenneth Patten bound over for two years for stealing a coat belonging to the Hon. Audrey Lyttelton, daughter of Lord Cobham, from the Hagley estate (December).

1943
Body discovered in Hagley Wood by four youths (18 April).
Police and Professor James Webster (of West Midland Forensic Science Laboratory) visit site (19 April).
Body extracted from tree by Professor J. M. Webster (20 April).
Search undertaken of area around deposition site (probably 21 April).
Bones and other items collected from search of vicinity passed to Webster (April 22).
Professor Webster issues report on behalf of West Midland Forensic Science Laboratory (23 April).
Coroner's inquest – report of which has not been retained (28 April).
Investigation into clothing found some 115 yards from body (28 April).
Initial police conference held (3 May).
Private Haywood provides statement to police advising that he had never contacted them regarding the disappearance of Mary Wenman / Lee (11 May).
Bill Fletcher and Nalie Smith interviewed at Halesowen Police Station in relation to earlier "missing person" letters. Within this, Fletcher admits to sending letting purporting to be from Haywood (14 May).
Regional conference held in Birmingham, where Professor Webster expands on his earlier statement (May).
Origin of victim's shoes established (May).
Report that Mary Wenman had been sighted at the Dog public house (Over, near Gloucester), in the company of Henry Beaver (probably 2 June).

Timeline

Date that John Swindon later claims to recall seeing couple enter Hagley Wood (16 June).

Una Mossop marries Alfred Hainsworth. Worcestershire CID write to Stockport County Borough Police requesting information on Dinah Curley and Mary Lavin; and to Pembrokeshire Police regarding the latter. (September).

CID formally write to Shropshire, Leeds and Dumfries police forces requesting information about John Edward (Jack) Lavin, in response to information obtained by Northamptonshire force (October).

Likely timing of first wall messages relating to "Lubella", in Halesowen area (autumn).

1944

John H. Jones visits *Birmingham Daily Gazette* newspaper offices to check on details of police investigation (25 March).

Police alerted to wall message for first time – in the fruit market area of Birmingham (28–30 March).

Allegation that a man in the Star public house at Halesowen (on 30/03/1944) claimed to know who had committed the murder (3 April).

Police interview John H. Jones at his home (5 April).

Unnamed prostitute tips police off as to the disappearance of colleague, Bella Lawley (7 April).

Following overheard pub conversation, police re-examine the reported domestic assault of 06/07/1942 (10 April).

Anonymous letter sent to Birmingham City Police suggesting the involvement of Arthur Edgington in the murder (11 April).

John Edward (Jack) Lavin formally interviewed at Gerald Road Police Station, London (18 July).

Florrie Porter murdered at Lickey End, Bromsgrove (October).

Police receive a letter from a "Mr Wood" claiming to be the author of the wall messages (1 November).

Discovery of handbag in Hagley Wood, near to site of wych elm (17 November).

Warwick Aston Plant claims to have contacted police with details of woman named Bella who had played the piano in his parents' pub and who subsequently disappeared.

Appendix A

Alfred Hainsworth transfers to Standard Aero's Aircraft Production Division, Ansty Aero.

1945
Murder of Charles Walton at Meon Hill (14 February).
Professor Margaret Murray presents her theories to the press – linking the murder of Charles Walton to the body found in Hagley Wood (February).
Alfred Hainsworth leaves Ansty Aero.
Samuel Allsop junior marries Mavis Jones.
The *Evening Despatch* carries the headline: "BLITZ ON BIRMINGHAM – You can blame Hans [Caesar] for this" (June).

1947
Jeremy Lygon Byford-Jones born, at Wenlock (December).

1948
Jeremy Lygon Byford-Jones dies (death registered at Wolverhampton).

1949
Meeting convened at Hagley Wood / Nimmings Field involving Tommy Williams, four other police officers and Eddie Shearwood (2 October).
Hull Daily Mail runs a story which hints at a significant breakthrough (4 October).
Vivienne Coss provides new evidence, relating to Kenneth Francis Patten. Eddie Shearwood provides information on possible Gipsy / Traveller involvement on overheard pub conversation (October).
John Swindon advises police of his sighting of couple entering Hagley Wood some six years earlier (7 October).
Julian Mossop moves to London.

1950
Jennifer Augusta Byford-Jones born at Wellington (March).
Robert Fabian publishes his memoir *Fabian of the Yard* which reprises the "Bella" case (and potential links to witchcraft), and spawns further newspaper articles.
Isabella Shemwell (Lawley) marries George Brittain.

Timeline

1951

Mr Leon Hughes of Hasbury raises a concern that the dead body could be that of "Billy" Gibson (21 February).
Jennifer Augusta Byford-Jones dies.
Alfred and Una Hainsworth move back to Kenilworth.

1953

Alfred and Una Hainsworth move to Four Acres, Long Acre, Claverley.
Julian Mossop emigrates (August).
Wilfred Byford-Jones (*Quaestor*) writes two major articles for the *Wolverhampton Express & Star*, recalling the discovery of the body and surrounding events, some 12 years before (19/20 November).
Una Hainsworth writes first Anna of Claverley letter (dated 18 November).
First Victor Crumpton letter received by police (23 November).
Birmingham Daily Gazette reports: "Scrawl clue to 'Bella' is false" (28 November).
Una Hainsworth writes second *Anna of Claverley* letter (3 December).
Whittington Inn meeting between Una Hainsworth, Wilfred Byford-Jones and police (5 December).
Victor Crumpton loses his wallet whilst visiting Hagley Wood at 4 a.m. (7 December).
Within one of a number of letters sent to Det Supt Tommy Williams, Victor Crumpton includes the following: "I wish to dispose of (a) souvenir so would you accept same it will interest you." (15 December)
Una Hainsworth provides written statement to police (28 December).
Bill Wilson provides statement to police at Kenilworth Police Station regarding claims made by Una Hainsworth about Jack Mossop (30 December).
Zita Boyden begins letter-writing campaign, offering police spiritualist "advice" in solving the crime (late in year).

1954

Victor Crumpton readmitted to Barnsley Hall Hospital (4 January).
George Elwell makes a recording of himself under self-hypnosis, claiming that the victim was a Leeds woman by the name of Annie

Appendix A

Bradley. After publication of related article in the *Birmingham Daily Gazette*, Irish woman, Mrs Bradley, contacts police with concerns that this could relate to her missing daughter (January).

1956
ITV broadcasts programme which claims that the mystery had been solved (22 May).
Alfred Hainsworth's father dies, leaving a considerable estate.
Ladislas Farago's *War of Wits: The Anatomy of Espionage and Intelligence* published.

1957
Una Hainsworth and children travel to Canada to join Alfred, who had journeyed out there a few weeks before (February).
Hainsworth family returns from Canada (June).

1958
Quaestor article "shedding light on Kinver Inn meeting" published (16 January).
M. P. Pugh retires from role as Agent for Director of Public Prosecutions.

1968
Donald McCormick publishes *Murder by Witchcraft* (A Study of the Lower Quinton and Hagley Wood Murders). J. G. Bowers of Tipton contacts police regarding his own theories on the case.

1970s
First (of many) "Bella" messages allegedly appear on Wychbury Beacon.

1973
First of a series of articles within the *Black Country Bugle* revives the case. These include interviews with former police officer Richard Skerratt and a forestry worker, both offering some new insights into the case. As a consequence, two former Home Guard officers separately come forward with additional "new" information (18 September).

Timeline

1977
Wilfred Byford-Jones dies.

1978
Black Country Bugle runs a front-page headlined: "Bella in the Wych Elm Revived" (13 June). As a result, shoe mender Leonard Cogzell comes forward.

1979
Una Hainsworth dies.

1980
Ladislas Farago dies.

1988
Victor Crumpton dies at Malvern.

1993
First authenticated messages appear on Wychbury Beacon.

1994
Crime Stalker (*Casebook Bella*) broadcast on Central Television (14 September).

1998
Donald McCormick dies.

2002
Kenneth Patten dies in Surrey.

2005
Case formally closed by police (13 July).
BBC West Midlands screen *Inside Out* programme, revisiting the murder (September).
Nazi papers sold at auction which identify that Bridgnorth and Ludlow were identified as potential Third Reich UK headquarters in the event of a successful invasion.

Appendix A

2007
Joyce M. Coley publishes *Bella – An Unsolved Murder*.

2009
Paul Newman's book *Under the Shadow of Meon Hill: The Lower Quinton & Hagley Wood Murders* published.

2013
The Independent newspaper publishes Allison Vale's article – identifying Clara Bauerle as the victim (22 March).

2014
BBC Radio 4 episode of *Punt PI* first broadcast.
Bella in the Wych Elm: In Search of a Wartime Mystery by Andrew Sparke published (APS Publishing).

2016
Police case files released to the Worcestershire Archives.
The Sun publishes sensationalist article on the case, which claims that a diary has been found which includes the entry: "I put Bella in the Wych Elm" (November).

2017
Authors Alex and Pete Merrill commission Face Lab at Liverpool John Moores University to produce a facial depiction of the victim from the original forensic photographs of the skull. Their book *Who Put Bella in the Wych Elm? Vol 1* (APS Publications) is published later in the year.

2018
UKTV (Yesterday) *Nazi Murder Mysteries*, series 1, episode 4: *Who Put Bella in the Wych Elm?* first broadcast.
The Hollow Tree by James Brogden published.

2019
Who Put Bella in the Wych Elm? Vol 2 by Alex Merrill (with Pete Merrill) published (APS Publications).

APPENDIX B

Transcript Of West Mercia Police Case Closure Report

ALLEGED MURDER AT HAGLEY WOOD, DECEASED UNKNOWN 19 April 1943

Author: Detective Chief Inspector I Nicholls
(Report) Commissioned by: Detective Chief Superintendent T. Albutt
Report Date: 13 July 2005

Introduction

The purpose of this document is to record the review of the above file which pertains to the investigation surrounding the recovery of the remains of a female from within the naturally hollowed-out trunk of and [sic] elm tree located within Hagley Wood adjacent to the main Birmingham to Kidderminster Road. This road is now designated as the A456. The remains were first reported on 19 April 1943. It was estimated that the body had been so hidden for a period of not less than eighteen months.

When recovered the skeleton was disarticulated and certain bones were missing. The nature of the bones missing would induce a presumption that the absence was as a result of wildlife intervention rather than being removed at the time of or immediately after death. It was assessed that the individual has entered the cavity feet first, and the probability of this occurring willingly or intentionally was remote thus it was determined that this matter was an offence of murder.

It is, I contend, most certainly an unexplained death however in the absence of a specific cause of death or indeed any identified injuries which indicate the individual was subjected to trauma, the to [sic] that to

Appendix B

make the leap to a murder is questionable. However, in line with the current standards contained within the National Crime Recording Standards (Revised April 2004) specifically the "Balance of Probability" test, the balance is that the individual was subjected to unlawful actions, which lead [sic] directly or indirectly to her death.

Executive Summary

- Incident occurred at the height of Axis bombing of the West Midlands conurbation.
- The deceased has yet to be identified.
- Investigation centred on the identification of the deceased.
- Final resting-place of deceased still unknown.
- Investigation skewed by false reports.
- No further witnesses identified.
- Forensic opportunities examined however no advantages identified.
- Two potential suspects were identified as a result of information in 1953; one of whom was dead, the other remains untraced.

Investigation

The investigation of the offence centred primarily on the identification of the deceased, and through that process identifying any person whom may have been involved in the death.

The identification phase centred upon the shoes retrieved from the scene, circulation's [sic] appertaining to the deceased, and examination of missing persons, or persons allegedly missing.

To contextualise, the event occurred at a time when considerable bombing by Axis forces was occurring within the Birmingham / Wolverhampton / Coventry conurbation, and thus it was considerably more common for persons to be transient and obviously death without record was a more frequent occurrence.

During the course of the investigation, a number of factors caused a skewing of the resources involved.

The first issue, which took up considerable effort, was the series of chalked messages upon walls throughout the West Midlands conurbation from Wolverhampton, into the "Black Country" and also into the city centre of Birmingham. The chalkings were undertaken over a protracted period of time. The reason for and also the author/s of the chalkings were not established despite considerable investment.

Additionally considerable effort was expended attempting to identify the whereabouts of a Mary Wenman @ Lee@ Beaver [sic], a traveller who at one time resided close to the location where the cadaver was recovered. A soldier HEYWOOD,[260] who formerly was having a relationship with the woman and sought to re-establish the relationship, initiated this. By a number of guises he used the Police to initiate an investigation to ascertain her whereabouts. The reality of the situation came to light and HEYWOOD subsequently admitted the details.

Bella TONKS was raised as a possibility following a media circulation. The name "Bella" was seemingly derived from the chalk writings on the walls throughout the West Midlands conurbation and as such the link to the enquiry was questionable. That said, the individual Bella TONKS was identified as living under her maiden name in Heath Hays.

Ann FORREST, a traveller, was identified as having lived close to the deposition site, and was raised as potentially the deceased as a result of this. Enquiries traced FORREST in April 1944 as being alive and well.

Bella BEECH was drawn to the enquiry's attention following her disappearance from bombed premises in West Ealing, London. She had left the bombed premises to live in the Birmingham area, and contact had ceased. Enquiries traced this woman to a hospital in the London area where she was working as a nurse.

Bella LUER was a woman who moved from London to undertake factory work. The contact chain with persons in London was broken and thus she was raised as a possibility as being the deceased. Again the major factor was the term "Bella". Enquiries traced a Bella LUER as being a resident at Goring on Thames however this individual was not definitely linked to the Bella LUER who was formerly resident in the Stamford Hill area of London.

---

[260] It is only the police report that spells the name this way. Elsewhere, "Haywood" has been used. This includes by Fletcher himself when masquerading as his army colleague.

Appendix B

Violet GOODE was a female who had been involved in a relationship with Thomas Henry TRUMAN resulting in his relationship with his wife [May] Gladys TRUMAN failing. Subsequently TRUMAN returned to his wife and a spurious assertion was made that GOODE had been killed to make way for this return. GOODE was identified as being alive and well, working and living in Stourbridge.

Lines of Enquiry Unfinalised

Dinah CURLEY @ O'Grady [sic]
This line of enquiry commenced with the report of the above named person being missing by a woman, the recorded details of whom were Mrs M. Lavin, 56 Stanley Street, Manchester. This report prompted enquiries to trace both CURLEY and the reporter LAVIN. The thrust of the latter was following a labourer called Jack (John Edward) LAVIN.

Document 112[261] outlines page two of details of a number of persons reported missing for the time appropriate to the believed death, provides a number of persons albeit there is no reference to investigation into the circumstances of their disappearance.

From the information supplied there is insufficient to identify whether CURLEY aka O'Grady in fact existed. Enquiries to trace the person M. LAVIN failed to do so however there were a number of coincidences with the labourer Jack LAVIN. His wife was Mrs Mary LAVIN nee DOWLING. Their home was 40 Lawrence Street, Stockport, Manchester. The reporter of the missing person allegedly resided at 56 Stanley Street, Cheetham, Manchester however she moved in about 1941 to an address in 32 Robert Street, Cheetham, Manchester with a family called Lynch. The LYNCH family subsequently removed to an address in Haverfordwest. Jack LAVIN was employed on a contract in the St David's area of west Wales, residing at an address on the Fishguard to Haverfordwest Road. Whilst there he was joined by his wife Mary.

Enquiries in the Haverfordwest area for the reporter LAVIN identified an address of 73 Belle Vue Terrace, Haverfordwest until 30 March 1943

---

[261] See Appendix C.

Transcript of West Mercia Police Case Closure Report

from where she removed to an address of 9 Claremont, Ripon, Yorkshire. The LYNCH family removed six months earlier to an address in Kettering, Northamptonshire. Jack LAVIN was sought for non-payment of fines in Northamptonshire.

In respect of Ripon, to where Mrs M. Lavin allegedly moved following leaving Haverfordwest, coincidentally a Mr John Edward LAVIN resided at 9 Claremont, Ripon from 9 March 1943. The latter's previous address was recorded as being 40 Lawrence Street, Stockport.

Thus with all coincidences it is highly probable that the reporter for the missing person was Mrs Mary LAVIN, the wife of Jack (John Edward) LAVIN, despite denials by him of any knowledge and links to the 56 Stanley Street address. There is nothing on the file to indicate that Mary LAVIN was interviewed and challenged about these issues.

The reasons for the denial and the report being made remain unclear, however it is probable that it was personal gain, and that the alleged missing person CURLEY was a fictitious individual.

There are on file a number of communications which, it would seem prudent not to follow as the basis for the content is at best questionable.

Suspects

During 1953, his former wife, UNA HAINSWORTH, identified JACK MOSSOP as a potential suspect following a submission. MOSSOP, in later life was suffering from mental illness and died in a mental institution in 1942. In 1932 the relationship of MOSSOP and the now HAINSWORTH produced a son, Julian MOSSOP, who remained with his mother until 1949, when he went to London and there became involved in criminality. At the time of the discovery of the deceased, Julian MOSSOP was eleven years of age, living in Kenilworth and as such can be discounted as a suspect.

Mrs HAINSWORTH seemingly had some history, as it would appear that the removal from the Kenilworth address had left behind considerable debts.

Following their divorce and in the later part of his life, HAINSWORTH and MOSSOP met where he alleged he was losing his mind, suffering from mental images of a woman in a tree leering at him.

Appendix B

At this stage HAINSWORTH was obviously not aware of the Hagley body as it was yet to be discovered, and thought it was a delaying tactic for resolving issues.

With the discovery of the body and subsequent media attention in a pictorial, HAINSWORTH wrote a letter signing it "Anna". At that stage some assertions with regard to witchcraft had been made and she wished not to be associated with it.

The story she outlined was that a Dutch male called Van RALT (term also includes the spelling Van RAALT hereafter) came to her home in 1940. He was seemingly without regular employment albeit he had considerable funds. HAINSWORTH made an aside that Van RALT may have been a spy. This aside seems to be the basis for later conjecture that the death involved spies.

In March or April 1941, MOSSOP arrived home noticeably having had drank [*sic*] alcohol, and in an agitated state when he allegedly stated that he had been to the Lyttelton Arms with Van RALT and the "Dutch piece". (Presumably this meant a female either Dutch in nationality or associated with the Dutchman Van RALT). MOSSOP allegedly stated that the female had become awkward then passed out. Van RALT directed MOSSOP to drive to a nearby wood where the former stuck her into a hollow tree and left her there. It was allegedly stated that she would come to her senses the following day and the men returned to Kenilworth.

There was and still remains a public house in Hagley called the Lyttelton Arms, which was located on the main Kidderminster to Birmingham Road. More latterly with road enhancements, the public house now sits on a side road.

The logical route back towards Kenilworth from the public house would have been through Clent, to Bromsgrove, and thence into Warwickshire. This route is the opposite direction to the wooded area on the main Birmingham Road where the deceased was recovered.

It would appear that there was a link between Van RAALT and an act appearing at the Coventry Hippodrome in 1938, the performers being known as "Frick and Frack" however the grounds for such a link is undefined.

Checks of the nationality database subsequent to 1948 (probably in

Transcript of West Mercia Police Case Closure Report

1953 following the disclosure by Mrs HAINSWORTH) identify two Van RALT nominals.

The first is Pieter Van RAALT who landed in 1948, and had an address in London SE25, the second was a female who held a permanent address in London but occupied a teaching position in Nottingham. Significantly, the female, Laura Frances Van RAALTE had on 17 August 1940, vacationed in Malvern staying at the Beauchamp Hotel, and thus has arguably some relationship with Worcestershire.

There is nothing on the file to indicate whether it was possible in 1954 to establish whether Ms Van RAALTE was still alive, however there is a report concerning the individual using the present tense which would seem to indicate that in 1954 she was still surviving. If one is to take the post-mortem report of Professor WEBSTER as being precise, then in 1940. Ms Van RAALTE was over forty years of age and would just about fall outside the requisite parameters for the deceased.

Lines of Enquiry

Nomination of Suspects

Following the disclosure by HAINSWORTH, Jack MOSSOP and Van RAALTE appear to be worthy of review. If taken at face value, there are a number of factors, which would key in with the information known. Unfortunately it is now extremely difficult to clearly identify the degree of information which was released into the public arena which would allow for the story to be sewn together by HAINSWORTH.

In relation to the area of Hagley, HAINSWORTH may have had a degree of knowledge. When making the disclosure she was resident in Claverley, a small Shropshire village lying just outside the Wolverhampton conurbation. Hagley in those days would lie on a route between the Warwick, Shrewley areas and Claverley. It would appear that the public house was quite well-known and was a point to where persons would travel for a day out. It was a waypoint in the general area of Hagley and Stourbridge used as a means of direction or a marker for directions.

Appendix B

Review of Status of Crime

The status of the crime as an unsolved murder is based considerably on the post-mortem report of Professor Webster. In his field, Professor Webster was regarded as being pre-eminent, however with the passage of time, the identification of new concepts, and the modification of previously held beliefs may result in a differing perspective being placed upon the cause of death. Exploration of this concept has been undertaken and there is no advantage taking this forward.

Witnesses

Whilst the only identified witnesses survive, these individuals can only proffer information surrounding the discovery of the remains, some substantial time following the death. Over the passage of time no other witnesses have been identified despite the factor [sic] that the death was broadcast nationally in an investigative style program [sic] by John STALKER. The prospect of locating witnesses at this juncture is remote.

Media Appeals / Communications Strategy

The prospect of receiving information, which would move the enquiry forward following a general media appeal, is minimal. Indeed the prospect is that the appeal would generate considerable interest from the perspective of obsessionalist theorists and individuals as archived in the rear of the folder. The opportunity of working with an investigative journalist who seeks to undertake a program [sic] or a part program [sic] concerning the case is rather more appealing. This would potentially facilitate a mechanism of reawakening the public awareness, and those having genuine knowledge prompted to be in touch. That said, the case was subject to a television program [sic] produced by John STALKER, broadcast nationally, which resulted in no additional material being forthcoming.

Arrest Strategy

The passage of time, the demise of MOSSOP and the hitherto non-identification of Van RAALTE who would now be in the latter phase of this his life, if indeed he has not predeceased this report. At this time there are no other potential offenders identified, thus an arrest is not envisaged.

Transcript of West Mercia Police Case Closure Report

Search Strategy

The passage of time has rendered impractical a search otherwise than in the identification of a potential offender. It is highly likely that even after the passage of time, that [*sic*] the offender would maintain either media reporting or similar, and thus would be the subject of the search.

Interview Strategy

The interview strategy at this stage cannot be defined, but in the unlikely event of a suspect coming to notice this would be developed.

Identification Strategy

Identification of the deceased after this passage of time is somewhat difficult. There may well be opportunities to be explored in respect of DNA profiling and thereby gain a lineage match. Extensive enquiries to identify the resting place of the remains have thus far failed.

An interment would have taken place, however it is unclear as to where the remains would be buried, and where the ownership of the remains lies.

Forensic Strategy

Consideration has been afforded to the use of the expertise of a Forensic Archaeologist, Forensic Anthropologist, Forensic Environmentalist, Palaeontologist and an Odontologist. Additionally the advances in DNA techniques have been researched.

The Forensic Archaeologist may have been able to assist had there been any photographs of the scene recorded. At this stage I am unable to identify whether this was the case. Most certainly there is no record of such on the file. The scene has decayed over the passage of time as indeed has the tree, and thus no scene worthy of calling such remains.

The identification of the deceased has a potential to move the enquiry forward. This can potentially be achieved by virtue of DNA analysis of the remains, and extraction of the mitochondrial [*sic*] DNA. Furthermore the origins of the deceased could potentially be ascertained through analysis of the bone constituents thereby providing supportive structure to the assertions of HAINSWORTH.

The final resting place of the bones has yet to be ascertained. In such

Appendix B

cases, the remains were buried in a "pauper's" grave. Enquiries with the cemeteries within the Stourbridge and surrounding West Midlands's [*sic*] area have failed to identify the resting-place of the deceased. Thus without source material such forensic initiatives are flawed.

Conclusion

At this stage with the passage of time, there are no clear investigative leads. If the location of the remains were established, development of the DNA processes has not afforded investigative opportunities. Any person involved, if surviving, would be in excess of eighty years of age and the prospect of a prosecution would at best be remote.

I therefore make the following recommendations:

- The case is identified as being closed
- Consideration should be afforded to placing the documentation in the Worcestershire Records Office as an historic document

13 July 2005
I Nicholls
Detective Chief Inspector

Addendum

As per attached e mail communication between DCI NICHOLLS and DCS 333 on 28 July 2005, this file has now been declared closed and is not for henceforward to be regarded as a live investigation.

28 July 2005

APPENDIX C

List of Persons Reported Missing to (Birmingham Police) May 1940–August 1941

Missing person	Enquirer (reporter)	Date reported
Mrs Elsie Robinson 28 Peplow Rd Glebe Farm	Mrs Britten (Bristol)	Aug 1941
Mrs E. Parry 108 Lozells Road	W. Haynes (Tyne & Wear)	July 1941
Miss Evelyn Loveridge 2/263 Icknield Port Road	G. E. Stephenson (Middlesbrough)	July 1941
Mrs Mary Claypole 3/35 Ryland Road	Mrs Claypole (Sheffield)	July 1941
Mr & Mrs E. Anson Aston	Miss E. Fearn (Derby) 99 Pritchett Street	Aug 1941
Mrs Dodd 1/11 Frederick Road Aston	AC1 C. W. Capel (RAF Cranfield)[262]	June 1941
Mrs Crowe 78 Balsall Heath Road	Mr E. J. W. Crowe (Spalding, Lincs)	June 1941
Mrs Shaw & Mrs Townends 491 Moseley Road	Mrs Whale (Castleford, Yorks)	May 1941
Gwen Parish	Mrs M. Burns (Co Durham)	May 1941

---

[262] AC1 is the abbreviation for aircraftman first class.

Appendix C

Green Street Birmingham 9		
Patricia Scott Address n/k	Mrs D. N. Downham (Blackburn)	Dec 1941
Miss P. D. Montgomery Address n/k	John A. Montgomery (Newcastle)	Sept 1941
Margaret Johnson Address n/k	G. F. G Johnson (Leeds)	Sept 1941
Mr & Mrs Howlett Address n/k	H. A. Clarke (Muswell Hill, London)	Sept 1941
Ivy Morris Fuge (aka Morris) Address n/k	David R. Fuge (Swansea)	Oct 1941
Sarah Clague (aka Lewthwaite) Address n/k	Trooper T. W. Clague (42nd Armoured Divn)	Nov 1941
Annie Goldstein (aka Zeitlin, aka Biezansky, aka Shagrin) Address n/k	L. Goldstein (Stepney, London)	July 1941
Miss Helen Ormsby Address n/k	Dan J. Murtagh (Nottingham)	Aug 1941
Mrs J. Kelly Address n/k	Mr E. Head (Worthing)	Aug 1941
Elizabeth Kinsman Trench-Morris	Capt. P. N. Trench-Morris (Halifax)	May 1941
Dinah Curley aka O'Grady	Mrs M. Lavin (56 Stanley Street, Manchester)	May 1941
Mrs Gladys Herbinson[263] 1/60 Benacre Street	Mr D. Henderson (Huddersfield)	May 1940

---

[263] This is an unusual surname, and it may be that it was wrongly transcribed (particularly given the identity of the enquirer).

APPENDIX D

Sequential "Bella" Wall Messages[264]

1   Late summer–December 1943: "WHO PUT LUBELLER IN THE WYCH ELM". Chalked on wall in Haden Hill, Old Hill (within Worcestershire Police District). Notified to police 30/03/44.

2a   27–29/03/44: "WHO PUT BELLA DOWN THE WYCH ELM – HAGLEY WOOD". On wall in Upper Dean Street, Birmingham, on empty premises next to Messr Williamson. This was the first to be discovered, and notified to the police (28/03/44).

2b   27–29/03/44: "HAGLEY WOOD BELLA". Outside the premises of Messrs White very close by, soon after. (Notified to police either 28/03/44 or 30/03/44.)

3   12/04/44: "WHO PUT BELLA IN THE WITCH ELM HAGLEY WOOD JACK THE RIPPER? / JACK THE RIPPER / ANA BELLA DIED IN HAGLEY WOOD?" On wall adjoining premises of Walter Somers of Mucklow Hill, Halesowen (copycat hoaxer suspected). Notified to police the same day.

4   31/07/44–01/08/44: "HAGLEY WOOD LUBELLA ADDRESS WAS OPPOSITE ROSE & CROWN HASBURY". Underneath railway arch (Sun Passage) at Heath Town, near Wolverhampton. Notified to police 01.08.44.

---

[264] Those that were reported to, and considered to be significant by, the police. The dates shown are those when it is believed that they originated.

Appendix D

5a   01/08/44: "ADDRESS WAS OPPOSITE ROSE AND CROWN HASBURY HAGLEY WOOD LUBELLA". Chalked on a five-bar gate in Shelton Lane, Belle Vale. Spotted by police officer the following day.

5b   01/08/44: " HAGLEY WOOD LUBELLA WAS NO PROSS". On wall underneath an arch, nearby (also Shelton Lane). Spotted by police officer the following day.

6a   29–30/10/44: "HAGLEY WOOD LUBELLA / ADDRESS WAS 404 LOWER HASBURY / HALESOWEN". In Station Road, Old Hill (Halesowen), on wall extending from the railway bridge to the entrance of Messrs W. H. (William Henry) Palmer & Co. First noticed by police on 02.11.22.

6b   29–30/10/44: "404 LOWER HASBURY / HAGLEY WOOD LUBELLA / ADDRESS WAS". In Coombe Hill (just off Station Road). First noticed by police on 02/11/22.

APPENDIX E

List of Customers Calling at Williamsons Early Monday, 27 March 1944

(shortly before discovery of wall messages; as recorded in police files)

Mr Dinwiddy	182 Triscot Rd, Frankley Beeches, Northfield, Birmingham
Mr H. Edmonds	Halesowen Road, Old Hill, Nr Birmingham
Mr Guest	19 Quinton Road West, Birmingham 32
Mrs Hackett	35 Bromsgrove Street, Birmingham 5
Mr C. Jones	721 Hagley Road West, Birmingham 32
Mr H. E. Jones	225 Lakey Lane, Hall Green, Birmingham
Mr Manley	177 Lodge Road, Winson Green, Birmingham
Mr Parsons	556 Bristol Road, Selly Oak, Birmingham
Mr Pibworth	131 Pottery Road, Warley, Birmingham
Mr Revill	106 Tudor Street, Winson Green, Birmingham
Mr Sharpe	83 Turves Green, Northfield, Birmingham
Mr G. W. Smith	131 Winson Green Road, Birmingham
Mrs Sutton	351 Monument Road, Birmingham
Mr Taylor	5 Swinford Road, Selly Oak, Birmingham

NB A further memo advises that a police officer undertook a follow-up visit on Thursday 30 March 1944 (at 2 p.m.). He saw the manager of Whites, interviewed the warehouseman, and took a list of all lorry drivers who had called at the premises on the evening of the 29th and morning of 30 March. This identified that they came had come principally from the Midlands (Blackheath, Coventry, Stourbridge, Wolverhampton, Wednesbury, Smithwick, Hednesford, Walsall and Dudley), with additional representation from Newcastle-under-Lyme,

Appendix E

and with two vehicles from Shrewsbury. The memo does not identify the police officer in question, although it would appear to be the same individual who was notified about the behaviour of J. H. Jones. It contains only sheet two (sheets one and three – and possibly others – seem to be missing).

APPENDIX F

Summary of Police Enquiries at Addresses in Hagley Road, Hasbury, 2 August 1944

Timber Yard: occupied by John T. Willetts & Sons (timber merchants).

No. 390: occupied by Ernest Willetts, his wife and one child.

No. 392:[265] occupied by Walter Willetts and wife (but none of their children). The family had been living here for the last 40 years. Walter probably the father of the incumbent of number 390 (although this was a large family).

No. 394: occupied by Harry Moore, wife and three daughters (probably all adults). Family had been at this address for last 30 years.

No. 396: occupied by Colin Edward Withers, wife and (very young) child. Edwards was at this time away from home in the armed forces; family had been at this address for five years.

No. 398: occupied by Hilda Argent (widow) and one small child. The Argents had moved in 12 years previously, but the husband had been killed in action in 1941

No. 400: occupied by Alfred Thomas Hardwick, wife and three children – resident for the past six years.

No. 402: occupied by Albert Allsop, wife and daughter. Albert had been at this address for last 35 years.

---

[265] The police report did not quote the number 392, but from other evidence supplied this is a reasonable inference. It is possible that this was at one time part of No. 390.

Appendix F

No. 404: occupied by Samuel Allsop (resident for 56 years) and wife. *(NB At the time of the initial investigation, there was no mention of the son – Samuel Charles Geoffrey Allsop [born c.1921] – who would have been living there when on leave from the RAF.)*

No. 406: occupied by Arthur James, wife, daughter and son-in-law. James and his wife had been here for the last 12 years.

No. 408: occupied by Mabel Basterfield (widow), for the last 30 years. Her son was also living with her at this address.

No. 410: occupied by John Laight, his wife and three small children, over the past five years. Laight was at the time away, serving in the armed forces.

APPENDIX G

Transcript of Victor Crumpton Letter

Supt S Inight [sic]

23 Nov 1953[266]

Sir,

I resided with my family at St Kenelm's Hall Romsley, Halesowen for over 25 years but returned to Old Hill 1940, therefore found great pleasure reading your deductions in "Wych Elm Case", through the medium of "Quaestor" the Express & Star.

Several years ago "Staffs County Police" Old Hill were put to much inconvenience with "chalking on a wall" at Belle Vale (Barrs Road end). PC B Horrobin who after months of vigil whilst on night duty with various colleagues, himself caught the offender; there was no conviction – so no record. According to PC Horrobin's own graphic account to me, it was about 4 a.m. and his second visit this night to area; with no results. Suddenly footsteps were heard coming up road from Halesowen direction so the officer in his place of concealment commanded good outline of wall in darkness.

On reaching wall this person (MALE) halted and started to write with chalk on latter, at this point the officer crossed the road and jumped on the culprits [sic] back causing him to faint away, due to shock.

This particular person came from Halesowen and was going to Netherton (via Belle Vale) in time for early turn at Ironworks

Should you wish to contact Mr Horrobin, he is now Sgt Hilltop West Bromwich.

Yours sincerely,
Frederick Victor Crumpton

---

[266] The address and date are not fully legible, but police records strongly suggest that it was written then, and that the address Crumpton was writing from was 35 Harcourt Road, Old Hill, Staffordshire.

APPENDIX H

Transcript of Statement of Vivienne M. Coss

[Provided at her home at 27 Hoarstone, West Hagley, and taken by DS Thurston in the presence of T. N. Williams on 11/10/1949. Occupation given as housewife, and "apparent age" 28 years.]

About the middle of October, 1942, I was employed by a Mr T. F. Parsons of West Hagley for the most part delivering milk in the West Hagley area. During this time I met a man who was later known to me as "Pat Graham". (I subsequently found that this was not his correct name.)

This man stopped me one morning at Hagley whilst I was driving my employer's van and made a comment about the front wheels of my van wobbling. I told him that I was aware of this fact and that my employer was not able to get another van. He then asked me the name of my employer, and following this conversation he went to see my employer, and later did work on my vehicle and another van owned by Mr Parsons. He appeared to have a good knowledge of vehicle maintenance.

When this man first stopped me, he was accompanied by a Land Army girl by the name of "Sheila" who was employed at Hagley Hall. This man subsequently became friendly with my employer and I often saw him around the dairy. There were times when this man "Pat" had little else to do and he often accompanied me on journeys in my van.

One noticeable thing about "Pat" was that he was always singing an R.A.F. ditty: "My wife she died, I laughed 'till I cried, because I was single again". He told me that his fiancée was a former racing motorist and that she was killed in a crash. He said that he was getting over her death a little, but he would never forget her screams when she was killed as he was present in the pits at the time, I mention this because of his queer behaviour.

He was frequently to be seen in the Hagley Hall grounds, and mentioned that he was on a month's leave from Rolls-Royce where he worked, and that he was staying with friends at Hagley. He said that he had a van hidden in Hagley Woods, but his firm did not know that he

Transcript of Statement of Vivienne M. Coss

had brought it away and he did not want anyone to know.

"Pat" was often seen wearing a white mackintosh which was later found to have been stolen from a stable at Hagley Hall. At this time, I had a red setter dog named "Pat", and when I mentioned this to "Pat Graham", he said he was very interested in animals and he did in fact borrow my dog to go, as he said, to Hagley Woods for some shooting.

This man was very plausible, but I became somewhat suspicious of him and it came as no surprise to me when I heard that the Police wanted to see him.

It happened one day either about the end of October or the beginning of November, 1942, I was at Mr Parson's dairy, when Lord Cobham's car drove up and I believe a Police Officer was in it. He said that he wanted to speak to "Pat Graham", but "Pat" was not there. I went out on my milk round and subsequently called at my home for lunch, leaving my van outside the house. I told him that the Police were after him, and he said, "I know, it must be about those tyres I got without a permit". He asked me if he could come inside whilst he thought things over.

He was allowed to come in the house, and he then asked me if I would do him a favour. He said when it got dusk would I drive him in the van somewhere and would I lend him my red setter dog. I was reluctant to do this, or to lend him my dog, and when I asked him where he wanted to go, he would not tell me but said that he would ... *[the rest of this sentence is illegible]*

Later, however, I agreed to take him, and he stayed at the house until it got dusk. It would then be about 6pm.

We got into the van and took the dog with us. I drove off and then asked him where he wanted me to take him. He didn't say exactly where he wanted me to take him. He didn't say exactly where we were to go, but he kept directing me until we got to Hagley Hall, he then asked me to pull up at the entrance to Hagley Wood Lane. This is the lane which adjoins that part of Hagley Wood where later in April 1943, the skeleton of a woman was found in a tree.

During this journey, he was singing hysterically, and had a very queer look about him. I became very nervous and upset by his behaviour.

He got out of the van and told me to drive straight back to the dairy, and not to tell anyone that I had brought him out there. I promised him that I would not do so.

He then walked away up Hagley Wood Lane, and I saw him disappear into the darkness with my dog.

Another peculiar thing was, that as he got out of the van, a 'bus went by and he appeared to hide his face from the people in the 'bus.[267]

I then drove straight back to the dairy where I saw Mr Parsons. Mr Parsons remarked as to the length of time I had kept the van and also remarked on the fact that I was not looking too well. I did not tell him anything about where I had taken "Pat Graham".

I went home and next morning I went to collect my van, and Mr Parsons met me with my dog. He told me that "Pat Graham" had brought my dog back at about half past ten the previous night.

I did not see "Pat Graham" again until a short while afterwards, but I cannot remember whether it was a few days or a few weeks later.

He came to the dairy one day, and I noticed that he was very much smarter in his appearance. He asked me what was happening, and I told him that as far as I knew the police were still after him. He said that he had been away to Manchester driving taxis.

He then went away and I did not see him again until some Court proceedings at Stourbridge when he was charged with stealing a mackintosh. His correct name was then disclosed as Kenneth Francis Patten.

After the Court, he came to see Mr Parsons, and the last I ever saw of him was when I left him talking to Mr Parsons.

I recollect that when I dropped him that evening at Hagley Wood Lane, I asked him why he was going there, and he replied that he could not possibly tell me, but that one day I might know.

When in April 1943, the skeleton of a woman was found in a tree in Hagley Wood, I did not connect the incident of taking "Pat Graham" to the wood with it, because upon reading the report, I saw that the body was stated to have been in the tree at least eighteen months, and it was only about six months prior to the finding that I had taken "Pat Graham" there.

The incident however, had remained in the back of my mind and when recently I saw that the case had been re-opened it brought the matter up again, and I decided to inform the Police.

---

[267] This would presumably have been on the Kidderminster–Birmingham Road, at the corner with Hagley Wood Lane (no buses would have entered Hagley Wood Lane itself).

APPENDIX I

Transcript of First Anna of Claverley *Letter*

Claverley
Nr Wolverhampton

18/11/53

My Dear Quaestor,

Finish your articles regarding the wych elm crime by all means they are interesting to your readers but you will never solve the mystery.

The one person who could give the answers is now beyond the jurisdiction of earthly courts.

The affair is closed and involves no witches, black magic or moonlight rites.

Much as I hate having to use a nom de plume, I think you would appreciate it if you knew me.

The only clues I can give you are that the person responsible for the crime died insane in 1942, and the victim was Dutch and arrived in England illegally about 1941. I have no wish to recall any more.

[The last paragraph has been crossed through, but appears to read:]

I am no hoaxer. What happened to our mutual friend Mike Shurey [? — unclear] did he return to Brau Hay [? — unclear]

Yours sincerely

Anna

APPENDIX J

Transcript of *Second* Anna of Claverley *Letter*

3.12.53

Dear Quaestor,

Had so much publicity not been given to "Anna" I would have contacted you before.

I will meet you and officers of the Worcestershire CID at "the Dick Whittington"[268] (it is beyond the Stewponey[269] from Wolverhampton) tomorrow night (Friday) at about 8:30pm and maybe I can help them with their investigations if they are still interested – subject to my conditions to which I think they will agree your my [sic] criteria, will not advertise this meeting in your press.

You have had many wild goose chases during the last few days maybe this will be the last or the beginning of many who knows?

At the "Whittington" they have a back room [to] the left of the entrance called the "Priest's Hole".

Sincerely,
Anna

---

[268] Now the Manor House of Whittington, Kinver.
[269] Stourton is situated either side of the A458 road, at the junction of the A449 (between Kidderminster and Wolverhampton. The name originally related to the area west of the River Stour, but now incorporates the former Halfcot. The Stewponey inn was formerly situated at the crossroads, until it was demolished to make way for housing. Stewponey remains a local name for the area.

APPENDIX K

Statement Provided to Police by Una Ella Hainsworth 28 December 1953

[NB This does not reflect verbatim the contemporaneous notes recorded by officers. A significant omission is Una Hainwsorth's contention that she met van Ralt "only twice". Una Hainsworth's address is given as: Four Acres, Long Common, Claverley.

I was married to JACK MOSSOP in 1932 and we went to live at the Bridge House, Wombourne. At that time he was studying to be a surveyor. The only child of our marriage was born in 1932 and he was christened Julian and at the present time, he is somewhere in America.

My husband joined the A.S.T. in 1937 as a Pilot Officer and was stationed at Hamble, near Southampton.

In 1938 he commenced work for the Armstrong Siddeley Works Coventry and subsequently he went to work at the Standard Aero Works at Coventry (Banner Lane).

It was in 1940 that a man named "VAN RALT" came to our house No. 39 Barrow Road, Kenilworth. I believe this man was Dutch and as far as I know he had no particular job, and I have a suspicion that he was engaged on some work that he did not wish to talk about, but in my opinion it might have been that he was a spy for he had plenty of money and there were times that my husband appeared to have plenty of money after meeting him.

It was either in March or April, 1941 that my husband came home noticeably white and agitated. [270] This was at about 1 a.m. in the morning and he asked me for a drink. I made a comment that I thought he had had enough as he had been out all day but I gave him a drink. He then said he had been to the Lyttelton Arms with "VAN RALT" and the

---

[270] It appears that the typed copy originally read "the worse [for wear]" but this was changed to "white and agitated".

Appendix K

"Dutch Piece" and that she had got awkward. My husband was driving the car, which belonged to "VAN RALT" she got in beside him, "VAN RALT" was in the back and then she fell over towards my husband, and he said to "VAN RALT" that she had passed out. "VAN RALT" told him where to drive to and they went to a wood, stuck her in a hollow tree. "VAN RALT" said she would come to her senses the following morning, and as far as I know, my husband came home. He came home in "VAN RALT's" car which was a Rover.

I lived at Kenilworth until December 1941 and between April and December, my husband appeared very jumpy and it was noticeable that he had more drink than usual, and appeared to have more money to spend. He was nearly always away from work and this led to my suspicion that in some way, he was obtaining money and may have been meeting "VAN RALT". I should mention that my husband had an old Standard car of his own and he used to go off for days on end and I did not know where he was.

When I left my husband in December 1941 I went to Henley in Arden, and we[271] lived there for ten years. We lived at Nuthurst House, Shrewley, Near Henley in Arden, and we finally returned in 1951 to Kenilworth and came to our address in August, 1953.

I saw my first husband JACK MOSSOP at Kenilworth on three occasions after I was forced to leave him in December, 1941 and tried to get my possessions including furniture from the house and on one of these occasions, it would be the last time I saw him, he told me what I thought at first, was a further story to put me off and it was as follows; that he thought he was losing his mind as he kept seeing the woman in the tree and she was leering at him. He held his head in his hands and said "it is getting on my nerves, I am going crazy". It was about June 1942 when I heard that he had been taken to the Mental Hospital at Stafford where he died in August 1942. I was not informed of his death at the time and I did not attend the funeral because of this. The first I knew was when my present husband told me that an application had been made at the works claiming money due to him and sending a doctor's certificate.

---

[271] Assumed to mean her and Alfred Hainsworth.

Statement Provided to Police by Una Ella Hainsworth (28/12/53)

I had no knowledge whatever of the Hagley Murder until an article appeared in the Express and Star newspaper, neither had I read anything before which could in any way be connected with the incident I have told you about. I have not discussed the matter with anyone and it was not until I was reading the details and bearing in mind the possible date when the woman met her death that I, in any way, connected this with my husband's statement to me in March or April, 1941, and because of the articles referring to witchcraft etc., I decided in the first place to write a letter and sign it "Anna". I put sufficient clues in the letter which should have helped to have identified me and it was only because of the subsequent appeal in the newspaper and because I felt I ought to say what I know of this matter that I decided to arrange to meet you. I cannot add anything further and because I am now married again with three small children I hope that what I have said to you will only be used to aid the course of justice and it is this which has prompted me to take the action I have. I was not treated too well by my husband and do not wish in any way to rake up the past but if what I have told you will help you in this matter, then the foregoing statement has been made by me voluntarily and with that end in view.

I, of course, have no proof, that what I have told you now is the truth, but bearing in mind my husband's condition and what he said to me at the time, I have done my best to recall it to help in the enquiry.

APPENDIX L

Bibliography, Film, TV and Radio Broadcast Detail

Books (Factual)

War of Wits: The Anatomy of Espionage and Intelligence – Ladislas Farago (Hutchinson & Co.), 1956.

Murder by Witchcraft – Donald McCormick (Arrow Books), 1968.

Black Country Ghosts & Mysteries – Aristotle Tump (Harry Taylor), 1987

Bella – An Unsolved Murder – Joyce M. Coley (History into Print), March 2007.

Under the Shadow of Meon Hill: The Lower Quinton and Hagley Wood Murders – Paul Newman (Abraxas & DGR Books), February 2009.

Worcestershire Murders – Nicola Sly (The History Press), 2009, 2012 (Chapter 22 – Who put Bella in the Wych-elm?).

Bella in the Wych Elm: In Search of a Wartime Mystery – Andrew Sparke (APS Publications), 2014 and 2016.

Who Put Bella in the Wych Elm?: Volume 1 The Crime Scene Revisited – Alex Merrill with Pete Merrill (APS Publications), 2018.

Who Put Bella in the Wych Elm?: Volume 2 A Crime Shrouded in Mystery – Alex Merrill with Pete Merrill (APS Publications), 2019.

Books (Fiction)

The Hollow Tree – James Brogden (Titan Books), 2018.

Film / DVD

Bella in the Wych Elm – Carnie Features (2018).

TV

ITV broadcast (title unknown) – screened 22 May 1956.

Crime Stalker (episode; Central TV). First shown September 1994.

Inside Out (BBC West Midlands). Broadcast September 2005.

Nazi Murder Mysteries: series 1, episode 4 (*Who Put Bella in the Wych Elm*) – UKTV (Yesterday). First shown December 2018.

Radio

Punt PI: BBC Radio 4; series 7, episode 4 (*Who Put Bella in the Wych Elm?*). First broadcast 4 August 2014.

Index

Abel, Frederick Rowlinson 171
Abel, Rhoda Gertrude 171
Abel, Una see Una Hainsworth
Alcester Chronicle 208
Allard, Norah Elizabeth see Norah Brittain
Allso family 156–7
Allsop family 38, 39, 156–7, 160, 249
Allsop Isabella 161
Allsop, Samuel sr 42, 160–3, 264
Allsop, Samuel, jn 42, 160–3
Anderton, David 82
"Anna of Claverley" see Una Hainsworth
"Anna of Claverley" letters 67–69, 87, 185, 213, 215, 218–9, 226, 227
Armchair Science 35, 120
Askwith, Richard 277

Bache, Insp (Halesowen) 34, 39, 123
Bache, John 29
Badger's Sett pub see *Gipsy's Tent*
Baird, Capt J 211
Baldacchino, Carl 276
Basterfield, Harry 94, 96, 160, 226, 237–8
Bauerle, Clara 79–81, 197–8, 277
Bauerle, Karla Sofie 198
Beaver, Henry 26
Beaver, Mary see Mary Wenman
Beech, Bella 45, 154
Beech, Donald 45
Beech, Emily 45
Benbow, PC 19
Bird, Sir Robert 211
Birmingham Citizens' Society 23, 139
Bird, Sir Robert 211
Birmingham Daily Gazette 4, 6, 7, 32, 34, 35, 47, 114, 164, 165, 224
Birmingham Post 195
Black Country Bugle 8, 92–6, 123, 203, 236, 238–9, 240, 242–3
Blest, Mrs 249–51
Bolton, Hannah 24
Bond, George 31–2
Bottomley, Peggy 149
Bowers, J G 215
Boycott Arms, Claverley 168, 169, 184
Boyden, Zita 82–86, 158, 204–5, 225, 231
Bradley, Annie 85–86
Bradley, Mary 85, 123, 204
Brick Bridge see *Waggon & Horses*
Brickmakers Arms 178, 179
British Jeweller 193–5
Brittain, George 155
Brittain, Norah Elizabeth 155
Brogden, James 278
Bromyard Camp 140–1
Brown, Evelyn see Evelyn Loveridge
Bull, Edith 137
Butler family see Smiths
Butler, Arkus see Arkus Smith
Butler, Daniel 59, 137
Butler, Ivy 59
Butler, Margaret see Margaret Evans
Byford, Mary Elizabeth 207
Byford-Jones, Cynthia 212–3, 220, 235
Byford-Jones, Wilfred 66–8, 73–4, 82, 92, 95, 121, 183, 185, 186, 206–35, 236–7, 240–3, 258, 259, 274
Byford-Jones, Wilfred Louise 207

Caesar, Hans Paul 75–7, 79, 95, 193–5, 197, 199–200, 226
Chambers, Harry 224

Index

Churchill, Sir Winston 211
Claypole, Mary 142
Closure Report 24, 99, 108, 109, 124, 129, 142, 147, 183,
Cogzell, Leonard 95–96, 124, 238–9
Coley, Joyce 29, 89, 97, 99, 100, 261, 263
Comins, Frederick 150
Coss, Vivienne 61–63, 122, 148–152, 266–7
Coventry Hippodrome 187–8, 274
Cox, John 32, 33
Cremer, Mme 78–79, 196
Crime Stalker 98, 243
Cross Keys, West Hagley 24, 272
Crown, Iverley 185
Crump, Charlotte ("Lollo") see Charlotte Mossop
Crump, George 168
Crump, Mary Ann see Mary Ann Jenkins
Crumpton, Rex 49
Crumpton, Frederick 48
Crumpton, Laura 48
Crumpton, (Frederick) Victor 47–50, 127, 128, 163–5, 219–21, 225, 227, 249–53, 272
Curley, Dinah 23, 24, 122, 142–148
Cutler, Percy 25

Daily Sketch 89, 221
Davies, Clara see Clara Shemwell
Davies, Dr 96, 239
Davies, PC John A 50, 250–1
Dawson, Winifred Louise see Winifred Byford-Jones
Deacon, Richard see Donald McCormick
Dickenhoff, Karl see Hans Caesar
Dickson, Frances 27
Dixon, Joyce 106
Dorrill, Stephen 195

Douch, Arthur & Alice 176
Douglas-Osborn, Peter 88–89, 98–99, 200
Douglas-Osborn, Sqd Ldr William 7–8, 88–89, 200
Dowling, Edward 144
Dowling, Mary 144, 145
Draco, Vic 189
Dronkers, Johannes Marinus 78–79, 197
Dronkers, Frau 78–79, 197
Drummond, David 27
Drummond, Ellen 27

Edgington, Arthur W 46–47, 119, 249
Edinburgh Gazette 172
Edmonds, Horace Henry 34, 122–3, 165
Elwell, George 85, 204
Evans, (William) Alfred 140
Evans, Isabella 101, 140–141
Evans, Sarah 101, 140
Evans, Margaret 140
Evening Despatch 194

Fabian, Insp Robert Fabian 51, 257
Farago, Ladislas 75–7, 79, 193, 195, 197, 199, 206, 226, 240, 243, 258
Farmer, Bob 3, 4, 5, 115, 244
Fletcher, Pte William (Bill) 26–28, 55–7, 60, 121, 124, 137, 138–40, 147–8, 166–7, 262–3, 264–6, 273
Forrest, Ann 24, 25, 131–4
Forrest, Hamilton 25
Forrest, Harry 133
Forrest, James 25, 131–4, 269
Forrest, Mary Ann 25
Forrest, Swaley 25, 249
Frick & Frack (variety act) 73–74, 190–1
Fukken, Engelburtes see Jan Willem Ter Braak
Gardner, Gerald 54

Index

Garrett, Charles (and wife) 61–62, 267
Gatacre family 97, 240–3
Gatacre Hall 97–8
George Inn, Halesowen 57, 167, 273
Gibson, Arnold Howard 246
Gibson, Millicent ("Billy") 63–65, 121, 245–9
Gibson, Osborne 64–5, 245–9
Gifford-Hull, Michael 110
Gipsy's Tent pub 19, 25, 60, 132–3, 224, 273, 278
Goldfar, Sp PC 11
Goode, Violet 29–30
Graham, Pat see Kenneth Patten
Green, Michael 230
Gregory, Cynthia see Cynthia Byford-Jones
Grivas, Georgios 209, 210
Groebli, Werner see *Frick & Frack*
Grove, Geoffrey 93, 237–8

Hagley Hall 61, 63, 70
Hainsworth, Alfred (Jack) 174, 177–80
Hainsworth, Alfred sn 178–9
Hainsworth, Jill see Jill Mossop
Hainsworth, Una 67, 68, 69, 73, 75, 81, 82, 121, 125, 168–92, 193, 215, 216–7, 224, 227–34, 238, 240, 242, 243, 259, 266, 271, 274
Hall, Edward 29–30, 162
Hancock, DC 56, 139
Hand of Glory 52, 201–2
Harper, AG (chaplain) 26, 167
Harris, Dora 44–5
Harrison, Dr Wilson 34, 35, 166
Hart, Robert 3, 6
Haywood, James 98
Haywood, Pte 26–27, 124, 167
Heselton, Philip 204
Hill, WPC Florence 85, 187
Hill Tavern, Clent 57, 59, 167

Hindlip Hall 120
Hipkins / Hipkiss 84
Hodgets, A H 128
Holden, Mr 96
Hollow Tree, The 278
Hollyhead, Supt 5
Holt, Simom 277, 278
Horrobin, PC B 47, 118, 163, 165, 220, 227, 249
Hughes, Leon 63–65, 121, 245–6, 249
Hull Daily Mail 55, 87, 139
Hutton, Prof Ronald 98

Illey House Farm 28–9, 263
Illustrated London News 209
Independent, The 80, 203, 277
Inight, DS Sidney 7–8, 68, 163, 215
Inside Out 98, 244
Ivy House Inn / Hotel 170, 273

Jakobs, Giselle (Gigi) 197–8
Jakobs, Josef 79–81, 199
James family (farmers) 100, 138
James, Alfred 28, 264
James, Bella 38, 39, 122, 161
James, Mrs (landlady) 46, 155
Jenkins, Mary Ann 168, 169, 171, 181, 273
Jepson-Turner, Maria Belita 191
Johnson, Annie 185
Johnson, Cynthia see Cynthia Byford-Jones
Jones, Dave "Tatty" 277
Jones, Ehud 207, 208, 219, 220
Jones, John H 34–35, 120, 165–6
Jones, Lilian M 161
Jones, Mavis 160–3
Jones, Nigel 99, 199

Kedward, DC 31
Kendrick family 156–7
King, George 55, 139

327

Index

King, David Halford 248
King, Milicent see Millicent ("Billy") Gibson
Kinver Inn see *Whittington Inn, Kinver*

Labour in Vain, Yarnfield 185–6
Lambourne, Sgt 5
Langley, PC William 136–7
Lavin, Jack 122, 142–148, 152, 265–6
Lavin, John Bernard 145
Lavin, John Edward 143
Lavin Mary 24, 122, 139, 142–148, 265–6
Law family 224
Lawley, Isabella (Bella) 45–46, 154–7, 159
Lawley, Beryl AK 155–6
Lawley, Frank W 155
Lawley, June Millicent 155
Laycock, PC 41–42
Lea, Lily 264
Lea, Mary see Mary Wenman
Lee family (travellers) 100–1, 137, 139, 140, 261, 263
Lee, Charles Henry ("Charlie Boy") 27, 101, 137, 140
Lee, DC John 34, 35, 36, 37, 39, 42, 139, 162
Lee, Mary see Mary Wenman
Lehrer 77, 78
Levaine, IJ 44
Lewis, Dorothy 24, 25, 131–3
Loveridge family 101, 134–8, 140, 141
Loveridge, Evelyn 141, 142 (nee Brown)
Loveridge, Frederick 142
Loveridge, John 134, 135, 136
Loveridge, Joseph 134
Loveridge, William 135
Luer, Bella 44, 154
Lund, John (biologist) 10–11, 16, 88, 98, 111, 113, 117, 125–6

Lund, Richard 98
Lynch family 145, 152
Lyttelton, Hon Audrey 148
Lyttelton Arms, Stourbridge 70, 71, 182
Lyttelton Arms / Hotel, Halesowen 55, 60, 139, 263, 273

McCormick, Donald 22, 52, 77, 78, 79, 81, 115, 193, 196–7, 198, 199, 203–4, 206, 226, 240, 243, 258
Maiden, Eliza 169, 171
Maiden, Sidney 169
Mander family 185, 186, 209, 217
Mander's factory 37, 159
Manor House of Whittington see *Whittington Inn*
Markham, Dr 115, 118, 260–1
Mauch, Hans Rudolf see *Frick & Frack*
Mellor, Louis 84, 204–5
Merrill, Alex & Peter 100–1, 106–107, 140
Merry, Harold 106
Mitre, Stourbridge 90, 91, 92, 223
Moore family 160
Morris, David 277
Mortimore, Millicent see Billy Gibson
Mossop, Charlotte ("Lollo") 168, 170, 224
Mossop, Eliza see Eliza Maiden
Mossop, (Edward) Percy 168–9, 174
Mossop, Jack 69–73, 97, 110, 121, 163, 168–92, 213, 217, 233, 237–8, 241–4, 249, 259, 271, 278
Mossop, Jill Kyra 175–7, 181
Mossop, Julian 121, 171, 174–5, 177, 178, 181, 182
Mossop, Louis 169, 170, 273
Mossop, Mary Ann see Mary Ann Jenkins
Mossop, Una see Una Hainsworth
Murder by Witchcraft see Donald

Index

McCormick
Murder, Mystery and My Family 106

Murray, Bridget 144
Murray, Prof Margaret 52–54, 55, 77, 110, 129, 158, 201–3

Nazi Murder Mysteries 98, 126, 244
Newman, Paul 197, 257
Newsam, Mr (manager Coventry Hippodrome) 187
Nicholls DI 109, 124
Nimmings Field 6, 56–7, 130, 137, 139, 140, 161, 263, 264, 265, 269, 280

O'Donovan, Judith 97, 184
O'Grady, Dinah see Dinah Curley
Oliver, Irene 237
Operation Cone of Power 54, 204
O'Reilly, Jean 144
O'Reilly, Michael 144
Orrell, Edward 248
Orrell, Millicent Evelyne 247

Palmer family 167, 264–5
Palmer, Charles 57, 167
Palmer, John (Jack) 57, 58, 167
Pardoe, Geoff 203
Parsons, TF (Dairy owner) 61, 122, 151, 152
Partridge, David 93
Pass, Leonard 21, 119
Patten, Kenneth 61–63, 121, 148–152, 263, 266–7
Patten, Sheila May 61, 149, 150
Payne family 156
Payne, Donald 5
Payne, Fred 3, 5
Paynter, Hilda Louise 246
Peck, Ted 189
People, The 44

Picks see *(Old) Lyttelton Arms*
Pheysey PC 208
Pitcher, PC Albert 38, 39
Plant, Doris Aston 89–92, 221–2
Plant, Warwick Daniel Aston 89–92, 123, 221–5, 266
Porter, Doris Aston see Doris Plant
Plant, Mrs 89–91, 223
Porter, Florrie 17, 118
Porter, Sara Annie 57
Potter, Alfred 51
Pound, PC Arthur J 18–9, 59, 63, 150
Pound, PC Jack 6, 8, 63, 93, 123, 150, 123, 236–7, 241
Pregnant Fish Theatre Co 277
Prosser, Ethel 22–23
Pugh, Mervyn Phippen 107
Punt PI 98, 113, 244

Quaestor see Wilfred Byford-Jones

Rathgeb, Franz 78, 196
Ray, Stanley Arthur 37, 159
Reece, Alfred 57
Reece, Mrs Flora 57–59
Renshaw, Sgt 34
Richardson, Alfred 44
Rimington, Stella 126
Roberts, Jessie Constance Hughes 248
Rose & Crown, Hasbury 37–40, 122, 156, 162, 220, 249, 264
Rowley, James 32, 33
Rutter, Thomas Lee 277
Ryder, DC Roger 278–9

Sanders (farmer) 19
Sealey, Arthur 161
Sealey, Bella see Bella James
Seignette, Elise Antoinette Eleanora 197
Shearwood, Eddie 55–6, 60, 121, 139–40, 156, 167, 263, 265

Index

Shelton Inn, Belle Vale 37, 272
Shemwell, Amy Isabel 154–5
Shemwell, Richard & Clara 154–5
Skerratt, Sgt Richard 6, 25, 93, 123, 236–7
Skinner, Mrs 45
Smith family 19, 101, 125, 129, 139–41, 261, 263
Smith, Annette Rosannah Thirza 171
Smith, Arkus (aka Butler) 19, 59, 137
Smith, Danny 59, 134
Smith, Ellen 59
Smith, Eugenia Stella 171
Smith, Herbert 134
Smith, Lallie 59
Smith, Lennie 59, 134
Smith, Nalie ("Titch") 26, 129
Smith, Rhoda see Rhoda Abel
Smith, William 134–137
Smith, Wisdom 59–60, 134–7
Sorohan, Mrs 145
South Wales News 179
Spaldings, Messrs 57
Sparke, Andrew 126, 277
Stalker, John 98, 243
Stanford, Mary Ann see Mary Ann Crump
Stanley, F St C 24
Star Inn (Hotel), Halesowen 27–28, 29, 140, 263, 273
Stephens, Lucy 73, 180
Stewart-Turner, W 193, 258
Strauss, Hon GR 211
Sun, The 278
Sunday Pictorial 33, 44
Sutherland, DC 21
Swindon, John 60, 226

Tate, Felix 57, 100, 130, 131, 269
Tate, Mrs Prudence May 57–8, 139
Taylor, Harry 92–6, 236, 237, 240
Taylor, May Gladys 29–30

Ter Braak, Jan Willem 76, 195, 199
Thomas, Major Charles 241
Three Crowns, Brierly Hill 89–90, 223, 224
Tit-Bits Magazine 20, 120
Tonks, Bella 45, 154
Tromans, Owen 276
Truman, Harry 29–30, 162–3, 249

Under the Shadow see Paul Newman *Of Meon Hill*

Vale, Allison 80, 197–8
Van Ra(a)lt 70–1, 173, 180–9, 233, 242, 249, 259
Van Raalt, Sydney 187
Vant, Violet Catherine 170
Venables, DC 29, 34, 165

Wafell, Lord 211
Waggon & Horses, Wombourne 171, 172, 180, 185, 186, 217, 219, 224, 273
Wall Messages 31–50, 153–167, 221
Walters, CF 222–3
Walton, Charles 51–2, 197.201, 203, 257
War of Wits 75, 195, 226
Watton, Rose 101
Wayside Inn, Alcester 84
Webster, Prof James 8–9, 10–16, 17, 18–19, 49, 88, 101, 105–117, 128, 135, 141 146, 151, 157, 181, 203, 230, 231, 247, 250
Wenman, Caleb 137
Wenman, Mary 26–29, 60, 85, 101, 134–40, 166, 262
Western Mail 179, 213, 215
Wheeler, Sgt Jack 6
White, Mr 31
Whittington Inn, Kinver 69, 73, 74, 232
Whyley, Leonard 64–5, 245, 249
Willetts, (Arthur) Ernest 39, 40, 160,

Index

162
Willetts, (Charles) Harry 57–8, 130, 139, 162, 264–5
Willetts, John 40
Willetts, Thomas 3, 4, 265
Willetts, Walter 39, 40, 110, 122, 160–2, 220, 264–5
Williams, Biddy see Vivienne Coss
Williams, Lloyd (Chief Con) 68
Williams, DI Thomas 7–8, 10–12, 21, 28, 32, 34–6, 39–40, 48, 50, 56, 60, 61, 63–64, 82, 85, 88, 110, 113, 119, 121–4, 125–6, 138, 162–5, 167, 215, 220, 221, 227, 229, 231–4, 250–3, 264, 265

Wilson, Bill 171, 174, 177, 181, 182, 189, 190, 191
Wolverhampton Express & Star 4, 5, 47, 66–8, 73–4, 88, 92–3, 108, 119, 123, 163, 207–8, 211, 212, 219, 227, 231, 234–5, 243, 275
"Wood, Mr" (writer of 42–43, 274 anonymous letter)
Wood, Douglas 220
Wood, Harry 220
Worthington, Harry 84
Worthington, John 84

Young, Francis Brett 209

www.ingramcontent.com/pod-product-compliance
Lightning Source LLC
Chambersburg PA
CBHW050514170426
43201CB00013B/1948